Political Culture and Foreign Policy in Latin America

SUNY Series in the Making of Foreign Policy:
Theories and Issues

Alex R. Hybel, Editor

Political Culture and Foreign Policy in Latin America

Case Studies from the Circum-Caribbean

Roland H. Ebel
Raymond Taras
James D. Cochrane

State University of New York Press

Published by
State University of New York Press, Albany

For information, address State University of New York
Press, State University Plaza, Albany, N.Y., 12246

Production by M.R. Mulholland
Marketing by Dana E. Yanulavich

Library of Congress Cataloging-in-Publication Data

Ebel, Roland H., 1928-
    Political culture and foreign policy in Latin America : case
studies from the Circum-Caribbean / Roland H. Ebel, Raymond Taras,
James D. Cochrane.
        p.   cm. — (SUNY series in the making of foreign policy)
    Includes bibliographical references and index.
    ISBN 0-7914-0604-0 (alk. paper). — ISBN 0-7914-0605-9 (pbk. :
alk. paper)
    1. Latin America—Foreign relations.   2. Political culture—Latin
America.   I. Taras, Ray, 1946–   . II. Cochrane, James D.
III. Title.   IV. Series.
F1415.E24   1991
327.8—dc20   90-9951
                                                                        CIP

10 9 8 7 6 5 4 3 2 1

Contents

Tables and Figures

Preface

Over the past two decades, a large body of literature has emerged detailing various aspects of the contemporary foreign policies and international behavior of the countries of Latin America. That is a most welcome development, for it sheds light and aids in understanding a long-neglected aspect of Latin American government and politics. Earlier on in the post-World War II period, scholars of Latin American politics rarely addressed the issue of foreign policy and international relations of Latin American countries—save for relations between those countries and the United States or their international politics expressed in various inter-American forums, especially the Organization of American States. Perhaps the scholarly premise was that Latin American countries had no foreign policies beyond those which were set by Washington. Or perhaps U.S. scholars of the Latin American political process simply viewed other aspects of that process as more important and, thus, more deserving of attention. Whatever the case, the situation has changed.

The literature of the late 1960s and beyond concerning Latin American foreign policy and international relations is of two sorts. Some of it provides micro (country specific) studies; others are macro (region-wide) studies. Both sorts of studies provide valuable insights and both address, among other topics, the sources of Latin American foreign policy and international behavior. Both confirm that policy and behavior are the product of a mix of external and internal factors or stimuli. The external stimuli most often pointed to have included: the international distribution of power; the influence (or lack thereof) of the United States, the USSR, and other major powers in Latin America; trends in the international environment (for example bipolarity, which gave way to loose bipolarity and even incipient multipolarity); the emergence of detente, its demise, and the asymmetrical superpower relations of the 1990s; Third World assertiveness; international economic recession, depression, and recovery; rise and decline in commodity prices; dependence on external actors; willingness and ability of external actors to interact with Latin American countries; and a number of other stimuli. Some authors go so far as to imply that there is very little or no indigenous foreign policy in Latin America. Those studies maintain that the foreign policies and international behavior of the countries of Latin America are either dictated or very heavily influenced by those countries' superpower sponsors or by events in the international environment. To be sure, these various external stimuli do exert a potent influence. But they lack an all-inclusive explanatory power.

External stimuli cannot explain Mexico's so-called "new foreign policy" pursued by former President Echeverría, nor can they account for why a very isolated Argentine junta (even if it vaguely thought it had Washington's backing) would launch the futile and fatal military conquest of the Falkland Islands. Important internal factors must also be addressed. Jennie Lincoln identified four sets of internal variables to be considered in explaining Latin American foreign policy decisions and international behavior. They were: national attributes; orientations of a particular regime; social forces within a country; and national experiences.[1]

National attributes refer to such tangibles as a country's size, resources, military capability, population, and level of development. Regime orientations have to do with such matters as the goals of a particular government, the attitudes and predispositions of a particular set of leaders, the regime's ideology or political philosophy and, perhaps, a given regime's development strategy. Social forces refer to group demands on a regime and the strength of various groups within a country. Lastly, national experiences focus on specific historical events or developments, for example, revolutions, democratic transitions, or the discovery of a natural resource (such as oil). All of these are important variables that, together with external factors, must be examined in order to explain foreign policy content and international behavior.

There is, however, yet another factor that merits attention; yet it has received little or no such attention in the study of Latin American foreign policy. That is political culture, which consists of subjective and objective orientations of a society to its political system, along with that society's political behavior. The link between political culture and the domestic political process is well established. Much less well established is the link between a country's political culture and its foreign policy and international behavior. Yet there is a link, even though it may, in some instances, be more muted than the link between political culture and domestic politics. There are two principal reasons for this. One, political culture, in large measure, provides the values, orientations, and sense of direction to decision-makers. Decision-makers who are deeply imbued with the values of, say, anti-*Yanquismo* or promotion of democracy at home are likely to mold and pursue policies that advance those values abroad. Here comes to mind Castro and Cuban foreign policy since 1959, on the first count, and Venezuelan and Costa Rican leaders and their foreign policies since democracy was firmly established in these states. Similarly, officials whose political value system include a deep commitment—even a sense of responsibility—to change the world fundamentally or reverse some offense to what is perceived to be national honor or *dignidad* are likely to pursue and shape—when opportunity is present—policies that advance those objectives. One can identify on the first count, Castro and Cuban foreign policy and, on the second, Argentine governments and their territorial claims on Chile in the straits of Tierra del Fuego and on Britain regarding the equally desolate, isolated, but highly valued Falkland/Malvinas Islands.

Two, it is not just officials or decision-makers that are influenced by a country's political culture; individuals, also, have a political culture that orients them to politics and political objects. For the individual, political culture establishes expectations about political behavior and sets broad limits about permissible behavior. For example, in most Latin American countries anti-*Yanquismo* is a prominent element of the political culture, and there is a corresponding expectation that government will take action to give effect to that sentiment, even if it may be closely related to the United States.

Many scholars, as we record in the chapters that follow, agree that a Latin American political culture exists that is based mainly on the colonial experience, that establishes norms concerning the organization of political authority, and that engenders expectations about governmental behavior. That culture is common to all of Ibero-America. Superimposed on that common political culture are a number of national cultures in Ibero-America. These cultures are differentiated from one another in terms of the nature of the political system. In this work we are as concerned with distinguishing between national cultures as we are with showing what they have in common.

This study is preliminary and exploratory, a first look at the link between political culture and foreign policy. The premise is *not* that political culture explains everything about Latin American foreign policy and behavior in the international system. Rather, the premise *is* that political culture is an important and neglected explanatory variable, one that has not been employed much in analyzing Latin American foreign policy and international behavior.

The study is not only preliminary and exploratory, it is synthetic. The book draws on existing literature on Latin American politics, foreign policies, and international relations in order to explore and further establish the link between political culture and international politics. And while we introduce some original paradigms with which to look anew at Latin American politics, our objective is to provide an introduction to this problematic. For case studies we have selected six small- and medium-sized countries located in the circum-Caribbean which have contrasting political traditions and political systems.

We would like to acknowledge the assistance of three graduate students at Tulane University who carried out secondary analyses of the political science literature used to identify the political cultures of the six countries featured in this study. Allison Stone Golcher undertook the preliminary analysis of the literature on Costa Rica (her native country) and Colombia, Mary Felise Smith-Peters completed the same task for Cuba and Nicaragua, while Elba de Lugo assisted in evaluating the literature on her native country, Venezuela. Two students also collected extensive material on the foreign policies of two of the countries: Steven Turner (Major, United States Army) for Guatemala and Mario de Castro for his native Colombia.

The authors are also grateful to a number of eminent scholars in the field of Latin American studies who commented on drafts of the manuscrpt. Howard Wiarda read an early version of the study and mixed telling criticism with needed encouragement. Individual chapters were strengthened by helpful critiques provided by Jorge Dominguez, Michael Morris, and Harry Vanden. Finally, the study was completed in March 1990, shortly after the Nicaraguan elections, and obviously does not consider subsequent events.

The authors also wish to thank Praeger Publishers for permission to use portions of a chapter entitled "Cultural Style and International Policy-Making: The Latin American Tradition" by Roland H. Ebel and Raymond Taras, published in John Chay, ed., *Culture and International Relations* (New York: Praeger Publishers, 1990); copyright 1990 by Jongsuk Chay.

Note

1. Jennie K. Lincoln, "Introduction to Latin American Foreign Policy: Global and Regional Dimensions," in Elizabeth G. Ferris and Jennie K. Lincoln (eds.), *Latin American Foreign Policies: Global and Regional Dimensions*. Boulder, CO: Westview Press, 1981, p. 6.

1

Political Culture and the Making
of Foreign Policy

In few other parts of the world is a region's culture perceived to be so distinctive, identifiable and, at the same time, so influential in the political process as in Latin America. For many observers of international politics, Latin America has become synonymous with *caudillaje* culture that is said to span the length and breadth of the continent. In turn, Central America is closely associated with military rule and the machismo culture it supposedly spawns. Despite the existence of such widely held stereotypes, few observers have searched for the linkage between these regional cultures and international policy making.

The principal objectives of this study are to identify the political culture found in Latin America generally and selected circum-Caribbean states in particular and, more importantly, to relate it to the type of foreign policies that have been pursued by these states. Before we can empirically investigate that linkage, however, we must make clear what we understand by the often elusive concept of political culture. The first part of this chapter traces the evolution of the term, the controversies that have surrounded it, and the paradigm that we are advancing. The second part addresses the question of linkage between deeply embedded cultural patterns and international policy making. Here we evaluate views on the impact that a national culture may have on foreign policy. We identify those independent variables that combine to make up a national culture and, then, evaluate their respective influence on the making of foreign policy in the Latin American nations chosen for this study. We hypothesize that both the configuration of such explanatory variables as well as the outcomes they produce will differ across states, but by adopting such a perspective we hope to arrive at a general association—not a causal relationship—between culture and international policy making. In this respect, we share the epistemological assumptions of Latin American scholar Peter H. Smith, who has observed: "My concern focuses on approaches that seek to identify specific connections between two or more variables and, *eventually* (italics ours), to construct workable models of causal processes." While this approach is often termed behavioral, in fact, as Smith argues, such a "focus deals with conceptualization, not technique."[1]

Let us begin by looking briefly at the concept of culture and its relationship to politics.

The Concept of Political Culture

After a period of relative disuse during the first part of the 1980s, the political culture approach to the study of politics has been making a comeback. Robert C. Tucker has stated emphatically that "The political culture approach is now deeply embedded in the culture of American political science,"[2] while Howard Wiarda has pointed out that "political culture is presently enjoying a renaissance. Samuel Huntington, Aaron Wildavsky, Harry Eckstein, and Lucian Pye—all among the leading figures in the profession—have recently published major books and articles using the political culture approach."[3] The common theme of diverse studies of the United States, China, the USSR, and Latin America, *inter alia*, is a focus on elements of national culture that are directly related to the political system. The politicized dimension of culture—not its more general anthropological aspects—has driven recent scholarship and has directed our research. In adopting the concept of political culture, we should state immediately that it extends beyond the parameters traditionally delineating the original concept. The term has become, after some initial scepticism, a widely accepted conceptual tool of political science.

There has been, however, a long-running debate among scholars investigating political culture as to whether the concept should encompass psychological orientations only, or should also include observed behavior. We recall that, according to a pioneer in this field, Sidney Verba, "The political culture of a society consists of the system of empirical beliefs, expressive symbols, and values which defines the situation in which political action takes place. It provides the subjective orientation to politics."[4] An earlier classic study, the path-breaking five-nation comparative investigation of political cultures by Almond and Verba, adopted a similar analytical framework. The authors made clear they "employ the concept of culture in only one of its many meanings: that of psychological orientation toward social objects."[5] Perhaps the most ambitious effort to operationalize such a limited understanding of the term was the comparative study of seven communist states undertaken by Archie Brown and Jack Gray. They viewed communist political culture "in terms of subjective orientation to history and politics, of fundamental beliefs and values, of foci of identification and loyalty, and of political knowledge and expectations." By decoupling subjective (psychological) from objective (behavioral) orientations, the research into Communist states could conclude that "differences of national political culture may have played a significant—perhaps even a decisive—part in the divergences in political behavior which have occurred."[6]

In a follow-up study carried out ten years later, Brown sought to justify such an approach by invoking the newer literature found in cultural anthropology which, too, displayed "a strong intellectual tendency to exclude from the scope of culture not only laws and formal institutions (which were sometimes included in the past) but also behavior patterns." As a result, Brown came to stress what he perceived as the fundamentally interdisciplinary nature of the study of political culture: "If political culture is considered as that part of a culture (in the newer anthropological sense) which bears relevance to politics, it can be particularly valuable as a concept which cuts across disciplinary boundaries and brings together, and organizes, insights to be found in the work of historians, anthropologists, social psychologists and sociologists (as well as of students of politics)."[7] Paradoxically, therefore, the operationalization of the concept of political culture—defined as it is by a political scientist such as Brown—places the field of political science on the analytic periphery and gives unquestionable preeminence to the disciplines of social psychology and cultural anthropology.

While the "subjectivist school" of political culture has, ironically perhaps (given the elusive and vague nature of its datum), proved to be an attractive alternative to those social scientists who wish to carry out empirical research, a number of eminent scholars have considered manifest political behavior an inseparable part of political culture. Samuel Huntington and Jorge Domínguez, for example, define a society's political culture as "the empirical beliefs about expressive political symbols and values and other orientations of the members of the society toward political objects."[8] These "other orientations" include, presumably, political behavior itself. Tucker has been more explicit and argued that a behavioral approach has the added value of comparing beliefs to actions, thereby distinguishing "ideal cultural patterns" from "real" ones. He goes even further by proposing that a nation's culture generally—not just its politics—should form the focus of analysis of the political culture approach:

> Political culture, politics as a form of culture, and politics as an activity related to the larger culture of society, might...be taken as the central subject matter of the discipline. Instead of treating political culture as an attribute of a political system, we would then view the political system of society in cultural terms, i.e. as a complex of real and ideal culture patterns, including political roles and their interrelations, political structures, and so on.[9]

In the field of communist studies, where the concept of political culture has most frequently been operationalized, the majority of scholars have opted for the combined subjective and behavioral approach. Thus, in his study of the Soviet Union Stephen White wrote: "Political culture may be defined as the attitudinal and behavioral matrix within which the political system is located."[10] Similarly, in his work on Czechoslovakia, David Paul understood political culture as "the configuration of values, symbols, and attitudinal and behavioral patterns underlying the politics of a society."[11]

While still focusing primarily on political rather than cultural variables, an even stronger argument for subsuming behavior under the concept of political culture was made by Richard Fagen in his research on Cuba. He noted that exclusive focus on existing subjective orientations "is useful in investigating and explaining how and why certain political institutions function or fail to function in specific national settings. It is much less useful, however, when the focus of inquiry is on the directed transformation of the institutions themselves." Moreover, Fagen emphasized how in a society undergoing planned political change, the ruling elite seeks to transform both the cognitive and overt behavior of its citizens. As a result, in any revolutionary system (such as Cuba), the ruling elite attempts "to create new values and behaviors in the context of new political settings." Even some time after the successful revolutionary takeover, "the emerging Cuban political culture should be viewed as still very dependent on the revolutionary environment itself, rather than on internalized and deeply ingrained values and patterns of behavior."[12] Under conditions of radical political transformation, the significance of a "snapshot" psychological profile of a country is limited. However such radical transformation has been exceptional in Latin America; we postulate that an underlying and enduring political culture can be identified in the region.

Indeed, Wiarda has defended the political culture approach to the study of Latin America even as the region, like other parts of the globe, has moved inexorably away from some of its authoritarian features towards democratization:

The more careful analysts of political culture have always rec gnized that, at least since the nineteenth century, two traditions—an authoritarian-corporatist one and a liberal-democratic one—have uneasily coexisted in Latin America, often alternating in power. At present, the liberal-democratic one is (temporarily?) ascendant. Second, while at the formal-institutional level...democracy in contemporary Latin America has triumphed, below the surface many institutions—the Church, the Army, labor relations, lord-peasant relations, the state structure—often remain dominated by authoritarian-corporatist-patrimonialist features.[13]

Scepticism about the political cultural explanation for Latin American political development is, Wiarda contended, strengthened by an ideological consideration: "What such explanations do is to place responsibility for Latin America's continuing underdevelopment directly on Latin America itself rather than allowing it to be ascribed (far preferable, from the Latin American viewpoint) to U.S. machinations, as in dependency theory." Finally, Wiarda pointed out that this approach is never held to be mono-causal anyway: "Not a single serious scholar who writes about political culture has claimed that this factor is important to the exclusion of all others."[14]

In order to minimize the perils of the political culture approach, our definition includes both popular opinion and popular conduct in the political arena. Apart from arguments advanced by Tucker and Fagen, such a broad approach appears justified given our need to evaluate the linkage between culture and foreign policy. If it is to have explanatory power, political culture should, in our analytical framework, subsume a wide- (rather than narrow) ranging set of variables related to national culture. In this way the variable set may correspond in magnitude to the macro-question before us: How does national culture affect particular state behavior in the international political system? Moreover, the distinction between attitudes and values, on the one hand, and behavior, on the other, is often murky and may overlap. For example, the classic *caudillaje* or machismo features attributed to much of Latin American society may involve both a state of mind, and actual conduct.

An important distinction to be made is the difference between political culture and political ideology. For us, culture denotes the more deeply imprinted patterns of a society—those attitudes, values, and beliefs that have been ingrained in a population from earliest childhood. Thus they are persistent, long-lasting, and much slower to change. An ideology, on the other hand, is a set of opinions and views that an individual or group may come to as a result of mature ratiocination. However, it is our belief that culture is stronger and generally more durable than ideology. For example, during the nineteenth century Latin American Liberals and Conservatives differed on a number of points of political doctrine or ideology. Nevertheless, the pattern of leadership of both groups tended to be that of *caudillismo*. In the case of the Liberals particularly, their cultural orientation towards strong personal rule was more deeply ingrained than their ideological commitment to republican political institutions.

A more recent example of the same phenomenon was the leadership style of Fidel Castro and Fulgencio Batista. Although the former belonged to the Marxist left and the latter to the authoritarian right, both were essentially *caudillos* who created a hierarchically structured and monolithic state based on the coercive power of the military. In that sense it can be said that both Castro and Batista were "as Latin as tortillas and beans."

Ideology, then, may make a contribution to a nation's or region's political culture and, depending on its character, may reinforce a cultural pattern (for example, the cultural congruence between authoritarian Marxism and the equally authoritarian Iberian political tradition). By the same token, competing ideologies may also serve to create or reinforce various political subcultures within a nation. However, it is our opinion that when ideology and culture are at odds, culture tends ultimately to prevail over ideology.

In summary, we postulate that a nation's or region's political culture is made up of three components: political values, attitudes, and behavior. Political values are the idealized norms of how a proper political system should be structured and operated. This often produces what Frank Parkin described as "the concept of a dominant value system."[15] Political attitudes are the reality-based orientations of people towards the political process. This is sometimes called the "modal" political culture. Political behavior is the way individuals and groups apply their political values and attitudes in concrete situations.

The dominant value system is primarily a part of the historico-cultural inheritance of a nation and stands above the particular values and attitudes of any specific social sector or political generation. As such it serves to moderate, filter or appropriate the more sector- or group-specific attitudes and values. However, because Latin America has historically been stratified into three broad class cultures—the elites, the "middle segments,"[16] and the masses—it is necessary to distinguish at least minimally between them. For example, Latin American societies generally possess a readily identifiable political class drawn from the middle sector of society which are most active in the process of *politiqueria* and whose values, attitudes, and behavior are transmitted downward to other segments of society. Consequently the importance of the values and attitudes of the political class is disproportionate to its size.

The analytical model of political culture used in this study is outlined in figure 1.1. We recognize that different social sectors have distinctive political attitudes and values, and that they behave in specific ways in the political arena. In addition, a dominant value system, based on national traditions and the consensual norms found throughout society, exists apart from sectoral distinctions. The national political culture is the end product of the interaction between dominant and sectoral values. Finally, national political culture influences not only domestic policy outcomes but also the international politics of the state.

FIGURE 1.1

Model of Societal Values, Political Culture and System Outputs

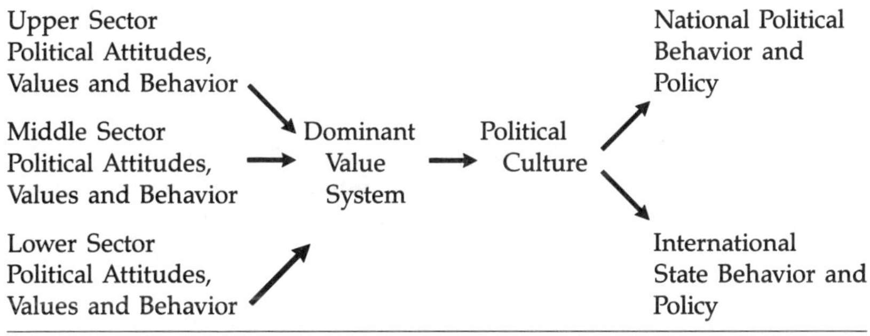

In chapter 2 we lay out what scholars conceive to be the basic characteristics of the dominant political value system of Latin America. We identify some of its competing value systems, distinguish between the values, attitudes and behaviors of the three class cultures, and distinguish the states which seem most fully to embody particular value systems or particular mixes of values, attitudes, and behavioral characteristics.

Paradigms of Domestic Politics as Foreign Policy Influences

We have examined the concept of political culture and the way it can be optimally applied to a study of Latin America. Our next objective is to examine the scholarly literature concerned with the linkage between political culture and international policy and behavior. Such hypothesized linkage has, explicitly or implicitly, underlain many theories developed by political theorists. By reviewing the major theoretical contributions to this subject, we hope to underscore the diversity of approaches that have been taken as well as the often amorphous, unsystematic, and prescientific nature of the enterprise. We conclude this chapter by proposing our own framework for studying the making of Latin American foreign policies.

Let us begin by identifying some of the domestic factors, related to political culture, that international relations specialists have regarded as crucial elements in the making of foreign policy. We will then be in a better position to isolate the impact of political culture—to hold it constant to the greatest degree possible—on international behavior.

The effort to establish an associational relationship between a country's domestic political system and its foreign policy orientation has either a long or a very short history, depending on one's perspective. The term political culture and the effort to employ it scientifically are of relatively recent origin, as we noted above. But references to warlike qualities of peoples and their effect on relations with other groups can be traced back to the writings of Homer. The concept of national character was a particularly fascinating topic for political theorists, and while it encompasses factors that extend beyond political culture (social norms and behavior, common response to a variety of stimuli—political and non-political), it also is a more limiting concept (its purported immutability, uniqueness, and predetermined quality). While corresponding in some areas (for example, political behavior) to the modern notion of political culture, therefore, it can only furnish us with a limited idea as to how theorists grappled with the linkage between culture and foreign policy.

The Greek historian Thucydides, in his *Peloponnesian War*, addressed virtually all the major theoretical linkages between national attributes, political systems, nature of leadership, and foreign policy that have confronted contemporary scholarship. He described at length the political psychology underlying the building of empires and the resort to wars, and he interpreted the outcome of conflictual relations between Athens and Sparta as necessarily following from the respective characters of the two peoples. Thucydides wrote of the "dash and enterprise," and intelligence and innovativeness of Athenians, compared to Spartans' "slowness and want of energy" and their conformity and devotion to the state. These attributes, in turn, were inextricably linked to the open character of Athenian democracy and the hermetic nature of the Spartan polity. Thucydides even considered the question of why the national character of the Athenians seemingly changed following the death of Pericles. A Thucydidian scholar, William Bluhm, has argued that

> Thucydides viewed political leadership as a function of the psychological tone of a community, and further that he believed that the tone of a community in turn depends upon social and political institutions. Thus it is Athenian democracy which is singled out as the cause, at one point in its development, of intelligent moderation in the Athenian people, and hence the Periclean leadership; and as the cause, at another point in its development, of frantic imperialism and thus of Cleon and Alcibiades....Thucydides quite clearly derives the personalities of leaders from national character, and relates national character in turn to social, economic, and political institutions.[17]

With regard to the specific question of foreign policies and empire building, Bluhm summarizes Thucydides' approach in these terms:

> Overstimulated passions paralyze the rationality of such [Athenian-type] societies and produce unduly aggressive or demagogic leaders and/or unduly timorous leaders, civil factions and selfishness, and megalomaniac foreign policies, all of which result in the destruction of the imperial power.[18]

Today, a student inquiring into Latin American politics may indeed speculate about the extent to which Fidel Castro, Juan Perón, or a particular military strongman has "overstimulated national passions" but still embodies or reflects a given national character and develops a foreign policy agenda appropriate to the qualities and drives of his people.

The relationship between national character and propensity to aggression has fascinated generations of observers since Thucydides' time. Writing at the apogee of the Roman Empire, Tacitus surmised:

> The Germans have no taste for peace; renown is easier won among perils, and you cannot maintain a large body of companions except by violence and war....You will find it harder to persuade a German to plough the land and to await its annual produce with patience than to challenge a foe and earn the prize of wounds.[19]

Racially grounded explanations of aggression (or lack of it) were not, of course, limited to the classical historians. Some eighteen centuries later, writing in post Congress-of-Vienna Europe, Carl von Clausewitz, in referring to victories achieved by Russia in 1812 and Prussia in 1813 against Napoleon, inferred: "these cases have shown what an enormous contribution the *heart and temper of a nation* can make to the sum total of its politics, war potential, and fighting strength." Conversely, internal failings can bring about the downfall of a state, as in the case of Poland: "Their [Polish leaders'] chaotic public life and their boundless irresponsibility went together, and thus they were swallowed up by the abyss."[20] For Clausewitz, therefore, *national spirit* helped determine a nation's international position. A modern-day Latin American example may be *caudillismo*, described in the next chapter.

In much the same vein but writing much later, Hans Morgenthau, one of the most influential postwar scholars on international relations, argued that "certain qualities of intellect and character occur more frequently and are more highly valued in one nation than in another."[21] Morgenthau, like Clausewitz, was careful to avoid adopting the category of national character as the sole explanation for the behavior of a particular nation-state, but he, too, recognized that to avoid all reference to the distinctive cluster of attributes—including the *socio-psychological*—found in a nation was to deprive an explanatory paradigm of an important variable. In the period in which he was writing the concept of political culture had not yet become common currency in political science, but we may note that related ideas, such as alleged national styles (and certainly national character), were already in circulation. By the twentieth century, Quincy Wright's massive quantitative study of war culminated the long-held intellectual curiosity in the subject.[22] It gave rise to further empirical investigations whose evidence on cultural properties and aggression have been generally inconclusive.[23] Further theoretical refinement of the relationship between international conflict and the internal structure of states was provided by Kenneth Waltz, whose concept of the "second image" traced the effect that the internal organization of states had on decisions to initiate wars or to make peace.[24]

An international relations scholar who was a contemporary of Morgenthau and Waltz, Henry Kissinger, also debated how certain factors found in a particular nation-state influenced the type of foreign policy it pursued. In his well-known essay, "Domestic Structure and Foreign Policy," he focused on two variables that differed, often radically, from one country to another: 1) administrative structure, and 2) leadership groups. In examining administrative structure, Kissinger did not consider the broader question of the federal or unitary nature of a political system which could, in fact, affect the making and substance of foreign policy.[25] In Kissinger's view, national *bureaucracies* appeared to exert an influence that at times helped to rationalize foreign policy making and, at others, to subject it to arbitrariness: "The more elaborate the administrative structure, the less relevant an individual's view becomes—indeed one of the purposes of bureaucracy is to liberate decision-making from the accident of personalities."[25a] But the danger always existed that when controversy was engendered and choices had to be made, bureaucratic processes could break down and might then be replaced by subjective preferences: "It is a paradoxical aspect of modern bureaucracies that their quest for objectivity and calculability often leads to impasses which can be overcome only by essentially arbitrary decisions."[25b]

As Alberto van Klaveren pointed out, however, the bureaucratic politics perspective

> has never been very popular among Latin Americanists, which seems understandable given the high levels of centralization and power concentration that characterize political systems in the region. It certainly would be a misrepresentation to view the region's external policies as the result of bureaucratic infighting.[26]

Both because many are economically underdeveloped countries plagued with underdeveloped bureaucracies and information resources and because of cultural style, foreign policy consensus in Latin America was even more likely to be achieved through fits of national passion and capricious improvization. Especially in the "city-state" of Central America together with the Caribbean, it was the *caudillo* who often served as an unsatisfactory substitute for an effective national bureaucracy, or who overrode bureaucratic calculations in order to impose his quintessential mark on policy.

Kissinger identified a further contradiction that has even more direct implications for our study of Latin America. In foreign policy, as in the economic sphere, international state actors could be divided into the haves and the have-nots. Accordingly for Kissinger,

> Where the technologically advanced countries suffer from the inertia of overadministration, the developing areas often lack even the rudiments of effective bureaucracy. Where the advanced countries may drown in 'facts,' the emerging nations are frequently without the most elementary knowledge needed for forming a

meaningful judgement or for implementing it once it has been taken.[27]

Kissinger suggested that in states not possessing adequate information and bureaucratic structures, foreign policy consensus might be achieved through nationalist sentiment. An example of this could be the Argentine junta's decision to take the disputed Falklands/Malvinas in April 1982.

Kissinger's discussion of the respective role played by *leadership groups* in various countries is equally instructive. They were shaped by three sets of factors: 1) their experience during their rise to eminence; 2) the structures in which they operate; and 3) the values of their societies. Following the Weberian framework, Kissinger noted that societies founded on the prestige or charisma of leaders (who are themselves frequently revolutionaries—of either the left or right) are subject to more radical change than societies rooted in legal or bureaucratic criteria. Furthermore, for a variety of reasons many developing nations appear, in Kissinger's view, to be driven towards reckless foreign policies. Economic advance disrupts traditional political structures, domestic instability may be overlooked by emphasizing a radical foreign policy, national identity may remain uncertain, super-power rivalry guarantees the assistance of one of the adversaries regardless of the actions taken by a developing nation, and international politics provides an arena for both the dramatic measures impossible at home and the perpetuation of charismatic leadership. Kissinger concluded that foreign policy can be divided into two distinct styles and philosophical perspectives,[28] which we encapsulate in figure 1.2. From our earlier discussion we see that many of the least developed Latin American states fit the second category, while the more industrialized Southern Cone states undertaking the process of democratization, which until recently were *desarrollista* bureaucratic-authoritarian regimes (Argentina, Brazil, Uruguay), appear consciously to style their foreign policies on the first model.

To summarize, political writers have long recognized that distinctive clusters of attributes (including socio-psychological) exist in various nations; a composite of these traits may be said to make up a national character. In earlier times, writers did not make explicit the association between political culture and international relations while recognizing the influence that a "national style" could have on foreign policy making. Only with the behavioral revolution in the social sciences, however, was this dominant humanistic perspective replaced with a disaggregated social science framework. Recent scholarship

FIGURE 1.2

Types of Foreign Policy Styles and Philosophical Perspectives

	Modern State	Developing State
Approach to Order	Political	Revolutionary
Role of Actor	Statesman	Prophet
Function of Actor	Manipulation of Reality	Creation of Reality
Philosophical Perspective	Real World is External to Observer	Real World is Internal to Observer

Source: Adapted from Henry A. Kissinger, "Domestic Structure and Foreign Policy," in *American Foreign Policy.* New York: W.W. Norton, 1977, 3rd edn., pp. 46–48.

has sought to discover associations between independent variables connected with political culture and dependent ones related to foreign policy. One specific area where the effort has been most distinguished is in the series of studies concentrating on the ethnocentrism of political decision-makers, intelligence analysts, and national security advisors.

In his research Adda Bozeman focused on shortcomings in United States intelligence work in the Third World: "The case continues to be made—rightly I think—that we do not know just how non-Western societies tick; that our intelligence collection is weak in respect of them, and that this is due chiefly to our heavy intelligence concentration on the Soviet Union." As a result, whether it be Castro's Cuba, Sandinista Nicaragua, or any of a variety of other controversial regimes, "we did not and do not yet understand the 'mindset.' " The mindsets of both oftentimes complex non-Western nations and of the power-holding individuals ruling them need to be examined carefully, for here ultimate political power is frequently associated with personalities. But failure to understand other countries is never more pronounced, according to Bozeman, than in the differing approaches to the concept of the state found in non-Western societies. It is a fact that we must accept, however grudgingly, that "the modern Western state is conceptually and historically alien or uncongenial to the majority of the world's societies." Going further, we must learn to differentiate among the varieties of non-Western patterns of authoritarian rule: "rather than continuing the present tendency to lump authoritarian states together, we need to distiguish and evaluate them carefully in terms of the cultures and ideologies that condition their political structures and that help shape their orientations to foreign affairs." For Bozeman's general thesis was that "norms and values observed in a society's inner order—be it Western or non-Western—will inevitably be operational also in the society's relations with the outside world." While providing no empirical evidence to substantiate the thesis, he saw the need for conducting comparative transcultural research, especially by scholars engaged in the humanities: history, religion, philosophy, literature, and language. Only by such means can we hope to understand all the factors generating a particular nation's statecraft and intelligence, and in this way discover the overt and covert identities of non-Western states.[29]

Addressing another central aspect of foreign policy—strategy and, more specifically, *deterrence*—Gerald Segal described its linkage to national specificities. His discussion was limited to three nuclear nations, but it remains analytically instructive to consider how he drew the association. Geography, ideology, and institutions are the key variables indentified which shape the deterrence strategies of the Soviet Union, China, and the United States. Russia's geographical and historical heritage produce a felt national need to overinsure for defense. Deterrence strategy becomes based on denying victory to the enemy rather than on the threat of punishment to an aggressor. In China a history of border threats (especially from the north and from the sea), combined with an ideology that has fostered distrust of foreigners, has also helped shape a strategy of deterrence by denial. Where the two countries differ, according to Segal, is in their respective commitment to massive and minimum deterrence; the Soviets, possessing the industrial and technological capacity, have sought to overinsure with quantity, while the Chinese, conditioned by their human geography (a large rural population) and limited economic and technological base, follow a doctrine of minimum deterrence coupled with people's war. The author concludes that United States' mimicking of other states' deterrence strategy would be "ethnic chic" and, simultaneously, poor judgement. Given the historical, geographical, ideological, institutional and technological backdrop of the United States, a strategy of deterrence by punishment, made credible through the maintenance of a sizeable arsenal of intercontinental and intermediate-range nuclear weapons, appears as the logical deterrence product of national specificities.[30] In an analogous way we might seek to link differing concepts of national security and defense policies pursued by populous Latin American states with regional power aspirations (Argentina, Brazil), land-locked states (Bolivia, Paraguay), the Andean bloc, or the "city-states" of Central America.

Ken Booth demonstrated in an exhaustive way how the making of *strategy* by a particular state is very much the product of national style:

> By its very nature the theory and practice of strategy adopts a nationalistic view of the world. It is full of the concomitant value judgements of the traditional society of states. Perhaps above all activities, strategy is based on and devoted to an ethnocentric and nationalistic conception of international politics.[31]

Methods of recruitment into the strategy-making establishment, criteria for promotion, the logistical need for compliance with established normative homogeneity, all favor those individuals with ethnocentric preferences. Further, in strategic issues national interest overrides all other interests. As a result, "The strategic paradigm is rooted in ethnocentrism and...strategists are professional ethnocentrics."[31a]

Booth added that bargaining and negotiating styles are peculiar to national cultures. Too, the very understanding of war and violence has profound cultural connotations. In some parts of the world (Booth cited conflict in sub-Saharan Africa, but Latin American *opéra bouffe* wars also come to mind) "organized violence has sometimes been more a matter of theatre than of strategy. War and martial activities have had more to do with the meaning of manhood and the universe than with politics in a Western sense." Of even more direct relevance to our analysis, Booth contended that Latin American guerrilla movements could not be understood apart from their socio-cultural setting; thus, "Catholicism and machismo were more significant than the Clausewitzian philosophy of war."[31b]

Booth's conclusions were that "Personality, society and culture form a continuous whole. Society and culture affect perceptual interpretation, motivation, behavioral norms and the structure of man's expectations; man organizes his cognition and perception of reality in terms of cultural meanings and values."[31c] But in proposing a strategy "with a human face," the author warned of the pitfalls of cultural relativism—an approach diametrically opposite to ethnocentrism. Five sweeping assumptions characterize this approach: 1) the socio-political values of the two sides are scarcely distinguishable; 2) neither party can be regarded as either aggressor or defender; 3) both sides are equally right, equally wrong, or equally responsible for tension; 4) both sides' behavior originates in similar thought processes; and 5) the reduction of image distortion can be accomplished with equal ease on both sides. It is clear from Booth's account, however, that the primary danger in the link between national culture on the one hand and the international perceptions, policies, and behavior of a state on the other, stems from the "ethnocentrist thrust"—the disproportionate and consequently adverse impact of one's own culture on an international Weltanschauung.[31d]

We conclude this chapter with one final examination of the linkage between national culture and foreign policy making. Fritz Gaenslen carried out a content analysis of literature which seeks to explain general decision-making processes in China, Japan, Russia and the United States on the basis of cultural explanations. For Gaenslen, *cultural explanations* "account for differences in human behavior by reference to differences in the enduring, internal dispositions of individuals," although currently they do not represent a prominent method in mainstream political science. Structural explanations, a more popular approach, are grounded in differences in the structure of rewards and punishments of a given society. If the first type emphasizes how human beings are less malleable than is generally assumed, the second suggests that simply shifting the structure of rewards and punishments can produce malleability in individuals. By analyzing one thousand interpersonal disagreements depicted in contemporary Chinese, Japanese, Soviet Russian and American fiction, the author sought to demonstrate differences in decision-making procedures that, in turn, had important implications for foreign policy making.

Gaenslen concluded that the first three cultures (regardless of how highly differentiated they are) produce a fundamentally dissimilar type of decision-making process from the American. Generally the behavior of participants in decision making in the non-American cultures was more contingent on interpersonal relationships than that of Americans. Following from this, "given the slightest hint of intransigence or exploitation on the part of a fellow countryman, Chinese, Japanese, and Russians will be more likely than Americans to overreact with vengeance; and, given the slightest hint of goodwill, Chinese, Japanese, and Russians will be more likely to overreact with cooperation." The author sees this as evidence that participants from the three non-American cultures are "collectivists" who highly esteem interpersonal orientation, while American participants are "individualists" who score low on interpersonal orientation.

Differences between Americans and all others are discovered in the roles played by superiors and subordinates in the respective decision-making processes. Superiors in the non-American cultures stressed the importance of peer input, not that of subordinates; they saw the process as enhancing their own legitimacy in the eyes of subordinates; they preferred secretive methods; they cloaked goals in myth, ritual and ideology; and they sought to monitor and control subordinates closely. By contrast, American participants displayed precisely the opposite tendencies. With regard to the roles of subordinates, those in non-American cultures sought to push responsibility onto superiors; they generally searched for unanimity in making recommendations, and they were more reluctant than American subordinates to participate in the decision-making process in the first place. Again United States counterparts displayed opposite tendencies. In sum, "other things being equal, the advantage of superiors over subordinates is likely to be greater for Chinese, Japanese, and Russians than for Americans; because of different cultural assumptions, Chinese, Japanese, and Russian superiors are likely to have at their disposal a resource not possessed to the same degree by their American counterparts."[32]

For our purposes we need not inquire into the data base, methodology, or generalizations (which appear to suffer from the ethnocentrism Booth described) found in Gaenslen's work. Nor should we be concerned with the dubious linkages established among cultural traits, decision-making processes, and foreign policy making. What is important to learn from such research is the raison d'être for carrying it out at all. The author advanced a humanistic reason for paying attention to seemingly insignificant cultural differences: "if such differences exist, we should try to document them. If we fail to do so because no agreed-upon method for identifying cultural attributes exists, or because it is difficult to make cultural explanations convincing, we yield to mere convenience. Such convenience comes at the cost of adopting a theoretical position in which one assumes 1) that societies do not have a cultural aspect, or 2) that culture has *no* consequence for behavioral variables, or 3) that different cultures have the *same* consequences for these variables."[33]

This is the theoretical position we adopt in chapter 3 where we link Latin American culture with international state behavior, and in chapters 4 to 6 where we consider six country studies from the circum-Caribbean region. We have seen how scholars have recognized the influence—albeit not always explicitly nor in any systematized way—of the mix of factors making up a national political culture and a country's international relations. While there has been general consensus that cultural differences in political and social spheres need to be documented, however imperceptible they appear to be, specification of methodologies and conceptualizations has never proved as alluring an enterprise as the substantive one of empirically discovering differences.

Figure 1.3 seeks to synthesize and systematize the main factors discussed in this section. It outlines the process that begins with the defining of an ideal-type political culture that is intended to mold the national modal political culture. This latter culture—consisting of the attitudes, values, and political behavior of all segments of society—is in practice heavily dependent on the "supraculture" formed by the political class in the given society and, to a lesser extent, by certain political subcultures (such as those in existence in the capital city, in the universities, or among *indigenas*). The national culture, in turn, affects the structures and procedural norms of power—leadership, bureaucracy, decision processes—that produce foreign policy outcomes. The paradigm offers a simple chain of influence that affects a country's international politics and posits no causal relationships. It is helpful in establishing the elusive link between political culture and foreign policy. Let us now examine the chief characteristics of Latin American political culture.

FIGURE 1.3

A Process Paradigm of Political Culture and International Relations

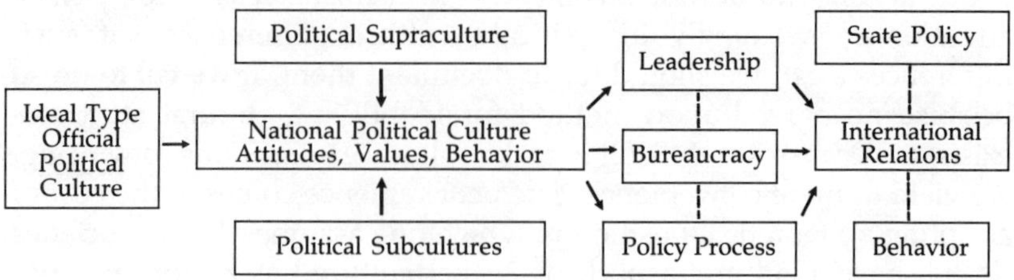

Notes

1. Peter H. Smith, "Political History in the 1980s: A View from Latin America," in Theodore K. Rabb and Robert I. Rotberg (eds.), *The New History: The 1980s and Beyond.* Princeton: Princeton University Press, 1982, p. 6.

2. Robert C. Tucker, *Political Culture and Leadership in Soviet Russia.* New York: W.W. Norton, 1987, p. 3.

3. Howard J. Wiarda, "Political Culture and National Development," *Fletcher Forum of World Affairs*, 13, no. 2 (Summer 1989), p. 199. The recent political culture literature includes: Samuel P. Huntington, "Will More Countries Become Democratic?" *Political Science Quarterly*, 99 (1984), pp. 193–218. Harry Eckstein, "A Culturalist Theory of Political Change," *American Political Science Review*, 82

(September 1988), pp. 789–804. Lucian Pye, *The Mandarin and the Cadre: China's Political Cultures*. Ann Arbor, MI: University of Michigan Center for Chinese Studies, 1988. Probably the most productive and, at the same time, most innovative scholarship on political culture has been carried out by Aaron Wildavsky. See his "Choosing Preferences by Constructing Institutions: A Cultural Theory of Preference Formation," *American Political Science Review*, 81 (March 1987), pp. 3–21. Richard Ellis and Aaron Wildavsky, *Dilemmas of Presidential Leadership*. New Brunswick, NJ: Transaction Publishers, 1989. Michael Thompson, Richard Ellis, Aaron Wildavsky, *Cultural Theory*. Boulder, CO: Westview Press, 1990. One of the authors of the present book participated in the NEH Summer Seminar on Poltical Culture directed by Wildavsky at the University of California, Berkeley, during summer 1989. For one possible critique of cultural theory, see Raymond Taras, "Cultural Theory, Collective Mentality, and Conflicting Ways of Life Under Socialism: When Fatalists Become Something Else," unpublished paper presented at the NEH Seminar, summer 1989. In particular, the problem of "conversion" from one way of life (culture) to another does not appear to be fully addressed by cultural theory. On the other hand, this important longtitudinal issue is also not fully debated in the present study of Latin America.

4. Sidney Verba, "Comparative Political Culture," in Lucian W. Pye and Sidney Verba (eds.), *Political Culture and Political Development*. Princeton: Princeton University Press, 1965, p. 513. For an overview of the early debate on the concept, see Dennis Kavanagh, *Political Culture*. London: Macmillan, 1972.

5. Gabriel A. Almond and Sidney Verba, *The Civic Culture: Political Attitudes and Democracy in Five Nations*. Princeton: Princeton University Press, 1963, p. 13.

6. Archie Brown and Jack Gray (eds.), *Political Culture and Political Change in Communist States*. London: Macmillan, 1979, pp. 10, 253.

7. Archie Brown (ed.), *Political Culture and Communist Studies*. Armonk, NY: M.E. Sharpe, 1985, pp. 154–155. The author admitted that his understanding of political culture represented a minority position in this volume of essays. But for a similar approach to Brown's, see Zvi Gitleman, "Soviet Political Culture: Insights from Jewish Emigres," *Soviet Studies*, 29, no. 4 (October 1977), pp. 543–564.

8. Samuel P. Huntington and Jorge I. Domínquez, "Political Development," in Fred I. Greenstein and Nelson W. Polsby (eds.), *Handbook of Political Science, vol. III: Macropolitical Theory*. Reading, MA: Addison-Wesley, 1975, p. 15.

9. Rober C. Tucker, "Culture, Political Culture, and Communist Society," *Political Science Quarterly*, 88, no. 2 (June 1973), p. 182.

10. Stephen White, *Political Culture and Soviet Politics*. London: Macmillan, 1979, p. 1.

11. David W. Paul, *The Cultural Limits of Revolutionary Politics: Change and Continuity in Socialist Czechoslovakia.* Boulder, CO: East European Quarterly, 1979, p. 3.

12. Richard R. Fagen, *The Transformation of Political Culture in Cuba.* Stanford: Stanford University Press, 1969, pp. 5–6, 157.

13. Wiarda, "Political Culture and National Development," p. 198. For more on the impact of corporatism on Latin American political culture, see Wiarda, *Corporatism and National Development in Latin America.* Boulder, CO: Westview Press, 1981. Also, Mitchell A. Seligson, "Political Culture and Democratization in Latin America," in James Malloy and Eduardo Gamarra (eds.), *Latin America and Caribbean Contemporary Record*, vol. 7. New York: Holmes and Meier, 1989.

14. Wiarda, "Political Culture and National Development," pp. 197–198.

15. Frank Parkin, *Class Inequality and Political Order.* London: Macgibbon and Kee, 1971, p. 82.

16. John P. Gillin, "Some Signposts for Policy," in Richard Adams et al., *Social Change in Latin America Today.* New York: Harper and Row, 1969, pp. 24–28.

17. William T. Bluhm, "Casual Theory in Thucydides' *Peloponnesian War*," *Political Studies*, 9 (February 1962), p. 25.

18. Bluhm, p. 33. See also his other propositions summarizing Thucydides' comparative psychological analysis.

19. Tacitus, *On Britain and Germany.* Baltimore: Penguin, 1948, pp. 112–113.

20. Carl von Clausewitz, *On War.* Princeton: Princeton University Press, 1984, pp. 220, 375; our italics.

21. Hans J. Morgenthau, *Politics Among Nations: The Struggle for Power and Peace.* New York: Alfred Knopf, 1964, p. 126.

22. Quincy Wright, *The Study of War.* Chicago: University of Chicago Press, 1965.

23. See the Correlates of War series, in particular, Melvin Small and J. David Singer, *Resort to Arms.* Beverly Hills: Sage Publications, 1982. For data on the lack of a relationship, see R.T. Green and G. Santori, "A Cross Cultural Study of Hostility and Aggression," *Journal of Peace Research*, 1 (1969).

24. Kenneth N. Waltz, *Man, the State and War.* New York: Columbia University Press, 1959. Chapter IV. Waltz's "first image" of international relations located the cause of war in the nature and behavior of human beings, while the "third image" centered on how the interstate system encouraged or discouraged aggression.

25. For a discussion of this topic, see the special issue, "Foreign Policy in Federal States," *International Journal*, XLI, no. 3 (Summer 1986).

25a. Henry A. Kissinger, "Domestic Structure and Foreign Policy," in *American Foreign Policy*. New York: W.W. Norton, 1977. 3rd edn., p. 25.

25b. Kissinger. "Domestic Structure and Foreign Policy." p. 23.

26. Alberto van Klaveren, "The Analysis of Latin American Foreign Policies: Theoretical Perspectives," in Heraldo Muñoz and Joseph S. Tulchin (eds.), *Latin American Nations in World Politics*. Boulder, CO: Westview Press, 1984, p. 14.

27. Kissinger, "Domestic Structure and Foreign Policy," p. 25.

28. Kissinger, "Domestic Structure and Foreign Policy," p. 25.

29. Adda B. Bozeman, "Statecraft and Intelligence in the Non-Western World," *Conflict*, 6, no. 1 (1985), pp. 13, 17–21, 25–26.

30. Gerald Segal, "Strategy and 'Ethnic Chic,' " *International Affairs*, 60, no. 1 (Winter 1983–84), pp. 15–30.

31. Ken Booth, *Strategy and Ethnocentrism*. New York: Holmes and Meier, 1979, p. 22.

31a. Booth, *Strategy and Ethnocentrism*, p. 29.

31b. Booth, *Strategy and Ethnocentrism*, pp. 79, 74.

31c. Booth, *Strategy and Ethnocentrism*, p. 144.

31d. Booth, *Strategy and Ethnocentrism*, p. 176. For more on "mirror-image theory," see James E. Dougherty and Robert L. Pfaltzgraff, *Contending Theories of International Relations*. Philadelphia: J.B. Lippincott, 1971, p. 226.

32. Fritz Gaenslen, "Culture and Decision Making in China, Japan, Russia, and the United States," *World Politics*, 39, no. 1 (October 1986), p. 95.

33. Gaenslen, "Culture and Decision Making," pp. 81, 95, 99, 102.

2

Latin American Political Culture

Political culture consists of the values, attitudes, and behavior of a nation in the political arena. Its influence on a country's foreign policy is generally recognized, though seldom carefully measured. In this chapter, we describe the main features of Latin America's political culture, and in chapter 3 we link these features to the international politics of the region.

The Dominant Value System

Latin America is what Louis Hartz calls a "fragment culture,"[1] that is, it is an offshoot of its Iberian mother culture. As such, certain characteristics of the late fifteeth- and early sixteenth-century political culture of Iberia were brought to the New World where they were implanted in virgin soil and subsequently flourished to a greater degree than they did in the mother country. Thus, as a generalization, it might be said that contemporary Spanish America is "more Hispanic" than is contemporary Spain. Howard Wiarda has made the point that the major movements that produced modern Western culture—the Reformation, Industrial Revolution, Enlightenment and the democratic revolutions of the eighteenth century—largely bypassed the Iberian world.[2] It is probably also accurate to add that during the twentieth century Spain (and to a lesser degree Portugal) has been more influenced by these movements emanating from the rest of Western Europe—particularly the scientific and industrial revolutions—than has Latin America. The impact of Protestantism, industrialization, and science in the latter area has largely been a post-World War II phenomenon.

What were the specific cultural traits that the Spanish conquerors brought to the New World "fragment" that embedded themselves so completely in the political life of the nations of the region?[3] In brief they were hierarchy, authoritarianism, patrimonialism, corporativism, political monism and paradoxically, political rebelliousness and resistance to authority. These cultural traits have taken different forms during different historical periods and under different socio-economic circumstances. However, in spite of massive social, economic and political change, they have proved remarkably durable, as we seek to demonstrate in this study.

To understand the nature of the political culture so strongly implanted in Latin America, one has to understand the character of the Conquest itself. What Latin Americans have called *La Conquista* was really a continuation of *La Reconquista*, only carried on in overseas areas ranging from Buenos Aires to Manila Bay, and from northern California to Tierra del Fuego. The political and military patterns utilized to effect the reconquest of the Iberian peninsula were simply transported, after the defeat of the last Moorish stronghold of Granada in 1492, to the New World as a means of achieving new conquests.

During the *Reconquista* two contradictory patterns of political organization were utilized by Spain to achieve its objectives: 1) a policy of local self-rule and decentralized military organization on the advancing frontier; and 2) a policy of centralization and monocratic rule in territories firmly under the control of the crown. Thus, two competing cultural strains arose in the Spanish empire concurrently: a culture of political centralization and authoritarianism so ably documented by Claudio Veliz, and a culture of decentralization and resistance to authority.[4] The first was the political culture of Madrid, the second the political culture of the frontier. The first was essentially Thomistic and organicist, stressing the values of order, stability and hierarchy.[5] The second was essentially localist and stressed the use of various stratagems to avoid control from Madrid as much as possible.[6]

The political values of the crown and the central authorities of Madrid were, theoretically at least, based on the political philosophy of St. Thomas Aquinas. Very briefly, for the Spanish Thomist the good society was the well-ordered, hierarchical society made up of governmentally sanctioned social constituents, each playing its proper function in an organically integrated society. The end of social order was the achievement of the common good (*bien común*)[7] as defined by the theologians and moral philosophers of the day and legislated and administered by a social and governmental elite. The means of attaining that end, according to Louisa S. Hoberman, was the creation of a hierarchically organized polity that encouraged complementarity rather than competition, and sought order and balance.[8]

To achieve order and balance, a complex system of social and political institutions was envisioned, designed to reflect the traditional Hispanic principles of governance: political monism, organicism, legal idealism and patrimonialism. Political monism was reflected in the hierarchical structure of the polity and its excessive bureaucratization. At the apex of the social and governmental order was the monarch who, with the guidance and assistance of the governing elite which held seats on the various royal councils and advisory bodies, was the chief guardian of the order and common good of the society. As such, he was above the positive law (*ley*), but subject to the higher or natural law (*derecho*) as discovered by the theologians and moral philosophers.[9] Below the peninsular elite and presiding over the affairs of the colonies was a highly structured bureaucracy which, formally at least, had a strong directive and interventionist role in the colonies. Social, economic, religious, and political affairs were extensively regulated by centrally and minutely drafted rules and regulations.

Political monism was reinforced by legal idealism which, in contrast to the Germanic tradition which stressed custom and the law of the folk, emphasized the ideal and the universal.

> Spanish legal theory stressed the abstract concept of justice rather than the preservation of custom or tradition; it sought to institutionalize abstract ethical goals rather than pragmatic possibilities. It sought to create 'an earthly *sumum bonum*' rather than a '*plurum bonum*' intrinsic to the Protestant tradition. In this tradition, law, of necessity, flows from above. It is to reflect the correct principles of social and political organization as determined by philosophers and theologians. It is the duty of the monarch to determine, on the basis of these principles, the law of the land. The Crown (and later, the state) is the law-giver, not the people.[10]

Organicism was reflected in the recognition and protection of certain powerful corporative groups such as the church, the military, the craft and commercial guilds, the landed estates, and the Indian communities. These organizations were charged both with controlling the activities of their members and with defending their interests before the organs of the state. As such they performed both a governing role and a restraining role on the government.

The potential rigidities of organicism and bureaucracy were counterbalanced to a considerable extent by patrimonialism under which functionaries of the colonial bureaucracy were considered to be under the monarch's personal authority. Flexibility was achieved by the creation of overlapping jurisdictions, by issuing ordinances that could later be rescinded, and by the exercise of the moderating power. As Moreno writes,

> The operational outgrowth of the royal moderating function was the introduction into the system of an apparent element of flexibility. If a tribunal of justice, or an administrative council, or the monarch himself took an action that adversely affected someone, the affected party could always appeal, in the name of ethical principles, for redress to the king in his moderating capacity. . . . Although the monarch held absolute political authority, his claim to it was supported by his commitment to allow challenges to its use that he, the monarch, would hear and rule upon.[11]

The Hispanic tradition of political monism, organicism, legal idealism, and patrimonialism has forged the dominant political value system of Latin America. This value system, which Glen Dealy has termed "monistic democracy,"[12] stresses order, stability, leadership by elites (whether ideological, economic or military), fear of competition, abstract planning, and constant attempts—albeit often abortive ones—to create the good society from the top by governmental fiat.

There was also, to use Richard Morse's suggestive terminology, a "Machiavellian" side to the Thomistic vision—a rebellious, localist, lawless side to the Hispanic concept of governance.[13] This resulted from a number of factors emanating both from the nature of Hispanic Thomism and from the nature of the Conquest. First of all, Thomism postulated the right of revolution if the government did not act on behalf of the common good. And how was it possible for any group of decision makers located in Madrid always to determine the "common good" of an empire so far flung and economically and ethnically diverse as the Spanish dominions of the sixteenth and seventeenth centuries when speed of communication was measured in weeks and months?

Local resistance to authority—even rebellion—became the political way of life in much of the empire. Thus, although the Spanish imperial system was formally centralized and bureaucratized, functionally it was highly decentralized and loosely governed. C. Hubert Haring has argued that the Spanish imperial government was one of checks and balances, not secured primarily by a rigid and clearcut separation of power, but by "a division of authority among different individuals and tribunals exercising the same powers."[14] Thus the two contradictory and paradoxical political traditions of Latin America grew up side by side: the authoritarian, bureaucratic and monistic tradition so well described by Claudio Veliz and Glenn Dealy; and the decentralized, rebellious, "power contender" tradition described by such writers as Haring, Robert Scott and Charles Anderson.[15]

These two traditions, although varying in form and content in different periods, have vied for dominance throughout the one hundred seventy five years of Latin American independence. The past fifty years have seen Latin America "fragmented" by competing political monisms—Marxism, developmentalism, Peronism, falangism, etc.—which begin their political life as Machiavellian movements of disorder and rebellion (often in the name of pluralism) only to impose an authoritarian, hierarchically structured monistic system upon their societies when they come to power. Political monism in Latin America, therefore, has both its Machiavellian and Thomistic manifestations.

FIGURE 2.1

The Two Faces of Hispanic Political Monism

The Thomistic Face	The Machiavellian Face
Search for the *bien comun*	Ideological rigidity
Unity	Rebellion
Hierarchy	Bureaucratic authoritarianism/ reactionary despotism
Organicism	Power contenders
Legal idealism	Resistance to law (*Obedezco pero no cumplo*)
Patrimonialism	Clientalism
Centralism	Excessive red tape (*Papeleo*)

Figure 2.1 attempts to present a schematic comparison of their most salient features. Standing alongside the two monistic traditions is a third—pluralistic democracy.[16] Although its roots go back to the democratic revolutions of the eighteenth century, until the last forty years it functioned primarily as an abstract intellectual ideal (whatever the formalistic borrowings of American, French and British institutions) and, with a few exceptions, never penetrated deeply into the Latin American political culture. However, since the end of World War II it has increasingly been able to mount a serious challenge to the dominant monistic tradition. The extent to which one can talk about a "democratic culture" taking root in such countries as Venezuela and Colombia, as opposed to simply the emergence of specific and often short-lived democratic regimes in countries like Argentina, Brazil, Peru or Guatemala, is hard to determine with certainty. However, the democratic tradition of peaceful electoral competition between ideological or programmatic

parties, loyal opposition, incremental decision-making reflecting bargaining and compromise, peaceful interplay between the governmental and/or societal institutions, and the subjection of the executive to the rule of law remain the weaker, less developed aspects of the Latin American political culture. In fact, Howard Wiarda has elaborated a Latin American model of democracy which seeks to capture the peculiar "Rousseauan" characteristics of the Latin American democratic tradition as it has evolved under the sway of the more dominant monistic tradition.[17]

FIGURE 2.2

The Third Face of Hispanic Political Monism

The Thomistic Face	The Latin Democratic Face
Search for the *bien comun*	* Limitations on political and human rights when required for the common good
Unity	National Front Agreements and other power-sharing arrangements
Hierarchy	Presidential dominance; subordinate legislature and courts
Organicism	* Guaranteed representation through state-recognized associations or corporative groups
Legal idealism	Ideological political parties and movements
Patrimonialism	* Clientalistic relationship between state and masses guaranteeing minimum welfare
Centralism	* Authoritarian (but not totalitarian) president/subordinate legislature

* Adapted from model presented in Howard Wiarda, "Democracy and Human Rights in Latin America: Toward a New Conceptualization," *Orbis* (Spring 1978), pp. 149–156.

Figure 2.2 attempts schematically to relate the pluralistic-democratic equivalents in Latin American culture to the Thomistic value system. With the political and military collapse of the Spanish empire in the decade between 1810 and 1821, the Thomistic base of the Latin American political culture—particularly its monarchical and bureaucratic structures—was destroyed. Most Spanish administrators and other *peninsular* elites returned to the mother country with their traditional authority, governing expertise, and economic capital, leaving the colonies largely in the hands of the military commanders of the independence movement, the *criollo* politicians, and the local and provincial leaders of the various corporative groups—the church, the landowners, artisan *gremios*, and commercial *consulados*. These social sectors, which at one time had been held together, at least formally and to a limited degree psychologically, by the imperial governmental structures, largely disintegrated into warring political factions. It is out of this socio-political environment that the *caudillo* emerged. As William Beezley writes,

> To unite the warring elements and to preserve society from anarchy on the local and national levels called for a strong man who could stand above the quarrels, attract the loyalty of the people, and crush his opposition. To maintain this type of power a person needed to control the military as well as the administrative, legislative, and judicial branches of government. The colonial period had provided a convenient heritage of just such a consolidation of authority in one person. The stage was set for the caudillo, a man who could remain aloof from the controversy among ideologies and institutions.[18]

Caudillismo represented the monistic tradition in a post-colonial setting. Although often regionally rather than nationally based, the *caudillo* was, in effect, a substitute monarch whose legitimacy was based on charisma rather than tradition. Even the ideological liberals who led the rebellion against Spain and who theoretically espoused democracy largely governed through personalistic *caudillos* rather than through well-established republican institutions. *Caudillismo* was also a reflection at the regional and national level of the patron-client relationship which had evolved in the countryside during and after Spanish colonial rule.[19]

The conservative *caudillos* of the first half of the nineteeth century, while building their personal power largely on clientalism, often sought to strengthen the traditional Hispanic corporative institutions—particularly the church, the Indian community, and the hacienda—which were seen as major buttresses of the traditional order.[20]

The period of oligarchic republics (roughly from 1865 to 1916) was formally republican in organization, although somewhat less corporative than the conservative period which preceeded it and was marked by intense elite factionalism. This "oligarchic" period largely perpetuated the major features of post-independence Hispanic socio-political monism: rigid social stratification, special privileges for certain sectors and groups (particularly the church, the landowners, and the military), rule by personalist liberal *caudillos* (such as Justo Rufino Barrios, José Santos Zelaya, Bartolomé Mitre, and Benito Juárez), and an ideology to take the place of sixteenth-century Thomism, namely, positivism.

In some respects the populist period that followed the oligarchic republics (roughly 1916 to 1964) represented a break with the monistic tradition. Brought into being as a result of economic modernization and urbanization by the growing middle classes, Latin American populism was oriented, in theory at least, toward constitutionalism and greater political and economic participation—at least for the urban middle sectors. These were, in Guillermo O'Donnell's terms, "inclusionary regimes."[21]

However, populism, while enjoying some early successes in redistributing income and opening up new avenues for social mobility, ultimately failed to alter Latin America's hierarchical society; and lower-class mobilization was largely managed by clientalist and corporative techniques.[22] And who could deny that the major populist leaders were either personalistic (Vargas, Perón, Arbenz) or party (Yrigoyen, Figueres, Cardenas, Kubitschek) *caudillos*?

Three additional types of regimes, following generally on the heels of populism, constitute our final examples of the monistic tradition. Bureaucratic authoritarianism represents military monism in the name of *desarrollista* ideology. Governed from the top by a single military figure (except for Uruguay) and usually assisted by a military council, these "exclusionary regimes" were obviously bureaucratic in their approach to governance, socially and economically elitist, and at times corporative. Similarly, the type of regime Enrique Baloyra calls "reactionary despotism" was structured in very much the same way, except that they sought to implement the agro-export model rather than deepening industrialization.[23] Finally, the Marxist or popular revolutionary regimes are clearly marked by their bureaucratic rule, elitism, general lack of competition and, in the case of Nicaragua from 1979 to 1984, very clear corporatism.

The Machiavellian monistic tradition has probably received less attention than the Thomistic variety. Suffice it to say that most of the revolutionary moments, ranging from the 26th of July Movement, the

Sandinistas, and the FMLN on the left to the Argentine Anticommunist Alliance, the Guatemalan *Mano Blanca*, and the Salvadoran *ORDEN* on the right, have had as their goal the imposition of a monistic regime on their respective societies based on some kind of utopian vision or ideology. The forced conversion of the masses did not cease with the demise of the Spanish empire.

In summary, the dominant value system of Latin America has been, and continues to be, what has been called political monism—a constant search for a harmonious, non-competitive social blueprint that can be imposed from the top. However, any monistic system, because of its resistance to political competition, differences of opinion, and thus to change, tends to be brittle and thus subject to fragmentation, disintegration, and collapse. This gives rise to certain behavioral patterns which in some ways constitute separate political cultural sub-traditions in their own right. The first is a powerful insurrectionary tradition that sees violence as the only way of bringing down an entrenched monistic regime where the electoral alternative is not available. However, the challenging groups usually seek to impose an alternative monistic vision of their own. Latin American political life, thus, has tended to oscillate, as Richard Morse suggests, between periods of Thomism and Machiavellianism.[24]

This has stimulated a second behavioral tendency, namely, an amazing institutional inventiveness in the area, as Latin American political elites have sought to control the oscillation. However, most of the institutional creativity has been of a monistic nature, ranging from political territorial monopoly arrangements (Uruguay) to quasi-hegemonic party systems (Mexico, Nicaragua) to power-sharing agreements (Colombia). In some cases, institutional experimentation has been used to consolidate domocracy: the weak presidential system of Costa Rica, the collegial executive of Uruguay, and the National Front Agreement in Colombia after 1972.

The third pattern is the use of the "democratic interlude" to resolve a political impasse. Pluralistic democracy is often accepted by the antagonistic forces of Latin American societies as a kind of middle ground between the excesses of extreme monism (bureaucratic authoritarianism, for example) on the one hand, and insurrectionary chaos on the other. Although compromise, bargaining, delay, and acceptance of the politically possible rather than the ideal is not generally satisfactory to many groups, it is often seen as necessary to reducing violence, obtaining foreign aid, or getting rid of a tyrannical regime. The military also often accepts the democratic opening as a means of retiring from the responsibilities of social and economic management.

The search for a democratic interlude explains why democracy seems to come in "waves" and after reaching a high point on the political shore recedes back into the ocean of Latin American history, once again leaving the people on the land the task of deciding which monistic group or movement they will follow. A summary of these national political cultural traditions appears in figure 2.3.

FIGURE 2.3

Latin American Political Culture Patterns During the Last Half Century

Stable Monism	Alternating Monisms	Altern. Monisms w/Dem. Interludes	Democratic Tradition w/Mon. Interludes	Stable Democracy
Mexico	Nicaragua	Argentina	Chile	
Paraguay		Bolivia	Colombia (to 1972)	Colombia (from 1972)
		Brazil	Costa Rica (to 1948)	Costa Rica (from 1948)
Cuba (from 1959)		Cuba (to 1959)	Uruguay	
		Dominican Republic		
		Ecuador		
		El Salvador		
		Guatemala		
		Honduras		
		Panama		
		Peru		
		Venezuela (to 1957)		Venzuela (from 1957)

The Class-based Political Subcultures

Within the dominant political value system of Latin America it is possible to identify a number of class-based or sectoral constellations of political attitudes and behavioral patterns. Since the turn of the century, the middle classes probably have been the most active, if not always the most powerful, political sector in Latin America. This derives largely from the tremendous surge in urbanization and the resulting rise of populist movements in the region. A number of writers have sought to capture the essential character of the political culture of this sector. Social anthropologist John Gillin, writing in 1960, identified ten "middle segment values" which he believed were barriers to modernization and development: personalism, machismo, dignity, familism, hierarchy, patronalism, tangible materialism, transcendental values (*Arielismo*), emotion as the fulfillment of self, and fatalism.[25] Similarly, Glen Dealy, in his model of Catholic or *"caudillaje* man" (which he extends to a wider range of countries outside of Latin America), uses slightly different terms and comes up with a shorter list of traits, but they largely encompass the same attitudes and behavior patterns identified by Gillin. In Catholic or *caudillaje* culture the dominant value is power, in the same way that in Protestant or capitalistic culture it is wealth.

> Catholic man pursues public power the way Protestant man strives for private wealth. In the one context there is a political referent for life's activities, in the other an economic referent. Both world views generate extremely rational worldly activity. One might ask, for example, what are the functional equivalents within caudillaje society for capitalist man's economic virtues of hard work, frugality, and reinvestment of capital? Immediately come to mind the virtues of leisure, ostentation, and instant gratification through the spending of one's capital. . . . [I]n the case of caudillaje man certain agreed-upon, essentially public or political virtues are demanded; for capitalist man, certain agreed-upon economic virtues emerge. Both fulfill the function of personal self-realization. And each carries its own 'signs' or 'indicators' of individual excellence which are readily recognizable.[26]

To achieve power, *caudillaje* man requires a cohort of associates and supporters. "The common man of caudillaje society knows that power depends upon friendship, that there are certain means of acquiring, holding and losing friendship, and that without it one is lost." What are these means of pursuing power through friendship? They are dignity, generosity, manliness, grandeur, and leisure.[27]

The *caudillo* as a political type emerged, as Richard Morse, William Beezley, Marvin Goldwert, and others have suggested, from the breakdown of the colonial "Thomistic Synthesis."[28] *Caudillaje* man, as a personality type, has its roots in historic *caudillismo*, but is perpetuated by the fact that contemporary political monism is inherently unstable and subject to disintegration, and *caudillaje* personality traits have particular "survival value" under such conditions. Thus, Latin America's dominant political value system—the search for a monistic synthesis—gives rise by its very nature to the *caudillaje* personality, particularly among the middle sectors which are the most highly activist politically.

Charles Anderson provides us with an operational picture of *caudillaje* man in his study of Central American political parties during the high point of middle-class populism in that region. He argued that the "Central American political party is the instrument through which the middle sectors strive to attain a power capability which will be recognized by other contenders in the political process, thereby winning for them admission to the arena in which the power structure is determined by manipulation among those possessing important power capabilities."[29] Political parties are particularly useful instruments for the middle classes, because they are the ones which have the "ability to manipulate the personal and institutional relations of a complex society."[30]

As the unique political instruments of the middle classes, parties serve a number of purposes: 1) to create programs and public services of particular interest to the middle sectors; 2) to provide their adherents with an opportunity to play an "heroic role" in the nation's life; 3) to provide an opportunity to display *dignidad* and "individualism"; and 4) "to seek identity through a political cause." Central American political parties also served, he argued, as job-getting and service-providing agencies.[31] As John Duncan Powell has suggested, with the surge of industrialization and urbanization in Latin America, clientalism was transferred from the hacienda to the government and other institutions of modern life.[32]

In summary, the *caudillaje* personality type is a reflection of the Machiavellian face of Hispanic monism. The basic Latin American political value system inherited from Hispanic Thomism remains the norm. However, because during and after the Independence Movement the centrifugal, localist and nuclear forces became dominant, the once-"recessive" Machiavellian traits producing *caudillaje* man became the dominant operative political behavior pattern—but usually in the name of and in search of the *bien comun*.

The Upper Sector Variant

The political culture of the Latin American upper class shares many attitudes and behavior patterns with the middle class. However, there are also a number of differences. First, because the upper sectors have, until relatively recently, been more secure in their social and economic status, they have been less politicized. Relying primarily on their personal contacts with other members of the elite, they have not felt the necessity of engaging in overt political activity as a means of achieving upward mobility or obtaining public or personal objectives. Rather than becoming highly active in political parties, upper sector interest groups have been the primary instruments of their political involvement. Because their social status has been secure, they have generally not needed public acclaim as the "indicator of excellence."

Second, the upper class is inclined to be familistic. Great attention is directed toward family activities and the enhancement of the family's holdings and general well-being. Thus, the elite remains largely uninterested in civic affairs broadly defined unless their interests are directly affected.

Third, the Latin American upper classes tend to be cosmopolitan rather than nationalistic. It is not uncommon for members of the elite to shop in Miami, vacation in Barcelona, study in Paris and bank in Switzerland. Thus, they are likely to be more conversant with the problems of the world (for example, the unstable international value of the dollar) than with the problems of their own countries. Because of their lack of politicization generally and their cosmopolitanism, the upper classes have looked to client groups to shelter them from the direct effects of lower-class mobilization. The client might be a political party, a personal dictator, a sympathetic state agency or ministry, the military, or, if all else fails, a "hit squad."

Fourth, the upper sectors have tended to be ambivalent on the role of government. Although they are disposed toward the belief that private enterprise makes a greater contribution to the well-being of their societies and that government, with its inefficiency and corruption, imposes a heavy burden, government is nevertheless viewed as performing a number of important functions. First, it is seen as serving as a buffer between the elite and the masses. A minimal welfare program, for example, is seen as a necessary concession to the needs and demands of the growing urban lower sector. Second, upper sector business groups look to government for subsidies, exchange rate concessions, and relief from import fees and other forms of taxation. Third, government is expected to provide at least some protection from world economic competition.

The behavior described above may have been moderated somewhat by the growing insurrectionary threat and the increased mobilization of the masses. Upper sector groups, particularly in Central America, have been drawn increasingly into partisan political activity. Personalities like Salvadoran businessman Alvaro Magana and the

Nicaraguan cooking oil magnate turned contra leader, Alfonso Robelo, might be considered typical of the *caudillaje* personality type drawn into politics from the business class.

The Peasant Variant

We have seen that the Latin American political culture tends to politicize the middle classes by providing them with a set of values through which its members are motivated to utilize the political system to achieve social and economic mobility while, at the same time, depoliticizing the upper classes by providing familistic and cosmopolitan norms. In the case of the Latin American peasant, the *caudillaje* pattern of behavior manifests itself in what might be termed "vicarious politicization" coupled with a low sense of political efficacy. To put it another way, peasants are often extremely interested in politics and can be motivated to engage in intense, even violent, political activity, yet be almost totally uninterested in and disillusioned with government or the prospect of meaningful collective action.

To understand this paradox, it is necessary to become aware of two conflicting elements in the culture of the Latin American peasant. One element is its emphasis on individualism and privatism. The Mexican peasant, Oscar Lewis has written, seeks security in a threatening world through the economic independence of the biological family. Because industry, thrift, and self-reliance are considered to be the highest values, involvement with others is viewed as leading to dependence. Among Mexican peasants the good man is one who minds his own business, takes care of his family, respects the dignity of others, fulfills his obligations, is not frivolous, and avoids quarrels. This same good man, however, is not expected to make a contribution to the welfare of the community. In fact, he demonstrates his good intentions by avoiding contact with others, since any display of interest in personal contact or group participation suggests that he has ulterior motives.[33] In Guatemala, however, the growing Protestantization of that country is breaking down this intense privatization considerably. Experience with congregational church polities coupled with the greater community-mindedness of Protestantism have considerably increased peasant participation in both national and local politics. Furthermore, the insurrectionary threat emanating from the once-passive Indian population motivated the Rios Montt government to attempt to draw them into the political process.

One of the most interesting attempts to build a theory to explain the personality of the Latin American peasant is George Foster's concept of the "limited good." He argues that the peasant perceives all goods, whether they be wealth, friendship, love, masculinity, or power, as existing in limited quantities. Thus, any improvement in the condition of one person can only be had at the expense of others. All of life, in fact, is viewed as a perpetual struggle with one's fellows and the world at large for what one considers to be his share of scarce goods and values. People who achieve more than the norm are a threat requiring corrective action. Those who fall behind are also perceived as a threat because of their supposed "rage" or jealousy. As a consequence the peasant is highly suspicious of others and reserved and guarded in his relationship with them. This reserve not only serves to ward off threatening situations posed by others, it insures that he too will not be perceived as a threat.[34]

The second and contradictory element is clientalism. John Duncan Powell argues that it is the fact that the peasant's world is characterized by "limited goods" and inhabited by people and institutions that have control over those goods that gives rise to the patron-client relationship. Clientalism, he argues, is one of the patterns of social relations (along with various kinship networks and poverty equalization mechanisms) that reduces the peasant's vulnerability to scarcity, calamity, and misfortune. Privatization in horizontal relations is, in effect, offset by the important role of clientalism in vertical ones.[35]

A cultural characteristic that stands in opposition to suspiciousness and reserve, however, is the campesino's love of excitement and action (*movimento*). Thus, he is greatly attracted by the speeches, parades, rivalries, and vendettas that Latin American political life produces. For him politics is primarily a spectator sport, and electoral campaigns are an exciting fiesta to relieve the dreary round of the agricultural year.

Although political efficacy is low, vicarious politicization coupled with economic insecurity can produce a condition of intense partisanship. Winning an election—particularly a local or regional election—means at least two things to the victorious faction. First, it opens up both jobs and business opportunities to the personal followers of the successful office seekers. Second, it enables individuals to achieve symbolic victories over their personal enemies. Insurrectionary movements provide an opportunity for peasants to inflict more serious damage on their enemies.

The Lower Class Variant

It is difficult to be precise about the political culture of the growing population of the lower-class barrios. In some communities migrants appear to establish contacts with kinsmen and fellow townsmen already living in the urban area as a means of cushioning the shock of adjustment to city life. In others, strong clientalistic relationships are developed to serve the same purpose. These social linkages give rise to a sense of community among the migrants from a given region or village.[36] However, in most countries the culture is much more individualistic.

Individualism among the urban lower classes is a logical development in an environment of limited economic opportunities. Whatever his initial contacts, the new arrival is ultimately faced with the task of providing himself with housing, a job, and the minimal amenities of urban life. Since industrialization and economic development have lagged behind the rate of urban growth, these goods are perpetually in short supply. The people of the barrios support themselves in a number of ways. The more fortunate obtain employment in factories and in the building trades; a great many more are forced to "hustle" a day's wage through petty commerce and street vending, domestic service, and odd jobs. In many working-class barrios the front rooms of the dwellings are converted into small stores which sell a miscellany of household goods and consumables. Barrio dwellers are, therefore, forced into competition with one another through sheer economic necessity. This helps to explain the spirit of *desconfianza* or distrust that prevails in many of these neighborhoods. As Louis K. Harris and Victor Alba write:

> Under these circumstances workers and their movement tend to occupy themselves solely with personal matters and show very little interest in politics. Few workers participate in the affairs of political parties, which explains why military coups, even though they tend to be opposed to the immediate interests of the workers, almost never meet active opposition in the form of strikes. Contrary to general opinion, Latin American workers are not revolutionary; rather, they are concerned with their immediate living conditions. If they do lose their passivity and become politically active they tend to become dependent upon personalities and parties rather than assume independent positions.[37]

Enrique Baloyra and John Martz paint essentially the same picture when they state that the Venezuelan lower strata are more cynical, less likely to vote, more anti-communist, less likely to support developmentalism, and less efficacious and capable.[38]

While individualism characterizes social attitudes within his neighborhoods, the barrio dweller seeks one or more patrons in the larger community to assist him in his fight to survive in the city. In his study of a lower-class barrio in Guatemala City, Bryan Roberts reports that the self-employed residents of San Lorenzo are linked in a network that extends to influential merchants and governmental officials who provide credit and markets. Persons of lower socio-economic status seek social contacts with those individuals throughout the city that can provide jobs, housing, loans, and legal counsel. Actually, the population of Barrio San Lorenzo, he states, is not stratified as much by social class as by access to persons of power.[39]

The fact that the people living in the lower-class barrios retain a mutual distrust for each other, plus the fact that they are dependent upon their connections with the sources of political and economic power scattered throughout the larger community, greatly reduces their sense of class consciousness or collective political power. Roberts argues that in a commercially-oriented city like Guatemala City there exist very few opportunities for groups to coalesce in opposition to one another, a condition necessary to produce class or group solidarity.[40] Barrio residents, thus, do not see the solution to their problems in mass organization, in political activism, or in violent confrontation. Rather, they are highly oriented toward achieving incremental changes through individual effort, although often facilitated by someone higher up in the social hierarchy.[41]

We have attempted to describe the political culture of Latin America in terms of a number of components:

1. The dominant value system derived from traditional Hispanic Thomism which we have termed "political monism." These values identified are the norm towards which the various movements and power contenders aspire.
2. Two competing value systems: Machiavellianism which derives its ethos from the desire to create an alternative monism, be it a Marxist, developmentalist, Peronist, or Peruvianist regime; and pluralist democracy, which is largely an Anglo-European import.
3. The *caudillaje* pattern of attitudes and behavior, which is the logical result of the tendency for monistic systems to break down and is a reflection of the Machiavellian value system. This behavior is seen as affecting those espousing the democratic value system as well.
4. The middle-class, upper-class, lower-class, and peasant variants of *caudillaje* culture.

FIGURE 2.4

The Latin American Political Cultural Prism

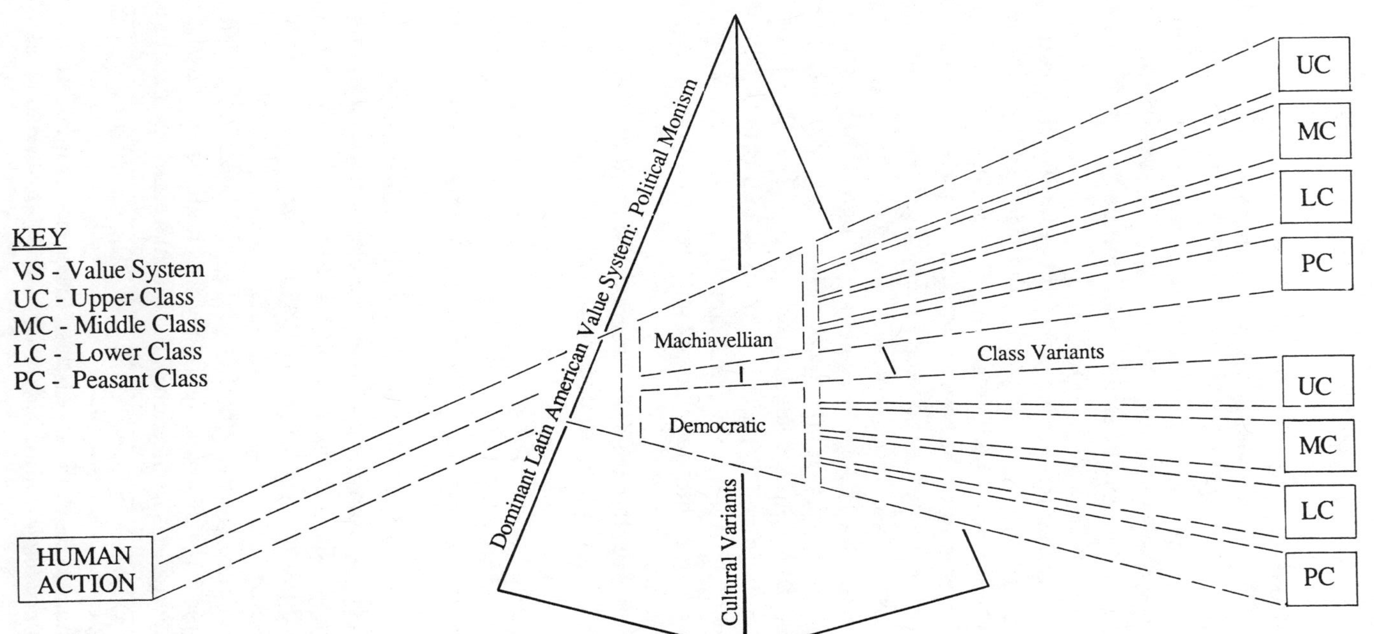

Source: Adapted from Fred W. Riggs, *Administration in Developing Countries: The Theory of Prismatic Society,* 1964, Fig. 1.2

As a means of understanding the interaction between these four components, it is useful to borrow the metaphor of the prism used some years ago by Fred Riggs to describe so-called "transitional societies."[42] Human action becomes "refracted" (or bent) as it comes into contact with various cultural traditions.[43] Figure 2.4 attempts to conceptualize this process in terms of a three-sided prism. From a political culture standpoint, human action is seen as, first of all, conditioned by the dominant value system of political monism; second, refracted once by the degree of Machiavellian or democratic elements coexistent with monism (or in competition with it); and, third, refracted once again by class into the various types of *caudillaje* behavior.[44] It should be remembered, however, that the ultimate goal of *caudillaje* behavior is to create a new monism to be presided over by the victors from among the various power contenders. We now consider what features of the Latin American political culture discussed in this section have the greatest bearing on Latin American foreign policy and international behavior.

Notes

1. Louis Hartz (ed.), *The Founding of New Societies*. New York: Harcourt, Brace and World, 1964, pp. 3–10.

2. Howard Wiarda (ed.), *Politics and Social Change in Latin America: The Distinct Tradition*. Amherst: University of Massachusetts Press, 1974, p. 6.

3. While there are many similarities (and some differences) between the Portuguese and Spanish conquest and colonization of the New World, the emphasis in this chapter is on Spanish America, not Brazil.

4. Claudio Veliz, *The Centralist Tradition in Latin America*. Princeton: Princeton University Press, 1980.

5. See Richard Morse, "The Heritage of Latin America," in Hartz (ed.), *The Founding of New Societies*.

6. For a summary of centralist and decentralist interpretations of Latin American governance, see Roland H. Ebel and James Henderson, "Patterns of Continuity in Latin American Society: Political and Historical Perspectives," *Annals of the Southeastern Conference of Latin American Studies*, VII (March 1976).

7. See Glen Dealy, "The Tradition of Monistic Democracy in Latin America" in Wiarda (ed.), *Politics and Social Change in Latin America*, pp. 80–90.

8. Louisa S. Hoberman, "Hispanic American Political Theory as a Distinct Tradition," *Journal of the History of Ideas*, 41 (April–June 1980), p. 201.

9. For a discussion of *ley* and *derecho,* see Francisco Jose Moreno, *Legitimacy and Stability in Latin America: A Study of Chilean Political Culture.* New York: New York University Press, 1969.

10. Ebel and Henderson, "Patterns of Continuity in Latin American Society," p. 95.

11. Moreno, *Legitimacy and Stability in Latin America,* pp. 31–32.

12. Dealy, "The Tradition of Monistic Democracy in Latin America," pp. 80–90.

13. Richard Morse, "Toward a Theory of Spanish American Government," *Journal of the History of Ideas,* 15 (1964), pp. 78–82.

14. C. Hubert Haring, *The Spanish Empire in America.* New York: Oxford University Press, 1947. Cited in John Leddy Phelan, "Authority and Flexibility in the Spanish Imperial Bureaucracy," *Administrative Science Quarterly,* V, no. 1 (June, 1960), p. 53.

15. Haring, *The Spanish Empire in America;* Robert Scott, "Political Elites and Political Modernization," in S.M. Lipset, (ed.), *Elites in Latin America.* New York: Oxford University Press, 1967; and Charles Anderson, *Politics and Economic Change in Latin America: The Governing of Restless Nations.* Princeton: Van Nostrand, 1967, Chapter 4.

16. See John D. Martz and David J. Myers, "Understanding Latin American Politics: Analytic Models and Intellectual Traditions," *Polity,* 16, no. 2 (Winter 1983), pp. 219–222.

17. A brief summary of the more important elements of his model would include the following characteristics of Latin American democratic practice: (1) authoritarian, but not totalitarian, presidential leadership; (2) a subordinate, yet consultative, national legislature; (3) limitations on political and human rights when required for the common good; (4) limited recognition of local and provincial rights and powers; (5) guaranteed political representation through state-sponsored or recognized mass associations and corporative groups; and (6) a clientalistic relationship between the state and the masses which guarantees a minimum degree of rights protections and welfare. Howard Wiarda, "Democracy and Human Rights in Latin America: Toward a New Conceptualization," *Orbis* (Spring 1978), pp. 149–156.

18. William H. Beezley, "Caudillismo: An Interpretive Note," *Journal of Interamerican Studies and World Affairs,* 11 (1969), p. 348. See also Torcuato S. Di Tella, *Latin American Politics: A Theoretical Framework.* Austin, TX: University of Texas Press, 1990, pp. 8–13.

19. John Duncan Powell, "Peasant Society and Clientalist Politics," *The American Political Science Review,* 64, no. 2 (June 1970), pp. 413–415.

20. See Ralph Lee Woodward, "Social Revolution in Guatemala: The Cabrera Revolt," in *Applied Enlightenment: Nineteenth Century Liberalism*. New Orleans: Middle American Research Institutue, Tulane University, 1971, pp. 64–70.

21. Guillermo O'Donnell, "Tensions in the Bureaucratic-Authoritarian State and the Question of Democracy," in David Collier (ed.), *The New Authoritarianism in Latin America*. Princeton: Princeton University Press, 1979, p. 292.

22. See Ronald C. Newton, "Natural Corporatism and the Passing of Populism in Spanish America," *The Review of Politics*, 36 (1974); and Powell, "Peasant Society and Clientalist Politics," pp. 415–417.

23. Enrique Baloyra, "Reactionary Despotism in El Salvador," in Martin Diskin (ed.), *Trouble in our Backyard*. New York: Pantheon Books, 1983.

24. Morse, "Toward a Theory of Spanish American Government," pp. 116–122.

25. John Gillin, "Some Signposts for Policy," in Richard N. Adams et al., *Social Change in Latin America Today: Its Implications for United States Foreign Policy*. New York: Vintage Books, 1960, pp. 14, 28–47.

26. Glen Caudill Dealy, *The Public Man: An Interpretation of Latin American and Other Catholic Countries*. Amherst: The University of Massachusetts Press, 1977, p. 7.

27. Dealy, *The Public Man*, pp. 8, 34.

28. See Roland H. Ebel, "Thomism and Machiavellianism in Central American Political Development." Paper given at the 44th International Congress of Americanists, Manchester, England, September 5–10, 1982. See also Morse, "Toward a Theory of Spanish American Government," pp. 118–122; William H. Beezley, "Caudillismo: An Interpretive Note," pp. 348–349; and Marvin Goldwert, *History as Neurosis: Paternalism and "Machismo" in Spanish America*. Lanham, MD: University Press of America, 1980, pp. 17–21.

29. Charles Anderson, "Central American Political Parties: A Functional Approach," *The Western Political Quarterly*, 15 (1962), p. 134.

30. Anderson, "Central American Political Parties," pp. 234–235.

31. Anderson, "Central American Political Parties," pp. 135–137.

32. John Duncan Powell, "Peasant Society and Clientalist Politics," *The American Political Science Review*, 64, no. 2 (June 1970), pp. 417–423.

33. Oscar Lewis, *Tepoztlan: Village in Mexico*. New York: Holt, Rinehart, and Winston, 1960, pp. 87–88.

34. George M. Foster, *Tzintzuntan: Mexican Peasants in a Changing World*. Boston: Little, Brown and Company, 1967, Chapter 6.

35. John Duncan Powell, "Peasant Society and Clientalist Politics," pp. 411–412.

36. Oscar Lewis, "Urbanization Without Breakdown: A Case Study," in Dwight B. Heath and Richard N. Adams (eds.), *Contemporary Cultures and Societies of Latin America*. New York: Random House, 1965, p. 434. See also William P. Mangin, "The Role of Regional Associations in the Adaptation of Rural Migrants to Cities in Peru," in Heath and Adams, *Contemporary Cultures and Societies of Latin America*, pp. 311–323.

37. Louis K. Harris and Victor Alba, *The Political Culture and Behavior of Latin America*. Kent, OH: Kent State University Press, 1974, p. 79. This picture is largely corroborated by Wayne A. Cornelius, "Urbanization and Political Demand Making: Political Participation Among the Migrant Poor in Latin American Cities," *American Political Science Review*, 68 (1974), pp. 1143–1146.

38. The Venezuelan lower class differs significantly from the generalization of Harris and Alba in the sense that they are less likely to support military coups than the "higher strata." In other words, they strongly support the democratic system in that country. See Enrique Baloyra and John Martz, *Political Attitudes in Venezuela: Societal Cleavages and Political Opinion*. Austin, TX: University of Texas Press, 1979, pp. 186–187.

39. Bryan Roberts, "Politics in a Neighborhood of Guatemala City," *Sociology*, 2 (1968), pp. 194–196.

40. Roberts, "Politics in a Neighborhood of Guatemala City," p. 186.

41. William Mangin, "Latin American Squatter Settlements: A Problem and a Solution," *Latin American Research Review*, 2, no. 3 (Summer 1967), pp. 76–77. See also Talton F. Ray, *The Politics of the Barrios of Venezuela*. Berkeley: University of California Press, 1969.

42. Fred Riggs, *Administration in Developing Countries: The Theory of Prismatic Society*. Boston: Houghton Mifflin, 1964, pp. 19–31.

43. Refracted light becomes "diffracted" when it is broken into the color spectrum. Riggs prefers this term to describe the ultimate result of modernization—the breaking up of a simpler "fused" society into a culturally "diffuse" one. See Riggs, *Administration in Developing Countries*, p. 23.

44. According to Funk and Wagnalls *New Standard Dictionary of the English Language* (1930), a ray of white light passing through a triangular prism is bent twice: once on entering and once on leaving.

3

Cultural Style and International Relations in Latin America

We begin this chapter by examining the various theories that have, explicitly or implicitly, been developed to relate Latin American cultural style with the international politics of the region. We then put forward five propositions that appear to govern the cultural style of Latin America's foreign relations. These include: 1) the relative absence of inter-state violence in inter-American relations; 2) the role of the United States as hemispheric *caudillo*; 3) the limited participation in foreign policy formulation; 4) the separation of foreign and domestic policy establishments; and 5) the economic dependence on advanced states. Finally we test these propositions empirically by describing the general features of international behavior in Latin America since World War II.

Cultural Theories of Foreign Policy

Of the variety of Latin American traits discussed in chapter 2, which ones appear to have the greatest general relevance to the area's foreign policy and international behavior? We would like to postulate that Latin American international behavior can best be understood as involving a contrapuntal relationship among three broad cultural orientations: international monism, clientalism, and nationalism. There is, in other words, a counterpoint between the "Thomistic" search for a stable world or regional order and, when that fails, a "Machiavellian" recourse to clientalism. Clientalism, in turn, generates what Milenky has called "reactive nationalism."[1]

As a means of understanding this pattern, three general environmental factors have to be considered. The first is the nature of the international system. In a very fundamental way it presents these nations with an environment, a *modus operandi* at odds with the region's political habits and traditions. That is, the lack of a sovereign decision-making center in the international system places a premium on the "democratic" habits and skills of bargaining, compromise, coalition building, etc. In this sense, Latin American nations are forced to operate in a much more free-wheeling, pluralistic environment than they are disposed to by their culture. Because of the need to develop the skills and expertise to operate in such a culturally "alien" environment, the foreign policy establishments of most Latin American countries have been more insulated from national politics (and from the behavioral norms and expectations of the national political culture) than the other ministries of government.[2] Foreign policy in the Latin American states traditionally had a much greater tendency to have a life of its own regardless of the regime in power. This, however, has been changing somewhat as more left-wing authoritarian governments have come to power. In countries like Cuba and Nicaragua (to 1990), foreign policy is less insulated from political and ideological considerations than under such *desarrollista* bureaucratic authoritarian regimes as Argentina, Brazil, or Uruguay.

A second factor is the historical political instability generated by Latin America's monistic political culture. Political monism is inherently unstable: it seeks to impose a top-down order on society on the basis of a political ideology or set of unimpeachable political objectives under the aegis of a charismatic leader or self-selected political elite. Unfortunately, every political monism spawns rival monisms anxious to impose their conceptions of the *bien comun* on the society. And, given the area's Machiavellian tradition, they are more willing to take to the streets or the hills to achieve that objective. Thus these countries, even the largest and intrinsically most powerful among them, have been among the weaker actors in the international system. As a result, Latin American diplomatic activity and doctrine has often oscillated between exaggerated assertions of national sovereignty and taking refuge under the protective wing of a more powerful international actor.

A third and related factor is the problem of dependency generally. Without in any way declaring ourselves to be *dependencistas*, it is clear that a combination of economic underdevelopment, relatively small size, and the nature of East-West political competition has made the Latin American nations more vulnerable to outside pressures and influences and, thus, has tended to drive many of them into the orbit of either the United States or, more rarely, the Soviet Union.

The attempt to escape dependency, as G. Pope Atkins has written, has often placed the Latin American states in a paradoxical position:

> Latin American states want to achieve or maintain independence in their international actions, but to do so they must be strong

in relation to the outside world; to become strong they must obtain some sort of assistance from the outside world toward which they wish to be independent, thus increasing the chances for a dependent relationship.[3]

Political instability and economic and technological dependency have served to reinforce in international behavior the pattern of clientalism that is so deeply ingrained in Latin American culture. One writer who addressed this phenomenon with graphic imagery was Norman A. Bailey in his essay of two decades ago, "The United States as *caudillo*."[4] Bailey contrasted the "lukewarm to frigid" response to United States attempts to curb Cuban subversion on the part of Latin American nations at the San José and Punta del Este Foreign Ministers' Conferences of 1960 and 1961, and the "unanimous and enthusiastic" backing the United States blockade obtained from the Council of the OAS during the Cuban missile crisis. What was equally significant, Bailey stated, was that during the first period "anti-Yankee sentiment seemed on the rise among the populace at large, and almost weekly riots and demonstrations in support of Cuba took place in one city or another of the region;" whereas during the second episode, "with the exception of La Paz, there was not a single important anti-U.S. demonstration or riot in any part of Latin America, whereas in some cities there were sizeable pro-U.S. manifestations."[5]

Bailey explains these contradictions, "none of which should have caused surprise in Washington," by the " 'patron' mentality" which had evolved through the centuries in Latin America:

"Strong" but benevolent leadership is the ideal of the Latin American in the national sphere. He is not, of course, a masochist, and if the government or *caudillo* attacks his liberties or what he considers his private concerns, he will resist. At the same time a "weak" government, no matter how benevolent and well-intentioned, is despised and obstructed, especially if it is not, in the individual's opinion, fulfulling its responsibilities.[6]

This psychology, he argued, carried over into the international sphere. Latin American nations want a strong but not overly intrusive *patrón* who will protect them from the uncertainties of international life. Great Britain fulfilled that role throughout most of the nineteenth century and the United States assumed it roughly at the time of the Olney Declaration.[7]

During the last decade of the nineteenth and the early part of the twentieth centuries, however, the United States violated the expected pattern of "patronal behavior" by its intervention in Cuba, Puerto Rico, Panama, Nicaragua, and the Dominican Republic. The Good Neighbor Policy, on the other hand, restored the United States to the position of the "beneficent *caudillo*."[8]

Bailey argued that up to the time he was writing, in 1963, the United States had had varied success in adequately playing the role of inter-American *caudillo*:

1. "In the afterglow of the Roosevelt Era" the *caudillo* role of the United States was institutionalized in the Rio Treaty of 1947 and in the Charter of the OAS (1948).
2. President Truman managed to fulfill American duties and responsibilities toward the region "but was not benevolent enough" for the Latin American taste.
3. President Eisenhower was perceived as being too weak to perform the proper *caudillo* role, while his alter ego, John Foster Dulles, was making too many demands on our clients.
4. President Kennedy was seen as insufficiently *macho* at the Bay of Pigs, but as a true and protective *caudillo* during the Missile Crisis.[9]

The proper role of America, as the international *caudillo* in the Western Hemisphere, Bailey contended, was to protect the client from the outside world while granting him a relatively free hand in his own bailiwick. Thus, the strongly held principle of non-interventionism in the internal affairs of states is compatible with strong United States patrimonial *caudillaje* leadership in the international sphere.

We might postulate that for Latin America a properly-working Inter-American system constitutes the "international" Thomistic synthesis. In it the United States plays the role of the beneficent *caudillo* (in Bailey's sense) or, from a traditionalist point of view, the role of the "beneficent monarch." Collective security and economic arrangements like the Rio Treaty, the Alliance for Progress, or the Caribbean Basin Initiative (and the principles and policies they seek to apply) constitute the *bien común* at any given time. Within the system, each state—in the "familistic" brotherhood of Spanish-speaking states—has its proper role to play, presided over and tended to by the United States through the bureaucracy of the various multi-national organizations. *Obedezco pero no cumplo* is the reaction of individual Latin American states to what are perceived as excessive or ill-conceived demands by the United

States. At a slightly higher level of resistance, middle class "reactive nationalism" (e.g., the Caracas demonstrations against Richard Nixon in 1958) comes into play. Full-fledged Machiavellian behavior is reflected in attempts by governments or movements to either lower the involvement of their nation in the Inter-American Thomistic system (the Arbenz regime) or withdraw it from the system altogether (the Sandinista regime). When the Inter-American system becomes "nucleated" (to use Richard Morse's term), the weaker states seek to protect themselves by drawing ever closer to a protective *caudillo*— whether the United States or the USSR.

Applying this conceptualization (or imagery) historically, it might be postulated that following the breakdown of the Iberian empires, the first international monism created by the Latin Americans was the Liberal Synthesis, which lasted from roughly 1860 to 1930. Presided over by the then dominant international *caudillo*, Great Britain, which provided its clients with capital, markets, and the *Pax Britannica*, the system was guided by the idealistic (Thomistic) docrine of comparative advantage and sought to achieve the *bien común* through the exportation of primary products and the importation of luxury goods. The conditions that made this system relatively successful for a period of Latin America's history were the low levels of mass consumption, politicization, and population growth.

The Liberal Synthesis was undermined during the last decade of the nineteenth century and the first two decades of the twentieth by industrialization, urbanization, and population growth due to advances in disease control, all of which served to politicize the urban middle classes and to create the beginnings of an urban proletariat. In addition, Great Britain had relinquished much of its *caudillo* role to the United States. The Liberal Synthesis was finally destroyed (except in Central America and the insular Caribbean, where it lingered on into the 1940s and 1950s) by the Great Depression, which thoroughly disrupted Latin America's "outward-oriented" economy. The fears and hopes of World War II tended largely to ward off the possible Machiavellian international behavior of the Latin American states resulting from the breakdown of the Liberal Synthesis (except for Argentina which flirted with the Axis Powers). After the war, fear of Soviet expansionism coupled with the idealism generated by Allied rhetoric and American economic and political dominance, caused the creation of what might be called a "developmentalist synthesis" under American leadership. The United States now fully assumed its role as, potentially at least, the "beneficent *caudillo*." The guiding idealistic doctrine was that of political and economic development; and the transfer of capital and technology was seen as the means of creating the international *bien comun.* "International familism" was also reflected in the movements of regional economic integration.

Once again, however, the developmentalist synthesis was undermined by what Helio Jaguaribe, Guillermo O'Donnell, and others have called the problems of populism: deteriorating terms of trade, inflation, industrial non-competitiveness, and hyperpoliticization.[10] These problems were exacerbated by the emergence of the intrusive multinational corporation which the United States was reluctant to control. The disintegration of the synthesis was further accelerated by the attractiveness of Marxist modes of analysis—the competing Thomism of the day—to university students and intellectuals. At the same time the United States was seen as abusing its *caudillo* status by intervening in the internal affairs of an "obstreperous" populist government—the Arbenz regime.

It is difficult to identify a single event undermining the developmentalist synthesis that had the impact that the Great Depression had had on the Liberal Synthesis. Earlier, the Cuban revolution was certainly of monumental significance. But possibly more important was the failure of the Alliance for Progress to achieve all of the results expected of it. This failure at region-wide economic development under the aegis of populist, quasi-democratic governments gave rise to various bureaucratic authoritarian regimes on the one hand, and insurrectionary movements on the other. There was also a search for an alternative to the traditional economic linkages between the United States and Latin America in the creation of the so-called Latin American Economic System (SELA).

The 1970s and 1980s have seen the Inter-American system become more chaotic with the emergence of competing international *caudillos* (the United States and Soviet Union) on the one hand and a variety of national *caudillaje*-type leaders on the other. Democratic *caudillaje*-type leaders have included Alan García, Napoleón Duarte, and Vinicio Cerezo; authoritarian ones have included Augusto Pinochet, Alfredo Stroessner, Daniel Ortega, and Fidel Castro. But still the search for the international *patrón* continues. America's budgetary crisis coupled with its intrusion into the Central American crisis of the 1970s and 1980s inhibits its ability to play the role of the beneficent *patron* effectively. Lack of economic growth and its military and political intrusiveness similarly impede the Soviet Union in playing that role. A number of so-called "regional actors" (Venezuela and Mexico principally; at times Peru, Argentina, and Brazil) have sought out a *cacique* (local *caudillo*) role, but the decline in oil prices, the world agricultural glut, and the debt crisis have undermined these attempts at leadership.

Thus, currently the Inter-American system is in flux. The new fledgling democratic regimes still primarily seek the protective wings of the American eagle, while beleaguered popular revolutionary regimes have sought the protection of the Russian bear. The larger states—Argentina, Brazil, Chile, and Peru primarily, Mexico to a somewhat lesser extent—are attempting either to go it alone or, until the recent decline of Russian power, to play the one *caudillo* off against the other. At the same time the combination of terrorism, narcotics smuggling, illicit migration, and the possible default on debt has served to reduce the capability of the United States even to operate as a *caudillo*, much less a beneficent one.

To what extent is the above description of Latin America's culturally based international policy and behavior in accord with reality? One useful summary of the international thinking of Latin American political and academic elites has been provided by Edward S. Milenky. Although published a decade ago, his survey paints an interesting picture of elite attitudes as they have evolved since World War II.

Most of the writers surveyed, first of all, see the international system in a largely hierarchical fashion with the United States as the dominant power vis-à-vis Latin America (figure 3.1).

FIGURE 3.1

Visions of the International System

Hierarchical View With U.S. as Dominant Actor	Hierarchical View With U.S. & USSR in Bipolar System	Multi-polar View
Silva Michelena	J. Jaguaribe	M. Kaplan
F. Herrera	Arujo Castro	O. Camilion
H. Godoy	J. Perón	K. Vasena
C. Furtado		
A.G. Frank		
O. Sunkél		
F. Cardoso		

Source: Milenky, "Problems, Perspectives, and Modes of Analysis: Understanding Latin American Approaches to World Affairs," in Ronald G. Hellman and H. Jon Rosenbaum (eds.), *Latin America: The Search For A New International Role.* New York: John Wiley & Sons, 1975, pp. 101–103.

All interpretations of the international power system, writes Milenky, "seem to offer Latin America limited options for action. The countries of the region are seen as closed out of the upper rungs of the international power structure and under United States hegemony or substantial influence."[11]

Most of the writers, furthermore, see their nation as the victims of powerful outside forces—typical clientalist attitudes according to John Duncan Powell.[12] Of the sixteen writers or research organizations cited on the matter of their countries' "national situation," only two (General Golbery do Couto e Silva and Helio Jaguaribe) saw certain nations (Argentina, Brazil, and Mexico) as having the potential for autonomous development.

> All of Latin America's international options as presented by a cross-section of its foreign affairs analysts, lead to the following conclusions. Regionalists and nationalists accept the status of Latin American nations as regional powers at best, as local powers if possible, and minimally as states capable of mastering their internal affairs.[13]

However, reactive nationalism is also central to the thinking of all of the writers surveyed:

> Latin American students of international affairs would have their nations seek a familiar catalogue of objectives: sovereignty and autonomy; national development and, if possible national power; and a respected position as actors, not objects, in world affairs.[14]

The one finding in the Milenky survey that does not quite fit our description of Latin American cultural orientations in international affairs is the postulate of an "organicist" desire to fit into an Inter-American system dominated by the United States as beneficent *caudillo*. He concludes that none of the analysts seek a return to the Alliance for Progress or Pan-Americanism. Nevertheless he asserts that a consensus does exist on the international role the Latin American governments should play in the region.

> Generally, Latin Americans see themselves as members of weak, externally penetrated societies in which great powers, multinational corporations, and international economic relationships play important roles. As a result nation-states in the classic sense of impervious units with a political supremacy over a defined territorial sphere do not exist. Latin American governments are seen as mediators between indigenous and nonindigenous actors and forces. These conditions are the product of underdevelopment and the low power position of Latin American nations in the world.[15]

In all discussions of political reality based on political culture, recognition has to be given to the fact that while any cultural pattern is highly persistent, culture is also subject to change. Latin America is currently experiencing a "democratic wave." Whether this development, which reflects a historically latent yet important tradition of the region, will last long enough to affect materially the national culture and the consequent international behavior of the nations of the area only time will tell. If it does persist, over the long term this should have the effect of changing the historic patron-client relationship between the United States and the Latin American states into one that lays greater stress on cooperation and mutual interaction. Concurrently, both the ability and inclination of the United States and the USSR to play the *caudillo* role may also be diminishing. The willingness of the two superpowers to reach settlements on such regional conflicts as Afghanistan, Angola, and Namibia is a case in point. This development may trigger major changes in Latin America's own international behavior.

Political Culture and Foreign Policy: Five Propositions

The previous section has outlined a general framework for understanding the cultural behavior of the Latin American states in international relations. This section will seek to apply this framework to a number of characteristics of Latin America's international behavior.

Relative Absence of Inter-state Violence.   Inter-state relations in Latin America have not been wholly free of violence. The so-called Soccer War in 1969 between El Salvador and Honduras, and the Argentine military action to incorporte the Falklands in Argentine territory are evidence of that. Boundary disputes between pairs of Latin American countries have, not infrequently, given rise to military posturing by one side or another and to occasional low-intensity warfare. The same is true of the battle between democrats and dictators in the Caribbean and Central America during the late 1940s and 1950s. Castro's efforts in the early and mid-1960s to foment violent revolution in other Latin American countries by training and equipping insurgents is further evidence of violence in Latin American inter-state behavior. Similarly, the Trujillo-sponsored attempt to assassinate President Betancourt of Venezuela reflects the existence of state-sponsored terrorism. Nonetheless, relations between Latin American countries have generally been remarkably free of sustained violence, especially given the number of long-standing, often emotionally charged disputes that exist in the region. Child identifies twenty inter-state conflict situations, real or potential, in the Latin America of the 1980s (figure 3.2).

FIGURE 3.2

Inter-State Conflict Situations in Latin America in the 1980s

Conflict	Parties involved	Type of conflict
Mexico-U.S.	Mexico, U.S.	migratory, resource
Caribbean	Caribbean states, U.S., USSR	ideological, resource, migratory
Hispaniola	Dominican Rep., Haiti	border, migratory
Central America	Central America, U.S., Cuba	ideological, influence, migratory
Honduras-El Salv.	Honduras, El Salvador	territorial, migratory
Belize	Belize, Guatemala, Britain, U.S.	territorial
Panama Canal	Panama, U.S.	territorial, resource
San Andres islands	Nicaragua, Colombia	territorial
Gulf of Venezuela	Colombia, Venezuela	territorial, resource, migratory
Essequibo	Venezuela, Guyana	territorial, resource
New River triangle	Guyana, Suriname	territorial, resource
Argentina-Brazil	Argentina, Brazil	influence, resource
Bolivia-Paraguay	Bolivia, Paraguay	territorial, resource
Northern Andes	Ecuador, Peru	territorial, resource
Central Andes	Peru, Bolivia, Chile	territorial, resource
Southern Andes	Argentina, Chile	territorial, resource, border, migratory
Maritime zones	Coastal states	territorial, resource
Falklands/Malvinas	Britain, Argentina	territorial, resource
South Atlantic	Argentina, Brazil	resource, influence
Antarctica	Treaty signatories	territorial, resource

Adapted from: Jack Child, "Inter-state Conflict in Latin America in the 1980s," in Jennie K. Lincoln and Elizabeth G. Ferris (eds.), *The Dynamics of Latin American Foreign Policies: Challenges for the 1980s.* Boulder, CO: Westview Press, 1984, p. 25.

Of course it cannot be assumed that because intra-Latin American relations have been so relatively violence-free in the past, they will remain so in the future. Indeed, the 1970s and 1980s have witnessed several developments that could portend greater violence in Latin American international relations. Thus two questions require examination: what has made Latin American international behavior so relatively violence-free in the past? What developments raise the possibility of greater violence in the future?

With reference to the first question, Kenneth Waltz's notion of "conflict within a loose association of states" can be very helpful.[16]

He holds that in international conflict situations countries have only three alternative responses: 1) they can integrate their activities in an effort to increase mutual well-being; 2) they can do battle over their differences; or 3) they can watch one another with wariness and suspicion and not battle it out but, rather, resolve their dispute through diplomatic means. The response chosen depends, as Waltz sees it, on how closely countries are joined, how interdependent they are. Countries are interdependent if they are dependent upon one another for various goods and services that they cannot provide for themselves or cannot obtain readily elsewhere. Traditionally, the Latin American countries have not been heavily dependent on one another, whether for trade, investment, security, tourism, or technology. The great bulk of the international interactions of Latin American countries have been with actors outside of Latin America.[17] In short, the fact that the Latin American nations have traditionally constituted "a loose association of states" whose basic necessities have come from outside the region has reduced the number and intensity of conflicts among them. Internal political violence which, at least in part, is predicated on the limited goods and resources available for distribution is reduced in an international environment where the major resources flow from such international "patrons" as the United States, the Soviet Union, or Western Europe. States in such an environment tolerate those with whom they have a conflict: they struggle for advantage, they posture militarily and verbally, and they may apply very small amounts of armed force against their antagonist. But they avoid full-scale armed hostilities.

In addition to co-existing in a loose association, several other factors have intervened to keep the violence—that is such a common feature in the domestic politics of so many countries of the region—out of their inter-state behavior during the 1940s, 1950s, and into the 1960s. First, the military and logistical capabilities of contending armed forces have been limited—quite sufficient for carrying off coups internally, but insufficient to mount sustained large-scale military actions against neighboring protagonists. In other words, the *desire* to use violent means in inter-state relations may have been present (as in domestic politics), but the *ability* to do so was lacking (unlike in internal politics). Second, this state of affairs was largely the product of American policy during that period. At the time, the United States was the near-monopoly supplier of military hardware to Latin America, a position that it deliberately sought.[18] And the United States used that status to maintain a rough military balance between contending states in order to prevent one of them from gaining the military superiority needed to annex territory or otherwise take advantage of a less powerful state. This can be thought of as another instance of the United States functioning as beneficent *caudillo* to maintain a regional *bien comun*, although over time many Latin American countries ceased to view a policy that strengthened the military, as against the civil, society as productive of their national *bien común*. Third, during the late 1940s, 1950s, and through the 1960s, the peacekeeping mechanisms of the Inter-American System, although not at all successful in resolving the root causes of inter-American conflict, were quite effective in bringing about an end to armed hostilities when they did occur, restoring the status quo "ante bellum." That, too, must be looked upon as an important restraint on the resort to violence in inter-state behavior in Latin America. Fourth, as Burr points out in a study of the territorial conflict between Argentina and Chile, there was usually—at least in these two countries—a climate of responsible opinion that counseled against resort to sustained full-scale armed conflict because of the damage that war would do to the development effort.[19]

Many of the factors that restrained armed conflict earlier either no longer prevail or prevail to a much lesser extent today. At the most general level the Inter-American System itself, along with its peacekeeping machinery, has weakened considerably in the 1970s and 1980s. The result may be that, in future, use of armed force in Latin American inter-state behavior may become more pronounced.

For one thing, the Latin American states are now less loosely associated than they were in the 1960s and 1970s. Beginning in the 1960s, direct interactions among Latin American countries have increased greatly, at both the official and non-official levels. Trade has increased somewhat, although not to the extent hoped for when the various movements toward economic integration in Latin America were launched. The countries are joined together in a number of regional and sub-regional organizations, such as the Latin American Economic System and the Andean Group. Government officials now include other Latin American capitals in their international travels, which until quite recently was rare. In the past, such travels were limited to Washington, New York, and perhaps some European capitals.

Interdependence has also been heightened by the internal conflicts within the nations of the region. Refugees, the existence of sanctuaries for guerilla groups in neighboring countries, and the flow of arms across borders have had the effect of internationalizing internal conflict. The result has been to increase the likelihood of inter-state warfare in such troubled areas as Nicaragua's borders with Honduras and Costa Rica. The United States has played the role of *caudillo* in these situations, both as disturber of the status quo and as pacificator. We should not discount the possibility, therefore, that the *caudillaje* pattern of behavior that has produced internal political violence in Latin America will increasingly come to dominate the region's international politics.

Child holds that the proneness of Latin America for inter-state violence has increased greatly since the early 1960s, further raising the spector that the violence that marks domestic politics may spill over to Latin American inter-state behavior.[20] He identifies several reasons why. One, the Caribbean basin conflict has become polarized along ideological lines. This began with the Cuban Revolution, Castro's alignment with the Soviet Union, his efforts in the 1960s to foment violent revolution elsewhere in Latin America, and the United States response to those developments.

Two, the last three decades have witnessed the emergence in South America, especially in the Southern Cone, of the "national security state"—emphasizing authoritarianism, nationalism, corporatism, and security under military rule. Child states that geopolitical thinking was the theoretical or intellectual underpinning of the "national security state." Southern Cone geopolitical thinking conceives of the state as a living organism struggling to survive, obtain space and resources, and project power and influence outward. Also, that geopolitical thinking, as described by Child, embraces a flexible concept of national boundaries: boundaries are not permanent lines of demarcation between states but instead are moveable. A country can push outward into the adjacent territory of a weaker country or one not vigilent in guarding its territory. Southern Cone geopolitical thinking, too, embraces the law of valuable areas which holds that if a country fails to occupy and exploit resource-rich areas of its territory, other countries can rightfully do so. These various ideas in Southern Cone geopolitical thought provide ample opportunity for resort to armed conflict. Although the "national security state" has largely passed from the scene with the transition to democratic government, what has not disappeared there is the presence and influence of geopolitical thought. It remains strong in the military and in some influential civilian sectors.

Three, remote or disputed border areas that were once regarded as lacking in practical value, even if possessing great emotional value, are taking on increased significance. The possibility that remote areas may contain valuable natural resources, together with the pressure created by rapid population growth, make such otherwise unimportant areas valuable and even now worth fighting for. A case in point was the 1969 war between El Salvador and Honduras. For decades prior to the war, landless Salvadorans in search of land encroached into relatively unoccupied Honduran territory along the Salvadorian border, territory that Honduras had traditionally not attached great value to. However, when in the 1960s the Honduran government was confronted by the political necessity of carrying out a land reform program that would benefit the peasantry without displacing the landed elite, the once largely ignored frontier land became valuable. Indeed, war followed to remove Salvadorans from land that could be turned over to Honduran peasants.[21]

Four, Latin American military capabilities have increased considerably since the 1960s. This is particularly true of the armed forces of the larger states, but it is also true of some smaller ones, for example, Cuba and Nicaragua. Expressed differently, the military and logistic capability to wage war has increased greatly, as Argentina demonstrated during its battle with Britain over the Falklands. Argentina showed that it could seriously engage a leading NATO ally, something it most certainly could not have done a decade or two earlier.

Five, the United States Government has lost its ability to impose limits on the kinds and amounts of military hardware that Latin American countries can obtain. This, in turn, has meant the end of Washington's ability to maintain a situation of military balance between competing states. During the 1960s, Washington adopted a number of restrictive measures on Latin American arms acquisitions, for example, proscribing the acquisition of sophisticated weapons and putting dollar limits on the military hardware that could be obtained.[22] In the face of these and other restrictions, most Latin American countries have turned to other supplier countries and obtained the hardware desired. Today, the United States is just one of many sources of arms for Latin America. Even small Central American countries, when faced with a cut-off of arms from the United States, have demonstrated an ability to get arms from other sources. It should be noted, too, that several Latin American countries have a significant domestic arms industry.

The U.S. as caudillo. Although U.S. officials have not used the term and probably have not thought that their actions were those of a *caudillo*, it is hard to question the proposition that the United States has historically acted as *caudillo* in Latin America and that it still endeavors to do so. Ample evidence also exists that Latin American countries, individually and collectively, have at various times wanted the United States to behave as *caudillo*. In performing such a role, the United States has sought to promote its conception of the *bien común* but, as often as not, that conception has not been shared by Latin American countries.

In the first place, agreement among Latin American countries as to what *bien comun* represents exists only at a rather abstract level: survival, security, development, and the like. On practical questions, competing conceptions of the common good tend to emerge. For a right-wing military regime, United States backing would indeed be regarded as that of a regional *caudillo* promoting the *bien común*. By contrast, a democratic country (such as Costa Rica) might view the United States action as that of *caudillo*, though not a beneficent one. Within a particular country there may be occasions when all sectors have the same conception of the *bien común*: United States transfer of control over the canal to Panama was universally acclaimed as promoting the Panamanian conception of the common good. More often, however, different sectors within a country have differing conceptions. For example, victims of human rights abuses during military rule in Argentina may have viewed the Carter administration's human rights emphasis as a United States *caudillo* action intended to advance the *bien comun*. The country's military leadership, on the other hand, saw the United States in quite a different light.

Respect for the United States as regional *caudillo* may be accompanied by the anti-*Yanquismo* sentiments often discernible in Latin America. These sentiments are the direct result of the U.S. seeking to function as hemisphere *caudillo* but, in the judgement of Latin American governments and publics, not effectively performing that role. For while the U.S. is sometimes recognized as the provider and promoter of the common good, quite often it is not, thereby exacerbating anti-American feelings in the region. The relationship between anti-*Yanquista* social attitudes and Latin American foreign policy responses go hand in hand.

Let us take a brief look at the history of United States involvement in the hemisphere. From early times the United States looked on Latin America differently from other regions of the world, and Lowenthal used the term "hegemonic presumption" to characterize this orientation. It rested on a long-held belief in United States decision-making circles (and to a degree, within the larger American public) that Washington could and should set the boundaries for what was acceptable political behavior on Latin America's part, and that it could and should insure that political forces opposed to the United States not gain power.[23]

The first manifestation of the hegemonic presumption was the Monroe Doctrine in 1823 when the United States enumerated certain hemispheric-wide rules that European powers were expected to adhere to. The doctrine was the first clear instance of United States *caudillo*-like behavior in the Western Hemisphere and, at the same time, could be viewed as its first effort to promote hemispheric welfare. Further manifestations came with additions to the doctrine made during the nineteenth and early twentieth centuries. In 1845, President Polk warned European countries against military intervention and diplomatic meddling in the Americas. In 1848, Polk forbade the transfer of Latin American territory to a European country or the transfer of a European colony in Latin America to another European country. A third extension came in 1895 when Secretary of State Olney, in the Cleveland administration, declared: "The United States is practically sovereign on this continent, and its fiat is law upon the subjects to which it confines its interposition." Olney was only voicing the thinking that gave rise to the original Monroe Doctrine.

The most extreme extension to the Monroe Doctrine was the Roosevelt Corollary issued in 1904. In it President Theodore Roosevelt assumed a hemispheric policeman's role for the United States and, then, he and several of his successors implemented the corollary by way of a series of United States military interventions, in effect military occupations, in a number of Caribbean and Central American countries. There are many other manifestations of the hegemonic presumption ranging from the Platt Amendment to the Cuban Constitution that authorized United States intervention in Cuban affairs, to United States efforts to manipulate the electoral outcome in Chile in 1970.

While the hegemonic presumption was hemispheric-wide from the outset, until the end of World War II the United States was able to function most effectively as regional *caudillo* in Central America and the independent Caribbean, and much less so in South America where it faced greater European political and economic competition. Indeed, the United States turned Central America into its backyard, just as it turned the Caribbean Sea into its own lake. The overriding concern of Washington in these areas has always been with security. To insure security the United States has continually sought political stability and the absence of foreign powers in the region, especially hostile foreign powers. A second concern is economic in nature. Domínguez states:

> [T]he desire for. . .hegemony has come from two essential goals.
> The first has been to assure that client states generally support
> the United States in its relations with extra-hemispheric powers.
> The second has been to assure that the flow of goods, services,
> and capital between the United States and these countries is
> relatively unimpeded.[24]

This ranking of objectives is noteworthy. Economic considerations may be important to the United States, but they are not dominant and remain secondary to security considerations.

It is possible to discover some Latin American support for the original Monroe Doctrine, which can be interpreted as a perception that the United States ought to act to promote the hemispheric *bien común*. Thus, several Latin American countries approached the United States about the possibility of entering into a defensive alliance. In similar fashion, in enunciating the Roosevelt Corollary and implementing it through a series of armed interventions to forestall possible European ones, the United States was convinced that it was pursuing the *bien común* for the area. However, Latin American countires—both those that were the target of intervention and those that were not—did not share that conviction. Prior to World War II, it is possible to identify something that all of Latin America regarded as in the common interest of inter-American relations—the pledges by the United States in 1933 and 1936 to refrain from intervention and the other steps the United States took to give effect to the Good Neighbor Policy.

Following World War II the hegemonic presumption became a hemispheric-wide reality for the United States. The United States truly became the "Colossus of the North" and constructed what Kurth labels the "hegemonic international system" in Latin America as a whole (not just in Central America and the independent Caribbean).[25] That system, according to Kurth, had four features: a military alliance (the Treaty of Rio); Latin American economic dependence on the United States; ideological commonality with the United States; and direct and indirect intervention by the United States. Concerning the latter feature of the hegemonic system in Latin America, Kurth writes:

> There is a general expectation among political elites and counter elites in the states comprising the system that there are certain diplomatic and political limits to a lesser state's behavior, the transgressing of which will provoke the great power to intervene in the offending state. One such transgression is the small state's imminent defection to a competing great power. A related transgression is the imminent displacement of a friendly regime within the small state by an unfriendly one.[26]

The hegemonic system established the United States as regional *caudillo* par excellence, and after World War II Washington acted as such with vigor.

That the United States could establish itself as international *caudillo* presiding over a hemispheric-wide inter-state system in the wake of World War II is attributable to the unchallenged power of the North American giant in Latin America at war's end. European countries—

both the defeated and the victorious states that had previously been engaged in South America—were displaced from there, and became preoccupied with their own post-war economic recovery. The same was true of Japan, which had previously been engaged economically in Latin America. The other immediate post-war great power, the USSR, was not yet in a position to challenge the United States in the hemisphere. Moreover, at the time Moscow regarded Latin America as largely "off-limits" because the region was so distant and so much in the United States sphere of influence.

Latin American countries anticipated that the United States would be the beneficent *caudillo* in the post-World War II era by providing United States government funds to underwrite Latin America's economic development. The countries believed this was due them as a reward for their wartime cooperation with the United States (an exception to such cooperation being Argentina). The Latin American countries were disappointed on this count, but continued to call on the United States to be the beneficent *caudillo* by putting forward a Marshall Plan for Latin America. In the late 1940s and 1950s, the United States emphasized anti-communism and security. It endeavored to marshal Latin American support for Washington's global policy interests and goals. When Washington did so, it perceived of itself as promoting the hemispheric *bien común*.

There was another manifestation of the Latin American expectation of a beneficent United States in the post-war period. That was found in the Latin American desire to revise and institutionalize the Inter-American Ssytem after the war ended, something the Latin American countries had resisted in the past. Latin America's preoccupation with economic development did not capture United States attention, at least not in the way or to the degree that its leaders wanted, until the Cuban revolution of 1959. Then, the United States began to change its economic policy toward the region. In the last years of the Eisenhower administration, the United States government committed large amounts of money to Latin American economic development. Then, in 1961, the Kennedy administration put forward the Alliance for Progress. These actions constituted, from the Latin American perspective, United States promotion of the hemispheric *bien común*.

Possibly one of the most important actions taken by Washington that was generally perceived by Latin Americans as pursuing the hemispheric *bien común* was the Kennedy administration's handling of the 1962 Cuban missile crisis. On that occasion, Kennedy clearly came across to the Latin American public as *muy macho*.

The *caudillistic* behavior of the United States in the post-World War II period manifested itself in several ways: the covert intervention against Arbenz in Guatemala in 1954, the organization and equipping of Cuban exiles to mount an invasion aimed at overthrowing Castro, and the landing of United States Marines in the Dominican Republic. None of these were regarded by *all* of the Latin American countries as promoting the *bien común*, but differing groupings of Latin American countries viewed each United States action as such. The states in Central America that worried about radicalism in Guatemala in 1940s and 1950s looked upon the United States actions as that of a beneficent *caudillo*. Those Latin American states that most feared and opposed Castro regarded the United States-backed 1961 Bay of Pigs invasion as an effort to restore the pre-Castro *bien común*. These were highly visible manifestations of the United States acting as *caudillo*.

By the late 1960s, the hemisphere-wide hegemonic system became less tenable, above all in the larger and more developed countries of Latin America. To be sure, from time to time during the past two decades the United States has sought to re-assert its role as hemispheric *caudillo*, as in the case of the campaigns to destabilize the Allende regime in Chile in the early 1970s and the Sandinista regime in Nicaragua in the mid-1980s.

There are several reasons why maintenance of the hemispheric-wide system has become untenable. Some have to do with Latin America itself (or large parts of it); others have to do with the evolution of the international system since the end of World War II; and still others have to do with the United States.

Understandably, the hegemonic system engendered some Latin American hostility and resentment because that system often failed to advance perceived Latin American interests and intensified an already-existing desire for greater independence. That objective is natural, given decades of economic, political, social, and cultural penetration—if not domination—by more powerful countries and is the product of a growing sense of nationalism. As Howard Wiarda observed about South America in the second half of the 1980s: "The tides of nationalism are gaining momentum in all countries of the region, rendering their relations with the United States more complex and difficult and decreasing their willingness to subordinate their foreign policies to United States badgerings."[27] Latin American nationalism represents in large part the desire to curb United States influence and the hegemonic system.

Internal changes in the larger and more developed countries during the late 1960s and 1970s partially account for the decline in the hegemonic system. Latin America has experienced a tremendous transformation since the early 1960s. While not the sort of transformation posited by the Alliance for Progress, it represented a transformation just the same.[28] There has been both economic growth and economic development. The capacity of the state has expanded greatly in virtually every Latin American country: accordingly, their governments have acquired a much greater stock of resources, including knowledge and technical expertise. Those changes, in turn, have allowed Latin American governments to assert previously unpossessd authority in various areas of public policy that had previously been beyond their grasp. Governmental institutions in Latin America have vastly increased their capacity to impact on society domestically and to shape their own international agendas. Political leadership has become more knowledgeable, assertive and active, and much less inclined to routinely follow the lead of the United States.

Atkins explains the situation that faces each Latin American country:

> Latin American states want to achieve. . .independence in their international actions, but to do so, they must be strong in relation to the outside world; to become strong they must obtain some sort of assistance from the outside world toward which they wish to be independent, thus increasing chances for a dependent relationship. Latin America's continuing dilemma, then, is this: how are nations to improve their capability position and modernize their societies while preventing inordinate influence in their economic and political systems?[29]

The approach that most Latin American countries have taken, since the mid-1960s, to that dilemma has been called the "diversification of dependence." Lincoln has characterized diversification of dependence as "a declaration of independence inviting diplomatic and economic exchanges from any part of the international system."[30] Latin American countries today are reducing—not wholly eliminating—dependence on one large, more powerful country (the United States) by significantly expanding their interactions with other international actors.[31] Cuba, which exchanged dependence on the United States for an even greater dependence on the Soviet Union, is a clear exception.[32]

Latin American countries may have desired a diversification of their international relations long before the mid-1960s, but it was not until then that the conditions necessary for diversification came into being.[33] Two of the conditions were the previously noted internal

political and governmental transformations. Another was the change
in the international system. The United States-Soviet detente in the late
1960s and early 1970s provided Latin American countries with greater
freedom to maneuver. Another change was increased Third World
activism and assertiveness. A third change was the recovery and re-
emergence as major actors of the European countries and Japan, as well
as the emergence of new international actors. Prior to World War II,
Japan and some European countries were deeply engaged in the South
American states. The world wars displaced those countries and allowed
the United States to assume the hegemonic position in all of Latin
America for the first two decades after the Second World War. With
post-war recovery, these countries have returned to the region. As
Stepan observes: "Germany, Japan, and to lesser extent Italy and Spain,
have all emerged as competitors of the United States in Latin America,
whether in selling cars or tying up long term contracts for scarce
materials."[34] Thus, the countries of Latin America have come to realize
that alternatives to an exclusive concentration of international interactions with the United States exist and can be pursued. Among the
new actors in positions of international significance after World War
II were the European Community, OPEC, and Israel.[35]

Soviet interest in Latin America has also increased significantly
since 1960. While concentrating on Cuba, the Soviet Union launched
a diplomatic offensive in Latin America, establishing formal relations
and economic links with a number of countries in the region. However,
it has not shown the willingness to sponsor other Latin American
countries—Allende's Chile, Sandinista Nicaragua, or Bishop's
Grenada—in the way that it did Cuba.[36]

These changes in the international system largely rendered
obsolete the assumptions that provided the foundations for the United
States hegemonic system. Those assumptions were: strategic and
ideological bipolarity, United States markets and investment as agents
of economic growth (at home and in the client states), and United States
confidence in military regimes as allies.[37]

United States behavior towards Latin America, particularly in the
1970s, also contributed to the decline of the hemisphere-wide
hegemonic system. That behavior stemmed from the reappraisal of
United States foreign policy following the debacle in Vietnam and the
resulting United States reluctance in the 1970s to continue to play the
world policeman role it had assumed at the start of the post-World War
II period. Further, as Stepan points out, "the traditional instruments
of U.S. influence in Latin America—e.g., economic and military
assistance—have had less potency in the 1970s and 1980s than in earlier

years of the post-war period."[38] Additionally, Wesson speaks of another factor that significantly constrained the *caudillo* role of the United States in the 1960s and 1970s—the lagging of United States will.[39] In other words, to be *caudillo,* beneficent or otherwise, the United States must have the determination as well as the resources to do so.

Significant variations exist among Latin American countries both in terms of their diversification of international contacts and in their capacity to expand international contracts. Generally speaking, those Latin American countries with the most to offer—large markets, attractive investment opportunities, demand for technology, political support on specific issues—are the ones in the most favorable position to establish new international relationships. Despite the growth in international opportunity and institutional capacity, some smaller, less developed Latin American countries have lacked the capacity to take advantage of new international opportunities.

Diversification, it should be noted, has two dimensions. The tangible one involves *actual* reduction in dependence on the United States. The other dimension is intangible and more psychological—a *feeling* of lessened dependence. An example of the latter dimension might be the confrontational tone of the 1969 Consensus of Vina del Mar in which Latin American countries collectively spelled out their economic policy demands vis-à-vis the United States. Another might be Brazil's recognition of the Cuban and Soviet-backed Popular Movement for the Liberation of Angola.

The United States continues to function as *caudillo* in its long-time backyard—the insular Caribbean and Central America. This is demonstrated by its various actions against the Sandinista regime in Nicaragua—the mining of Nicaraguan harbors, the trade embargo, and overt and covert support to the Contras in their campaign against the Sandinistas. While the members of the Association of Eastern Caribbean States viewed the United States action in Grenada as that of a beneficent *caudillo,* Ibero-America as a whole did not. Similarly, many states have not looked upon the United States approach to Sandinista Nicaragua as wholly beneficent, although some military and right-wing elements may have.

The future of America's *caudillo* role, even in the Caribbean basin, is open to question. The Reagan administration's failure to oust Manuel Noriega and its willingness to allow the demise of the Contras as an effective counterrevolutionary force cast doubt on United States will and capacity to shape events in even the smallest of the region's nations. But the success of Bush administration's military action in Panama in December 1989 and its support in February 1990 for the victorious

Nicaraguan Presidential candidate Violeta Chamorro may well demonstrate that the will and capability are, indeed, still there. On the other hand, however, the Latin American debt crisis (which has affected the largest countries most, notably Mexico and Brazil), combined with economic stagnation, have largely curbed further efforts at diversification of international relations and have again made the United States a more salient partner. The debtor countries have looked to the United States to help manage the debt and, ironically, expect it to function as beneficent *caudillo* on this one issue.

Participation in foreign policy making. Foreign policy in Latin America is an extension of domestic policy, and the foreign policy decision-making process in many ways resembles the process for making domestic policy decisions. The range of participants in foreign policy making is narrower, however, and has traditionally been the preserve of the elite stratum of society. G. Pope Atkins reports that although modernization and development have produced a middle sector that is interested and involved in domestic political issues, most of its members take little interest in foreign policy issues (though this might change in the future). The same is true of labor and, of course, the peasantry and the dispossessed. Public opinion, according to the same author, does not exert any significant influence on foreign policy decisions or actions.[40]

Who, then, actually makes foreign policy decisions in Latin America? The simple answer is, of course, the chief executive—a fairly accurate assessment up to the 1960s. Whether important issues of state or minor foreign policy issues were involved, the president, in conjunction with a relatively small coterie of officials, tended to make decisions on their own.

The importance of idiosyncratic, or voluntaristic, factors in the making of foreign policy should, therefore, be underlined. Not all Latin American chief executives have had the same orientation to foreign policy and international issues, and many have pursued their personal preferences. Wilhelmy identifies two sorts of presidents—the animateur and the referee. While the former takes an active role in formulating and implementing foreign policy, the latter gives lesser priority to such matters and leaves the initiative to other actors.[41]

Regardless of how much of an animateur a chief executive is, he can no longer single-handedly make or carry out foreign policy. The chief executive is usually a generalist rather than an expert in a particular area of public policy, such as foreign affairs. This means that he is dependent on others for technical specialized knowledge and for details.

That dependence significantly restricts the president's constitutional status as maker of foreign policy, especially as government and foreign policy agendas become increasingly complex. In the few Latin American countries—the Dominican Republic, Honduras, and Paraguay—where government and foreign policy agendas have remained relatively straightforward, the chief executive continues to enjoy sweeping autonomy in foreign policy.[42]

Traditionally, the greatest dependence a Latin American president has had is on the foreign minister and his staff. Other institutions also aid the president: key cabinet departments (such as the treasury, trade, tourism, and agriculture), the national bank and other financial entities, development agencies, and autonomous and semi-autonomous government agencies. As economic development became a priority and economic interdependence a fact of life, the foreign ministry was gradually bypassed or displaced by other government bodies responsible for these areas.

From the 1960s onwards, therefore, a more complex foreign policy-making process has evolved. Now, as Harold Eugene Davis and Larman C. Wilson point out, "The president must carry along with him the power structure through which he governs."[43] Alberto Van Klaveren elaborates further:

> [I]n general it is erroneous to view the foreign-policy making process in Latin America as a very simple and restricted process in which only two or three persons participate. For one thing, political systems in the region, democratic as well as authoritarian, include highly institutionalized bureaucracies and complex networks of interest groups that participate in the foreign-policy arena. For another thing, relatively high levels of development according to third world standards have imposed new demands upon what used to be traditional foreign policy establishments.[44]

The number of actors in foreign policy making has especially increased, in Van Klaveren's view, in the larger, more economically developed states, such as Brazil, Mexico, Argentina, and Venezuela. Let us examine this trend towards broader-based foreign policy decision making in a number of countries.

In the case of Brazil, Schneider has pointed to the dominant role played by the armed forces during the period of military rule from the 1960s to the 1980s. The senior command of the armed forces set the fundamental goals and established the boundaries of foreign policy, and though he was a member of that command the president could not act on his own. Thus, "The military is clearly the president's basic constituency; it is the group whose reactions to significant developments and policy initiatives are most assiduously sought out and anticipated by other groups and individuals."[45] At the same time, whether under military rule or not, the country's foreign policy traditionally rested on a broad consensus developed and presided over by the foreign ministry, as Selcher has noted.[46]

In reality, Brazilian presidents during the period of military rule may not have been as constrained as the foregoing might suggest. The armed forces were more preoccupied with the domestic restructuring of the country than with foreign policy issues, except when national security or their institutional interests were involved. By contrast, in recent years the economic and social modernization of the country and its enhanced role in the international economy has both created new publics concerned with foreign policy questions and has projected governmental agencies, once primarily concerned with domestic matters, into the international arena.

The same trend can be seen in Mexico. Although foreign policy has traditionally been the exclusive province of the president, events of the last two decades appear to be opening the foreign policy making domain to more actors. Brandenburg speaks of "the demands imposed on the President of Mexico by the 'liberal Machiavellian' " political system he heads. The president cannot forget in making foreign policy that he is the political leader of Mexico."[47] Accordingly, he must consult with other top Mexican political leaders and influentials, other members of the so-called Revolutionary family, before making any major foreign decisions or radical changes in policy. Ferris has pointed to the presence of more progressive senators in the Mexican upper house who are actively interested in foreign policy questions.[48] In turn Williams has recognized an expanded role of the Mexican military in the making of national security decisions, largely as a response to the influx of Guatemalan refugees in the southern border states and to problems associated with "narcotraffickers."[49]

If the entry of new actors into foreign policy decision-making processes has characterized much of Latin America since the 1960s, bureaucratic-authoritarian regimes have continued to concentrate power in the hands of the chief executive, at times with disastrous results. A case in point is Argentina. Tulchin has argued that the concern for institutional unity within its military, along with the right of each service to veto any action of the ruling junta, produced bottlenecks in decision making. It also cut the government off from civilian advisors:

Censorship in the press, the often murderous manner in which the armed services carried on their political dialogue outside the government, and the severe repression of public political activity virtually eliminated mediating mechanisms in the society and in the government bureaucracy itself through which the nation's leaders could assimilate information vital to their decision-making function.[50]

The military regime refused to be constrained by civilian actors in making the decision to seize the Falklands. Closed off from alternative sources of information and traditional actors in the bureaucratic complex, the Galtieri regime induced military disaster and collapsed.[51]

In Chile, the constitution of 1925 granted the president broad authority to conduct foreign relations but also established significant restraints on presidential powers. According to Manfred Wilhelmy, the balance-of-power framework created was to insure that the president manifested "moderate behavior" in carrying out the nation's foreign policy. Under the 1925 constitution, a trend towards technical specialization and bureaucratic fragmentation took place in a manner similar to Brazil or Mexico. However, with the seizure and consolidation of power by the Pinochet regime in the 1970s, recentralization of foreign policy decision making in the hands of the president recurred.[52]

Finally, the case of Peru suggests that even with the demise of military rule, incoming civilian presidents are not at full liberty to dismantle the foreign policy apparatus or ignore the foreign policy priorities established by the previous regime. Lincoln reports that when the Peruvian military returned government to the hands of civilians, President Belaunde Terry cut some programs established by the military because the country could not afford them. But he did not overturn those policies having to do with the military itself, above all, military spending and expansion.[53] That restraint was a mark of deference to a powerful veto group that had proved itself capable, in the past, of ousting civilian governments. The amnesties granted to the military by newly installed civilian rulers in Southern Cone states in the mid-1980s represented a domestic policy counterpart to preserving the prestige of the military.

We have discovered a general trend toward more diffuse and complex processes of making foreign policy in Latin America and have suggested under what conditions exceptions occur. Let us examine other pressures making for more participatory foreign policy establishments.

Latin American officials do not totally disregard the general public when reaching foreign policy decisions. Citizens establish certain parameters on foreign policy behavior that officials would only transgress at great risk. Thus, no Mexican chief executive could be successful without demonstrating his country's independence from the United States, whether through votes in the Organization of American States, foreign visits (such as de la Madrid's to Cuba in 1988), or in official discourse. Decisions not to break diplomatic ties with Cuba when the United States called for such action, not to suspend air links with the country, and to oppose the ouster of the Castro government from the OAS should be seen in this light.[54] In similar fashion, no Bolivian foreign policy maker could publicly abandon that country's claim to an outlet to the Pacific, nor could an Argentine foreign policy maker acknowledge British sovereignty over the Falkland Islands or abandon the Argentine claim. To be sure, these are very broad parameters that few leaders would be inclined to violate, but to the extent that they do exist they serve as constraints.

Another political constraint may be elected legislatures in democratic systems. While it is true that legislatures, even in the most democratic of Latin American countries, are not a major force in the formulation of foreign policy, they can sometimes hinder the executive in the conduct of foreign affairs. Two examples may illustrate this point: the Chilean legislature once withheld permission for President Frei to make an official visit to the United States; in turn, since 1958 Venezuelan executives have found their efforts to take the country into the Latin American Free Trade Association and, later, into the Andean Group, delayed by the legislature (working with certain economic interest groups).

If Latin American nations have differed in the degree to which participation in foreign policy making has broadened, the enormous expansion in the number of external actors has tended to increase the range of participation in foreign policy making. The existence of multinational corporations, international labor organizations, transnational party blocs, international human rights organizations and foundations, United States and Soviet military missions, and even international guerrilla and terrorist groups, have had the effect both of politicizing their counterparts within the Latin American nations and of stimulating direct action on their part when circumstances warrant it. International agencies, like the Inter-American Bank, the International Monetary Fund, and the World Bank, sometimes must be consulted in setting or carrying out policy. Who the president consults depends in large measure on the issue at hand: an issue dealing with political asylum or drug trafficking may be referred to justice or interior rather than the foreign ministry; an issue concerning foreign debt might be referred to the treasury, the national bank, and development agencies rather than the foreign ministry.

Finally, the *caudillo* role of the United States has for many decades shaped both the foreign and domestic policies of Latin American states. Lowenthal observes:

> The United States. . .considered it normal during the 1960's [and earlier] to have a major voice in the internal affairs of Latin American and Caribbean countries and a virtual veto on their foreign policies. Overwhelming U.S. power made it feasible for the United States to involve itself so deeply in regional affairs that no movement that might challenge U.S. domination could easily come to power or last long. Cuba, protected by its alliance with the Soviet Union, was the one exception.[55]

Thus, Latin American countries have been especially vulnerable to the penetrative type of international linkage in which members of one political system take a direct part in the political process of another political system.[56] And it is not just United States clients that have found their foreign policy behavior constrained by external linkages. That Fidel Castro did not speak out against Soviet imperialism in its suppression of political liberalization in Czechoslovakia or its invasion of Afghanistan is attributable to Cuba's extreme dependence on the USSR. Castro deferred to his *patrón,* even if that did nothing to enhance his position in the Non-Aligned Movement in which he aspired to a leadership role and in which anti-imperialism was the rallying cry.

In summary, two broad trends have been at work in Latin America to determine the nature and extent of participation in foreign policy making. One is the historical tendency to repose such power in the hands of the executive and a small group of advisors—primarily members of the diplomatic corps and the foreign ministry. Social modernization, economic development, and the growth of political communication, while not totally overwhelming this tradition, have nonetheless greatly expanded such participation both inside and outside the government. Thus, while the president's role in earlier decades was more unfettered and therefore more in keeping with what the political culture literature has had to say about presidential *caudillismo,* such behavior has had, of necessity, to become tempered as foreign policy agendas have become increasingly complex.

Separation of the foreign policy establishment. Traditionally the Latin American foreign policy establishment has been distinct from the domestic political process. In large part it consisted of the chief executive, the foreign minister, the bureaucracy of the foreign ministry, and diplomats posted abroad. However, due to the expansion of what foreign policy is thought to be, this insularity has been breaking down.

First, we can note that only rarely has the Chilean foreign minister been a national-level politician.[57] Atkins reports that, at times, political activists have been recruited to represent Chile in diplomatic posts abroad.[58] Second, several cabinet-level positions in Mexico have served as a "stepping-stone" to the presidency, but Secretary of Foreign Relations is not one of them. The same is true of Mexico's prestigeous ambassadorships to the United States, Britain, Cuba, France, the USSR, the United Nations, and the Organization of American States.[59] Third, when the military seized power in Brazil in 1964, the military leadership manifested a high regard for the staff of the foreign ministry, but not for personnel in other parts of the bureaucracy. Consequently, the military leadership did not intervene in the foreign ministry as it did in most other bureaucratic institutions.[60]

Undoubtedly, this separation from domestic politics has much to do with how diplomacy has been defined. That definition has been a narrow, traditionalist one and does not reflect the realities of foreign policy and international relations in the last quarter of the twentieth century. The definition of that mission in virtually all Ibero-American countries has been that of representing the country abroad and in international forums and building and maintaining cordial relations with other countries. That definition of mission has tended to take a highly legalist approach to foreign affairs (Castro's Cuba is an exception on both counts). The traditionally defined foreign policy establishment did not direct itself to such "specialized" or "technical" matters as international trade, economics, international finance, and science and technology. The narrow definition of diplomatic mission has had at least three consequences. First, the foreign policy establishment, because it interacts almost wholly with external actors, has had little opportunity to construct a domestic political constituency or power base or, even, to develop ties with politically significant domestic groups. Second, the issues of concern to the foreign policy establishment are generally not the center of national political debate. Third, as Atkins puts it: "Foreign ministries [i.e., the traditional Latin American foreign policy establishment] have been increasingly challenged by other bureaucracies in foreign policy administration"[61] That challenge has been successfully mounted by those bureaucracies that do have expertise in such areas as international trade, economics, international finance, science and technology, and other development-related subjects (education, health, urban planning, sanitation, housing, and agriculture). The bureaucratic actors that are challenging the traditionally defined foreign policy establishment are much less separate from the domestic political process. Indeed, they are part of it, for the issues they deal with are ones that are at the center of national political debate.

In most Latin American countries the foreign ministry is endeavoring to catch up and regain the central position it enjoyed in earlier decades when the traditional foreign policy establishment faced a less complex policy agenda. But the establishment faces an uphill battle, since it is now confronted by entrenched specialized bureaucracies that have established their command over certain issue areas and are not likely to surrender it willingly. Should the traditional establishment succeed in catching up and asserting itself in previously ignored issue areas, it is likely this will end its separation from domestic policies.

The separation from domestic politics is also influenced by the skills that the international political system demands of the foreign policy establishment. The realities of the international system, especially the absence of an authoritative decision maker, coupled with the subordinate power position of Latin American countries in the international system, put a premium on such skills as negotiation, compromise, cooperation, and coalition building. These are traits that do not figure prominently in the domestic political process of most Latin American states.

The degree to which the foreign policy establishment is separated from domestic politics is not uniform throughout Latin America. The separation is non-existent in Castro's Cuba and most fully developed in Brazil. In the latter country, diplomatic personnel are the products of the Rio Branco Institute, created and directed by the foreign ministry. Entry into the institute is by an examination that is biased in favor of the upper class. The socialization process instills a strong esprit de corps and a feeling of both difference from and superiority to other bureaucratic elements. Such an ethos leads to a pronounced sense of separation from the rest of the bureaucracy. Graduates of the Rio Branco Institute are, in fact, more professional than other members of the bureaucracy.

Economic dependence. One does not need to subscribe to dependency theory in order to acknowledge that Latin American countries are economically dependent on advanced countries. That has been true since the countries emerged as *de jure* independent entitites. The dependence on advanced states, or "center," was spelled out in the Prebisch thesis, or ECLA doctrine, concerning the causes of Latin American underdevelopment.[62] Economic dependence is as much a reality for the most developed Latin American countries as it is for the least developed ones. The nature of the dependence may differ from country to country: Brazil and Mexico need external markets for manufactured goods and access to relatively advanced technology and the international financial market; Guatemala and Honduras, at the other end of the spectrum, need access to external markets (especially the United States one) for primary products and semi-manufactured goods and a continued inflow of foreign investment. But dependence is a common reality and, contrary to Latin American expectations, development has brought more rather than less dependence on advanced countries.

Dependence has affected foreign policy behavior in at least two ways. First, in the early post-World War II years when Latin American countries were almost wholly dependent on the United States for investment capital, markets, and technology, when most Latin American governments were less assertive or less inclined to take independent initiatives than more recently, and when the United States was all-powerful in the hemisphere, virtually all Latin American governments backed United States foreign policy initiatives. Backing was given to the policy of containing the USSR, the formation of the United Nations, nonrecognition of the People's Republic of China, the establishment and survival of Israel, the effort to curb North Korean aggression against South Korea, and, with some reluctance, the United States conversion of the Organization of American States into an anti-communist alliance.[63] Some Latin American governments may have backed these United States initiatives out of conviction. But United States political clout in the region in the aftermath of World War II, as well as the imperative not to endanger the inflow of capital and technology or access to the North American market, go further in explaining the region's pro-American orientation to international affairs.[64] Support for United States global positions was undoubtedly seen by various Latin American governments as the necessary precondition for beneficent United States behavior towards Latin America's economic aspirations.

There are, to be sure, exceptions to adherence to the United States foreign policy orientation, the most obvious and dramatic being Cuba. That the Castro regime could take on the United States and survive is explained by the fact that it obtained the protection of the other superpower. It probably would not have survived had it embraced China. In this case the United States also failed to implement fully its *caudillo* role when it was still possible to avoid a confrontation with the USSR. In the early 1960s under Quadros and Goulart, Brazil constituted another exception, which was ended by a military coup that Washington welcomed and was prepared to assist.[65]

Second, the desire to escape from economic dependence has produced a quest in Latin America for autonomy. The means to attain that elusive goal has been seen as development. In fact, Coleman and Quirós assert that the main determinant of Latin American foreign policy and international behavior is the product of the particular economic development strategy that a government selects for itself.[66] These authors identify three contending development strategies that Latin American countries pursue: the conventional, the reformist, and the revolutionary. Each strategy demands its own foreign policy orientation.

The conventional strategy—what might be termed the traditional Latin American approach to attainment of development—emphasizes using the existing modern sectors of the economy and society: the urban industrial and agro-export sectors. While focusing on economic growth, little attention is paid to correcting inequalities in income or opportunity. The assumption is made that benefits from growth in the modern sector will, in time, filter downward and ultimately pull the less privileged sectors upward. While attainment of national economic autonomy may be a long-term objective, it is decidedly secondary to access to international markets and capital.

The convential strategy of development has been followed by all of the Latin American countries at one time or another. It was the prevailing strategy in the 1940s and 1950s. By the 1970s, nearly all countries had abandoned it, though a few of the small, least developed countries in Central America and the Caribbean (Guatemala, Honduras, El Salvador, and the Dominican Republic) still largely adhere to it. The traditional strategy is not directed towards ending the nation's dependence—at least in the short term—and dictates a foreign policy of close association with the United States and a virtual open door for United States private investment.

The reformist strategy has a different imperative: to end the vast gap between the modern and pre-modern sectors of society and create a single society that is integrated both economically and socially. This strategy of development aims at asserting national control over the economy. This quest for national economic control is primarily concerned with ending economic dependency. It is "a doctrine destined to serve the nation by making it not richer, but freer, by promoting not its material welfare, but its independence of foreign influence."[67] The origins of such nationalistic sentiment can be traced back at least to the Mexican oil expropriation in the early twentieth century. The sentiment became generalized throughout most of Latin America in the late 1960s and the 1970s when it was realized that the conventional strategy may have yielded some development but it had also engendered greater foreign control of the economy.

The reformist strategy requires a foreign policy quite different from that of the conventional one. Foreign investment is welcomed conditionally, but must submit to host-government regulations and must promote the development needs and desires of the host-country government. Further, foreign investors may be wholly excluded from certain sectors of the economy. Two laws enacted while Luis Echeverría was President of Mexico are illustrative of the reformist approach to foreign investment. The law on the transfer of technology was designed to alleviate the country's balance of payments deficit. It required that both foreign and domestic companies use domestically available technology, and it limited the export opportunities of firms that purchased costly foreign technology.[68] The other law, on foreign investment, established a more selective invitation to foreign investors than had previously been the case. It required that new foreign investment demonstate that it would serve such Mexican development objectives as creating new jobs and contributing to industrial diversification before being allowed to enter the country. An additional requirement pre-dating Echeverría was that of "Mexicanization"—the requirement that not more than forty-nine per cent of the capital or management of an enterprise be foreign.[69]

Probably the most stringent and ambitious regulation of foreign investment within the framework of the reformist strategy of development was found in Decision 24 (officially titled, the Common System for Treatment of Foreign Capital and on Trademarks, Patents, Licenses, and Royalties) of the Andean Group adopted in December 1970. The document established uniform rules governing foreign investment in Bolivia, Chile, Colombia, Ecuador, Peru and, when it joined the group, Venezuela. In the volatile and traditionally foreign-dominated area of natural resources, signatory countries could grant new concessions to foreign (i.e., non-Andean) interests until 1981 provided no depletion allowance was granted and the concession was limited to a twenty-year period. Establishment of new foreign-owned companies was prohibited in public service, insurance, banking and finance. To continue receiving local deposits, foreign-owned banks already operating in the region had to sell eighty per cent of their capital to domestic (i.e., Andean) sources within three years of the agreement taking force. Also, these institutions, together with firms dealing with publicity (radio, television, and newspapers), internal transportation, and domestic marketing, could no longer receive new direct foreign investment.

Various restrictions were placed on the manufacturing sector. The transfer of profits out of the region by foreign investors was limited to an annual amount of not more than fourteen per cent of their investment. Only domestic firms (at least eighty per cent capital participation by Andean sources) and mixed firms (a minimum of fifty one per cent host regional domestic ownership) had access to the benefits of the Andean Common Market. Decision 24 also encouraged disinvestment, or fade-out: foreign companies could become eligible to participate in Andean Group free trade only by converting to domestic or mixed ownership.[70]

Under the reformist strategy of development, some nationalization of foreign investment has occurred. Most often it has taken place in the areas of public services (utilities, railroads, airlines, radio) and natural resources (petroleum and mining). But governments have increasingly learned how to achieve the benefits of nationalization without the costs.

Countries following the conventional strategy have a foreign policy that centers on interaction with the United States in both government and private sectors. Those pursuing the reformist strategy seek diversification of international interactions and do not wish to exchange dependence on the United States for dependence on some other actor, as Cuba has. Rather, they have endeavored, with considerable success, to reduce dependence on one country (the United States) by establishing new diplomatic and economic links with other advanced countries, especially Japan, the European Community, some East European countries and, more recently, some of the nations of the Pacific Rim (such as Taiwan). Diversification has entailed finding new markets, sources of investment capital, and sources of technology. For many Latin American countries, particularly those in South America, the diversification of relations from the 1960s onwards marks a return to earlier practice, following a period of exceptional United States influence in the region in the immediate wake of World War II.

The foreign policy of the reformist strategy has manifested two other notable characteristics. One is greater association with Third World countries, especially in such multilateral forums as the Group of 77, UNCTAD, and the Non-Aligned Movement.[71] Two, foreign policy under the reformist strategy contains a strong element of nationalism, especially a willingness, and often even a domestic political necessity, to "take on" the United States in particular and the developed world in general. One illustration is the Consensus of Viña del Mar when the countries of Latin America collectively presented a series of economic demands to the United States. Another is President Echeverría's Charter of Economic Rights and Duties of States which was endorsed both by UNCTAD and the U.N. General Assembly (figure 3.3).

FIGURE 3.3

Echeverría's Charter of Economic Rights and Duties of Developed States

- The right of countries to use their natural resources as they wish;
- The right for each country to determine the role and responsibility of private capital;
- The obligation of states to forego military or economic coercion against others;
- The recognition that host countries have the right to define the rights of and limitations on foreign capital;
- The abandonment on the part of multi-national corporations of interference in host country affairs;
- The abandonment on the part of developed countries of trade discrimination against less developed ones;
- The establishment of fair, stable prices for primary products;
- The establishment of low interest rates and untied development financing.

Source: Guy Poitras, "Mexico's 'New' Foreign Policy," *Inter-American Economic Affairs*, 28 (Winter 1974), pp. 59–77.

A third example of Latin America taking on the United States was its criticism of the United States for its support for Britain during the Falkland Islands conflict. This was a case of Latin American countries expecting, for no justifiable reason, that the United States would act as beneficent *caudillo* by siding with Argentina. A fourth example was the refusal of many Latin American countries to go along with the United States grain sale embargo on the Soviet Union. A final example was Brazil's refusal, in the wake of United States pressure in the early years of the Carter administration, to drop the nuclear energy agreement between itself and West Germany. Such cases demonstrate Latin America's willingness to take on the United States while at the same time expecting it to provide for the *bien común*. It also demonstrates how difficult it is for either the United States or the Latin American nations to agree on what the *bien común* really is.

The revolutionary strategy is radically different from either of the others. Those strategies entail gradual change at differing paces. Furthermore, the two assume continued membership in the Western international economic system. By contrast, the radical strategy demands rapid and fundamental change domestically and equally fundamental change in international orientation and alignment. In addition to the goals it shares in common with the reformist strategy, the revolutionary one seeks economic and social equality in domestic society. What really sets the revolutionary strategy apart from the reformist is the means employed—extremely rapid change and a state-controlled and state-owned economy.

The foreign policy behavior of the revolutionary strategy as pursued by Castro's Cuba is a sharp break with the United States and with the Inter-American System and a movement toward the Marxist-Leninist bloc and the Non-Aligned Movement. Nationalization of foreign and domestic investment is also part of the foreign policy behavior of a revolutionary strategy. The foreign policy goal is to end all external dependence. In Cuba's case, however, it would be difficult to speak of achieving this objective; rather, Havana exchanged one external dependency for another, although this was not Castro's initial intention.

To date, of the Latin American countries only Cuba has fully embraced the revolutionary strategy of development and its foreign policy orientation. Nicaragua under the Sandinistas has embraced some elements of it, but that country's foreign policy behavior is much closer to that of the reformist strategy (as we discuss in chapter 6) than to the revolutionary one.[72]

Conclusion

This chapter has outlined the Latin American style in international decision making and has related it to some general features of its region-wide political culture. The nations of the area are seen as having to adjust their national political behavior patterns to an international political environment that often calls for different patterns of behavior. Thus, in this concluding section, we will seek to answer two interconnected questions: 1) To what extent is the generalized pattern of Latin American cultural orientations and behavior congruent with the requirements of the international system? and 2) What changes are taking place in contemporary Latin America that have an impact on this degree of congruence?

We began by postulating that because it lacks a sovereign center, international diplomacy places a premium on such democratic habits and skills as bargaining, compromise, and coalition building, whereas Latin America's traditional monistic culture has tended to produce either authoritarian modes of decision making or, when a monocratic regime breaks down, periods of intense conflict and violence. Yet, in their international behavior, the Latin American states have been marked by low levels of inter-state violence and foreign policy establishments that have absorbed the norms and skills of international bargaining.

We would give a number of explanations for this apparent incongruency. The first is a structural one: being a "loose association of states" without a history of extensive exchange of goods and services, Latin American nations have not been as prone to engage in intense inter-state competition and conflict as other areas of the world have been. Second, as economically dependent nations their primary international relationships have been as client states of an international *patrón* or *caudillo*—Great Britain in the nineteenth century, the United States since the 1930s, and more recently, as in the case of Cuba and Nicaragua, the USSR. Third, there was a tradition in many of the region's states to separate their foreign policy establishments from the national political system, thereby to a degree insulating them in their recruitment, socialization, training, and career structure from the national political system and its political culture. Because international politics was conducted in an arena very different from the domestic environment, the informal rules and norms that prevailed in domestic politics did not necessarily apply in foreign affairs.

Finally, two methodological biases need to be considered. One is the fact that much of the existent political culture literature is largely outdated, based on the Latin America of the 1950s and early 1960s; it does not address the transformation of political culture that has occurred since. The other is that the literature on Latin American political culture did not factor behavior in the international arena into its composite sketch; rather, political culture was derived exclusively from domestic political behavior. It is the explanatory power of both combined that offers us the greatest assurance that we understand the behavior of Latin American states in the international arena. Such methodological biases have had the effect of exaggerating the lack of fit between political culture and contemporary international politics.

Developments over the past four decades have changed the degree of reciprocity between political culture and international politics. To begin with, increase in trade and socio-political exchanges is not merely placing these nations in greater contact with one another, but also may be raising levels of competition between them. Central America is a prime example of internal and external warfare flowing from economic rivalry, population migration, and renewed political hostility beginning with the 1969 Soccer War.

Second, superpower rivalry brought many of these nations into the "cold war." As a result, domestic *caudillaje* behavior has become internationalized. This has taken place at the precise moment when the capacity of either the United States or the Soviet Union to create or maintain a regional *bien comun* has been greatly reduced.

Third, increased participation in international decision making by a welter of domestic political and governmental organizations has had the effect of introducing domestic issues into the foreign policy arena as never before. This is further complicated by the emergence of a world economic and political system which now so greatly penetrates these relatively weak national polities.

Fourth, the drive to break or substantially reduce dependency on the United States has had the effect of driving Latin American nations into the much more competitive global system.

It is impossible to predict whether the new contours shaping the environment of Latin American foreign policy making will produce a "spillover effect" in which the historic traits of Latin American political culture will increasingly come to dominate its international behavior, or whether the functional relationships as linkages of the global system will militate against national tendencies. These are matters that aggregate analysis cannot discern. The next three chapters take a contemporary look at six circum-Caribbean states possessing different national political cultures, and they explore the degree of congruence between these cultures and their international behavior.

Notes

1. Edward S. Milenky, "Problems, Perspectives, and Modes of Analysis: Understanding Latin American Approaches to World Affairs," in Ronald G. Hellman and H. Jon Rosenbaum (eds.), *Latin America: The Search for a New International Role*. New York: John Wiley & Sons, 1975, p. 100.

2. This would also tend to apply to central banks and governmental agencies dealing with international commerce and finance.

3. G. Pope Atkins, *Latin America in the International Political System*. 2nd edn. Boulder, CO: Westview Press, 1989, p. 78.

4. Norman A. Bailey, "The United States as Caudillo," *Journal of Inter-American Studies*, 5, no. 3 (July 1963), pp. 313–324.

5. Bailey, "The United States as Caudillo," pp. 313–314.

6. Bailey, "The United States as Caudillo," pp. 314–315.

7. On July 20, 1895 Secretary of State Richard Olney, at the time the United States was defying Great Britain concerning the Venezuelan boundary dispute,

declared: "Today the United States is practically sovereign on this continent and its fiat is law upon the subjects to which it confines its interposition." Bailey, "The United States as Caudillo," p. 318.

8. Bailey, "The United States as Caudillo," p. 320.

9. Bailey, "The United States as Caudillo," pp. 318–322.

10. Julio Jaguaribe, *Political Development: A General Theory and a Latin American Case Study.* New York: Harper & Row, Publishers, 1973, Chapter 22; and Guillermo O'Donnell, *The Bureaucratic Authoritarian State.* Berkeley: University of California Press, 1983.

11. Milenky, "Problems, Perspectives and Modes of Analysis," p. 103.

12. John Duncan Powell, "Peasant Society and Clientelist Politics," *American Political Science Review,* 64, no. 2 (June 1970), p. 411.

13. Milenky, "Problems, Perspectives and Modes of Analysis," p. 106.

14. Milenky, "Problems, Perspectives and Modes of Analysis," p. 103.

15. Milenky, "Problems, Perspectives and Modes of Analysis," p. 107.

16. Kenneth N. Waltz, "Conflict in World Politics," in Steven L. Spiegel and Kenneth N. Waltz (eds.), *Conflict in World Politics.* Cambridge, MA: Winthrop, 1971, pp. 454–474.

17. David F. Ronfeldt and Luigi R. Einaudi, "Conflict and Cooperation among Latin American States," in Luigi R. Einaudi (ed.), *Beyond Cuba: Latin America Takes Charge of Its Future.* New York: Crane, Rusak, 1974, p. 192.

18. See Edwin Lieuwen, *Arms and Politics in Latin America.* Revised edn. New York, Praeger, 1961.

19. Robert N. Burr, "Argentina and Chile," in Steven L. Spiegel and Kenneth N. Waltz (eds.), *Conflict in World Politics,* p. 175.

20. Jack Child, "Inter-state Conflict in Latin America in the 1980's," in Jennie K. Lincoln and Elizabeth G. Ferris (eds.), *The Dynamics of Latin American Foreign Policies: Challenges for the 1980s.* Boulder, CO: Westview Press, 1984, pp. 21–35.

21. See: Thomas P. Anderson, *The War of the Dispossessed: Honduras and El Salvador, 1969.* Lincoln, NB: University of Nebraska Press, 1981.

22. See Luigi Einaudi, Haus Heymann, Jr., David Ronfeldt, and Ceasar Sereseres, *Arms Transfers to Latin America: Toward a Policy of Mature Respect.* Santa Monica, CA: Rand, 1973; and James D. Cochrane "Latin America and Arms 1966–1975: Notes on Acquisitions and Sources of Supply," *Revista/Review Inter-Americana,* X, no. 2 (Summer 1980), pp. 156–172.

23. Abraham F. Lowenthal, "The United States and Latin America: Ending the Hegemonic Presumption," *Foreign Affairs*, 55 (October 1976), pp. 199–213.

24. Jorge I. Domínguez, *U.S. Interests and Politics in the Caribbean and Central America*. Washington: American Enterprise Institute for Public Policy Research, 1982, p. 29.

25. James R. Kurth, "The United States, Latin America, and the World: The Changing International Concept of U.S.-Latin American Relations," in Kevin J. Middlebrook and Carlos Rico (eds.), *The United States and Latin America in the 1980s: Contending Perspectives on a Decade of Crisis*. Pittsburgh: University of Pittsburgh Press, 1986, pp. 61–86.

26. Kurth, "The United States, Latin America, and the World,"p. 64.

27. Howard J. Wiarda, "United States Relations with South America," *Current History*, 86, no. 516 (January 1987), p. 1.

28. Abraham F. Lowenthal, *Partners in Conflict: The United States and Latin America*. Baltimore, MD: Johns Hopkins University Press, 1987, p. 49.

29. G. Pope Atkins, *Latin America in the International Political System*, p. 78.

30. Jennie K. Lincoln, "Introduction to Latin American Foreign Policy: Global and Regional Dimensions," in Elizabeth G. Ferris and Jennie K. Lincoln (eds.), *Latin American Foreign Policies: Global and Regional Dimensions*. Boulder, CO: Westview Press, 1981, p. 14.

31. James D. Cochrane, "Characteristics of Contemporary Latin American International Relations," *Journal of Interamerican Studies and World Affairs*, 20 (November 1978), p. 457.

32. Robert A. Packenham, "Capitalist vs. Socialist Dependency: The Case of Cuba," *Journal of Interamerican Studies and World Affairs*, 23, (Spring 1981), pp. 59–92.

33. What follows draws heavily on James D. Cochrane "Change and Continuity in Latin America's Post-World War II International Behavior," *Review of Latin American Studies*, 1, no. 2, pp. 1–16.

34. Alfred Stepan, "The United States and Latin America: Vital Interests and the Instruments of Power," in Ferris and Lincoln (eds.), *Latin American Foreign Policies*, p. 21.

35. To be sure, a number of Latin American countries moved away from Israel during the 1970s; some others have a significant military supply and developmental and technical assistance relations with the Middle Eastern state.

36. Cole Blasier, *The Giant's Rival: The USSR and Latin America*. Pittsburgh: University of Pittsburgh Press, 1983.

37. Kurth, "The United States, Latin America, and the World."

38. Stepan, "The United States and Latin America."

39. Robert Wesson (ed.), *U.S. Influence in Latin America in the 1980s*. New York: Praeger, 1982.

40. G. Pope Atkins, *Latin America in the International Political System*, p. 73.

41. Manfred Wilhelmy, "Politics, Bureaucracy, and Foreign Policy in Chile," in Heraldo Munoz and Joseph S. Tulchin (eds.), *Latin American Nations in World Politics*. Boulder, CO: Westview Press, 1984, pp. 45–62.

42. Yale H. Ferguson, "Analyzing Latin American Foreign Policies," *Latin American Research Review*, XXII, no. 3, 1987, p. 149.

43. Harold Eugene Davis and Larman C. Wilson, "Some Conclusions," in Harold Eugene Davis, Larman C. Wilson, et al., *Latin American Foreign Policy: An Analysis*. Baltimore, MD: Johns Hopkins University Press, 1975, p. 448.

44. Alberto Van Klaveren, "The Analysis of Latin American Foreign Policies: Theoretical Perspectives," in Heraldo Munoz and Joseph S. Tulchin (eds.), *Latin American Nations in World Politics*. Boulder, CO: Westview Press, 1984, p. 13.

45. Ronald M. Schneider, *Brazil: Foreign Policy of a Future World Power*. Boulder, CO: Westview Press, 1976, p. 68.

46. Wayne Selcher, "Brazil's Foreign Policy: More Actors and Expanding Agendas," in Lincoln and Ferris (eds.), *The Dynamics of Latin American Foreign Policies*,'' pp. 102–103.

47. Frank R. Brandenburg, *The Making of Modern Mexico*. Englewood Cliffs, NJ: Prentice-Hall, 1964, p. 318.

48. Elizabeth Ferris, "Mexico's Foreign Policies: A Study in Contradictions," in Lincoln and Ferris (eds.), *The Dynamics of Latin American Foreign Policies*, pp. 219–220.

49. Edward J. Williams, "The Mexican Military and Foreign Policy: The Evolution of Influence," in David Ronfeldt (ed.), *The Modern Mexican Military: A Reassessment*. San Diego: Center for U.S.-Mexican Studies, University of California, San Diego, 1984, pp. 179–199.

50. Joseph Tulchin, "Authoritarian Regimes and Foreign Policy: The Case of Argentina," in Munoz and Tulchin (eds.), *Latin American Nations in World Politics*, p. 191.

51. See Carlos J. Moneta, "The Malvinas Conflict: Analyzing the Argentine Military Regime's Decision-Making Process," in Munoz and Tulchin (eds.), *Latin American Nations in World Politics*, pp. 119–132 and, especially,

Joseph S. Tulchin, "Authoritarian Regimes and Foreign Policy: The Case of Argentina," in Munoz and Tulchin (eds.), *Latin American Nations in World Politics,* pp. 186–199.

52. Manfred Wilhelmy, "Politics, Bureaucracy, and Foreign Policy in Chile," in Munoz and Tulchin (eds.), *Latin American Nations in World Politics,* pp. 47, 51.

53. Jennie K. Lincoln, "Peruvian Foreign Policy Since the Return to Democratic Rule," in Jennie K. Lincoln and Elizabeth G. Ferris (eds.), *The Dynamics of Latin American Foreign Policies: Challenges for the 1980s,* pp. 137–149.

54. Martin C. Needler, "Mexico: Revolution as a Way of Life," in Martin C. Needler (ed.), *Political Systems of Latin America.* 2nd edn. New York: Van Nostrand, 1970, p. 41

55. Abraham F. Lowenthal, *Partners in Conflict: The United States and Latin America.* Baltimore: Johns Hopkins University Press, 1987, p. 31.

56. This definition is adopted from James N. Rosenau, "Toward the Study of National-International Linkages," in Rosenau (ed.) *Linkage Politics* New York: Free Press, 1969, p. 46.

57. Manfred Wilhelmy "Politics, Bureaucracy, and Foreign Policy in Chile," in Heraldo Munoz and Joseph S. Tulchin (eds.), *Latin American Nations in World Politics,* p. 54.

58. Orville G. Cope, "Chile," in Harold Eugene Davis and Larmen C. Wilson et al., *Latin American Foreign Policies: An Analysis,* p. 320.

59. See James D. Cochrane, "Occupants of Elite Positions in the Mexican Diplomatic Community," *Journal of Developing Areas,* 15 (July 1981), pp. 605–620; and James D. Cochrane, "Career Experience of Mexico's Ambassadors: The Case of Occupants of Seven Prestige Diplomatic Posts, 1935–1982," *South Eastern Latin Americanist,* 29 (Sept.–Dec. 1985), pp. 16–32.

60. See Alexandre de S.C. Barros, "The Formulation and Implementation of Brazilian Foreign Policy: Itamaraty and the New Actors," in Munoz and Tulchin (eds.), *Latin American Nations in World Politics,* pp. 30–44.

61. G. Pope Atkins, *Latin America in the International Political System,* p. 76.

62. Lowenthal, *Partners in Conflict.*

63. Jerome Slater, *The OAS and United States Foreign Policy.* Columbus, OH: Ohio State University Press, 1967, pp. 107–182.

64. Lowenthal, *Partners in Conflict.*

65. Phyllis R. Parker, *Brazil and the Quiet Intervention, 1964.* Austin: University of Texas Press, 1979.

66. Kenneth M. Coleman and Luis Quirós-Varela, "Determinants of Latin American Foreign Policies: Bureaucratic Organizations and Development Strategies," in Ferris and Lincoln, (eds.), *Latin American Foreign Policy: Global and Regional*, pp. 39–59.

67. Robert H. Swansbrough, *The Embattled Colossus: Economic Nationalism and United States Investors in Latin America*. Gainesville, FL: University of Florida Press, 1976, p. 11.

68. See Guy Poitras, "Mexico's 'New' Foreign Policy," *Inter-American Economic Affairs*, 28 (Winter 1974), pp. 59–77.

69. Poitras, "Mexico's 'New' Foreign Policy," p. 69.

70. See William P. Avery and James D. Cochrane, "Innovation in Latin American Regionalism: The Andean Common Market," *International Organization*, 27 (Spring 1973) pp. 195–197. Decision 24 subsequently was relaxed somewhat but not abandoned. Shortly after the military seized power in Chile, that country withdrew from the Andean Group. The reason was hostility to Decision 24.

71. The Inter-American countries belonging to the Non-Aligned Movement are: Argentina, Bolivia, Colombia, Cuba, Ecuador, Nicaragua, Panama, Peru. Source: *Atlas of United States Foreign Relations*. 2nd edn. Washington: Department of State, 1985, p. 30.

72. See Mary B. Vanderlaan, *Revolution and Foreign Policy in Nicaragua*. Boulder, CO: Westview Press, 1986.

4

Political Culture and Foreign Policy in the Circum-Caribbean: The Democratic Cultures of Costa Rica and Venezuela

This chapter is divided into two parts. In the first part, we describe the approach adapted for the empirical study of political culture and foreign policy in selected Latin American states, and we sketch the principal characteristics of the states chosen. The second part deals with the relationship between political culture and foreign policy in two Latin American nations with a fundamentally democratic tradition—Costa Rica and Venezuela.

Introduction

The approach. In chapter 2 we outlined the essential features of Latin American political culture in terms of four basic components: (1) the dominant value system which we termed "Thomism"; (2) two competing value systems—Machiavellianism and Latin American (Rousseauan) pluralist democracy; (3) the *caudillaje* pattern of behavior; and (4) the various class variants of *caudillaje* culture. For purposes of simplification, we can look at the six countries under study in terms of two fundamental cultural dimensions: (1) the Dominant Value System, which ranges from the Western Democratic type (WD) to the Latin American type (LA); and (2) the Dominant Behavior Pattern, which ranges from an essentially WD type to the *caudillaje* type. This yields a cultural matrix composed of four possible types of political culture as presented in figure 4.1.

In order to determine the type of political culture that dominates each of the six countries (the cell of the matrix in which each country fits), a technique called secondary analysis will be used. Pioneered by anthropologists working with large numbers of ethnographic studies in the Human Areas Research Files, "the term secondary analysis usually refers to studies based on a reworking of data from earlier research."[1]

FIGURE 4.1

Types of Latin American Political Culture

<table>
<tr><td>WD</td><td>WD Value System with Caudillaje Behavior Patterns</td><td>WD Value System with WD Behavior Patterns</td></tr>
<tr><td>LA</td><td>LA Value System (*) with Caudillaje Behavior Patterns</td><td>LA Value System with WD Behavior Patterns</td></tr>
</table>

Value System (vertical axis)

Caudillaje — Dominant Behavior Pattern — WD

*includes both Thomistic and Machiavellian variants
WD Western Democratic
LA Latin American

As employed in this study, the method involves three fundamental steps. First, a typology of political values and political behavior is created containing a set of categories of analysis composed of the essential characteristics, or features, of the value system or behavior pattern under consideration. Second, a series of operational variables is constructed to assist the analyst in identifying the attitudinal or behavioral patterns which are associated with each characteristic. Third, descriptions of national values and cultural behavior in the literature on the six countries are codified on the basis of the operational variables.

The typology and categories of analysis for the Latin American value system are those described as the "Two Faces of Hispanic Thomism" in figure 2.3. To provide a contrasting cultural category, a Western Democratic Value System type is also employed. To simplify the analysis, the Rousseauan Latin American face is omitted. The entire typology is presented in figure 4.2.

Figure 4.3 adds the operational variables used in codifying the data on national value systems taken from secondary sources.

FIGURE 4.2

Typology and Essential Characteristics of
Latin American and Western Democratic Value Systems

Latin American Value System		Western Democratic Value System
Thomistic Face	Machiavellian Face	
1. Search for *bien común*	1. Factional ideological rigidity	1. Negotiation and compromise
2. Unity	2. Rebellion	2. Pluralism
3. Hierarchy	3. Authoritarianism	3. Popular sovereignty
4. Organicism	4. Power contenders	4. Interest group liberalism
5. Legal idealism	5. Resistance to law	5. Obedience to law
6. Centralism	6. Red tape and corruption	6. Rational-legal administration

FIGURE 4.3

Operational Variables Used to Measure
Characteristics of National Value System

Value System	Characteristics	Operational Variables
A. Hispanic Thomism	1. Search for *bien comun*	a. Consistent rule by single party or movement
	2. Unity	a. History of bureaucratic authoritarian (BA), reactionary despotic (RD) regimes, or personal or one-party systems
	3. Hierarchy	a. Restricted voting b. Severe restrictions on parties and trade unions
	4. Organicism	a. Existence of formal corporative structures b. Informal corporative patterns of elite bargaining

FIGURE 4.3 continued

Value System	Characteristics	Operational Variables
	5. Legal idealism	a. Existence of a number of ideological parties, groups or movement b. Utopianism in public policy
	6. Centralism	a. Considerable governmental control over social and economic activities
B. Machiavellianism	1. Ideological rigidity	a. Existence of important ideological parties, interest groups, or movements
	2. Rebellion	a. History of insurrectionary movements and coups
	3. Authoritarianism	a. Historic domination by BA, RD, and dictatorial regimes b. Exclusion of parties and interest groups from political participation
	4. Power contenders	a. Excessive party and interest group fragmentation b. Frequent demonstration of power potential (strikes, coups, demonstrations, etc.)
	5. Resistance to law	a. Number of combat parties and anomic groups b. Significant use of mass action c. Circumvention or disobedience to law
	6. Red tape and corruption	a. Excessive numbers of bureaucrats b. Reports of bribery and bureaucratic inefficiency

FIGURE 4.3 continued

Value System	Characteristics	Operational Variables
C. Western Democratic	1. Negotiation and compromise	a. Effective legislative system b. Low level of ideological parties, groups, and movements
	2. Pluralism	a. Freedom to organize political parties and interest groups b. High degree of voluntarism in political organizations
	3. Popular sovereignty	a. Regular competitive elections b. Absence of coups
	4. Interest group liberalism	a. Opposition groups allowed to form b. Existence of avenues of articulation of interests
	5. Acceptance of and obedience to law	a. Low levels of coercion in political system b. Low levels of strikes, demonstrations, and insurrectionary movements
	6. Rational-legal administrative system	a. Organized civil service with rules governing recruitment and performance b. Low levels of corruption and private appropriation of government resources c. Governmental agencies operate outside capital city

Note: Some operational variables are naturally the measure of more than one cultural characteristic. How a nation will be categorized depends upon the total constellation of characteristics, not just one. For example, compare A-5-a with B-1-a.

Figure 4.4 sets out the two contrasting typologies for the behavior pattern dimension: the *caudillaje* and the Western Democratic behavior patterns. Figure 4.5 adds the operational variables.

FIGURE 4.4

Typology and Essential Characteristics of
Latin American and Western Democratic Behavior Patterns

Caudillaje Behavior Pattern	Western Democratic Behavior Pattern
1. Power as a major personal goal	1. Wealth and professional success as major personal goals
2. Tolerance for force and violence (*machismo*) in social and political relationships	2. Compromise and negotiation as norms for social and political relationships
3. Stress on personal dignity (*dignidad*) and prestige as ends in themselves	3. Stress on personal contribution to group and/or societal ends and goals
4. Cultivation of patrimonial and/or clientalistic relationships	4. Cultivation of organizational and/or group relationships
5. Personal appropriation of governmental office and resources	5. Trusteeship orientation toward governmental office and resources

FIGURE 4.5

Operational Variables Used to Measure Characteristics of
Caudillaje and Western Democratic Behavior Patterns

Caudillaje Behavior Pattern	
Characteristics	Operational Variables
1. Power as personal goal	a. Existence of numerous personalistic parties b. History of personal dictatorships c. Recruitment of "best and brightest" into politics rather than business
2. Tolerance for force and violence	a. High level of strikes and demonstrations b. High level of military coups and attempted coups

FIGURE 4.5 *continued*

Characteristics	Operational Variables
	c. High level of domestic political problems
	d. Significant curbs on human rights and civil liberties
3. Stress on personal dignity	a. High degree of party factionalism
	b. Existence of numerous personalistic parties
4. Cultivation of patrimonial/clientalistic relationships	a. Existence of numerous personalistic parties
	b. Patronage changes in bureaucracy, military, etc. at regime changes
	c. Reported clientalistic behavior in parties, bureaucracy, and interest groups
5. Personal appropriation of governmental office and resources	a. High levels of corruption reported in the literature

Western Democratic Behavior Pattern

Characteristics	Operational Variables
1. Wealth and professional success as major personal goals	a. Recruitment of "best and brightest" into business rather than politics
	b. Existence of more long-lived stable political parties
2. Compromise and negotiation as norms for social and political relationships	a. Low level of strikes and demonstrations
	b. Low level of military coups
	c. Low level of political assassinations
	d. High respect for human and civil rights
3. Stress on personal contribution to group and/or societal ends and goals	a. Low levels of party factionalism
	b. Existence of community groups manned by volunteers
	c. Business and professional leaders give time to community service

FIGURE 4.5 *continued*

Characteristics	Operational Variables
4. Cultivation of organizational and/or group relationships	a. Long-term commitments to political parties and interest groups b. Stable civil service system c. Low level of personalistic parties
5. Trusteeship orientation toward governmental office and resources	a. Low levels of corruption reported in the literature

It is not the position of the writers that these operational variables are quantifiable or that they represent mutually exclusive categories. Rather they serve as benchmarks around which the literature on the six countries can be organized. Ultimately each country will be rated on each of the variables so as to generate a score to determine which value system and behavior pattern best typifies its political culture. It will then be possible to place then in a four-cell matrix as shown in figure 4.1.

The countries. Six circum-Caribbean nations have been chosen as case studies for this comparative analysis of the relationship between political culture and foreign policy. The selection was based, first of all, on their relative geographic proximity to each other and to the United States. That is, they share in the commonalities of the Caribbean region, are exporters of primary products (largely to the United States), and have been historically dependent on the United States for markets, economic aid, national defense, and various cultural inputs (modern health care, educational materials, and so on). Although they differ in size, population, and levels of modernization when compared to such Latin American countries as Brazil, Mexico, Argentina, or Peru, they are relatively similar in size and population except for Colombia and Venezuela, which rank as medium-sized nations. Data on size and population are provided in table 4.1. The six countries also cover the spectrum of the five political cultural patterns discussed in chapter 2. Cuba since 1959 reflects the "stable monism" pattern; Nicaragua the "alternating monism" pattern; Guatemala a pattern of "alternating monisms punctuated by democratic interludes"; Colombia a "democratic tradition with occasional monistic interludes"; and Costa Rica and Venezeula each reflect over thirty years of "stable democracy."

Table 4.2 provides a summary of the ratings of each country on the three national value systems and the two behavior patterns outlined in the overall model.[2] A high rating score indicates the degree to which

TABLE 4.1

The Six Circum-Caribbean Countries

	Size (sq.Km)	Population	Percentage Urban
Colombia	1,138,338	27,880,000	73.7
Costa Rica	50,900	2,378,000	48.0
Cuba	110,300	9,718,000	87.7
Guatemala	108,889	7,527,000	32.7
Nicaragua	139,000	2,602,000	55.3
Venezuela	898,805	15,040,000	70.8

each of the types of national value systems and types of behavior patterns are reflected in the literature surveyed, based on the operational variables outlined in figures 4.3 and 4.5. A low score indicates that a given type of value system or behavior pattern is not highly reflected in the literature surveyed. A high score indicates that it is.

TABLE 4.2

Profiles of the Six Political Cultures (in Rating Points)

	Dominant Value System			Behavior Pattern	
	Hispanic Thomism	Machiavel-lianism	Western Democratic	Caudillaje	Western Democratic
Colombia:					
1948–1974	11	18	6	19	12
1974–	5	15	11	17	14
Costa Rica	3	7	23	8	18
Cuba:					
1933–1958	11	20	4	19	4
1959–	18	8	11	11	12
Guatemala	11	19	4	20	2
Nicaragua:					
1934–1979	11	11	4	21	7
1979–	13	14	9	11	7
Venezuela	4	10	20	11	16

It is clear from the table that two countries clearly manifest a Western Democratic national value system: Costa Rica and Venezuela.

One other country, Colombia, although predominantly Machiavellian in its value system, shows signs of developing a more Western Democratic political culture since the ending of the National Front Agreement in 1974. The other three countries appear to manifest a predominantly Latin American value system, with Cuba (since 1959) being primarily Thomistic in its value orientation while Guatemala and Nicaragua are primarily Machiavellian. The six countries are placed in the political culture matrix in figure 4.6.

FIGURE 4.6

Political Cultures of the Six Countries

(Three-Dimensional Matrix)

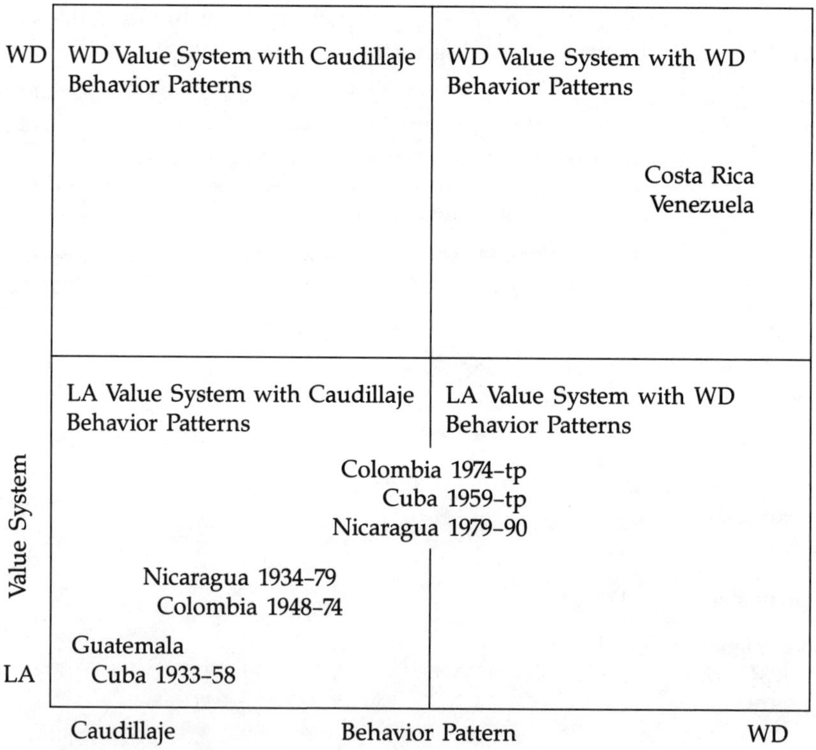

WD Western Democratic
LA Latin American
tp to present

With respect to their *behavior patterns*, Costa Rica and Venezuela both reflect a predominantly Western Democratic pattern although they also demonstrate some *caudillaje* characteristics. Colombia and Nicaragua currently are slightly more *caudillaje*, though not excessively so. Guatemala is strongly *caudillaje* in its behavior. Cuba is also historically a *caudillaje* culture, although in an interesting way it appears to be becoming less so since the Castro regime became institutionalized.

In summary, Costa Rica and Venezuela have political cultures that manifest both a Western Democratic value system and a Western Democratic behavior pattern; Cuba, Nicaragua, and Guatemala have cultures that are essentially Latin American in their value systems and *caudillaje* in their behavior patterns; Colombia seems to be moving slowly from a Latin American to a Western Democratic value system while retaining substantial elements of its traditional *caudillaje* behavior patterns. Except for Colombia, these results are in general agreement with the scores on the revised Fitzgibbon-Johnson index entitled "U.S. View of Democracy in Latin America, 1947–75" (table 4.3). They are also in substantial agreement with the "Bollen Political Democracy Index" for 1960 and 1965 except for Guatemala, which was in somewhat of a "democratic phase" in 1960 (table 4.4). Costa Rica and Venezuela ranked quite high on the two indexes; Cuba, Guatemala, and Nicaragua quite low; while Colombia finds itself lodged between them. With these data in hand, let us now turn to a brief profile of the political cultures of the two democratic states—Costa Rica and Venezuela—and relate this to respective behavior in the international arena.

Costa Rican Political Culture

Costa Rica has a higher literacy rate, a more homogeneous population, higher living standards, and a larger proportion of medium-sized farms and lower proportion of *minifundia* than do the other Central American countries, producing in turn the greatest degree of political stability in the region. "The contrast is so striking that there is a tendency to exaggerate it," Murkland has written.[3] Hubert Herring goes further:

Costa Rica...shares honors with Uruguay as the most soundly democratic in faith and practice of all Latin American states....The few dictatorships in Costa Rican history have been short-lived. Political parties are few and active; political discussion is avid.[4]

In Gaetano Cerosimo's study of elite opinion of the Costa Rican national character, respondents identified the following basic national

TABLE 4.3

Revised Fitzgibbon-Johnson Index:
U.S. View of Democracy in Latin America, 1945–1975

Country	Rank 1945	Rank 1950	Rank 1955	Rank 1960	Rank 1965	Rank (c) 1970	Rank 1975
Argentina	9	15*	15	4	7	14	5
Bolivia	16	13	12	15	16	15	15
Brazil	12*	5	4	6	10	17	16
Chile	3*	2	3	3	2*	2	18
Colombia	**3***	**6**	**9**	**5**	**5**	**5**	**3**
Costa Rica	**2**	**4**	**2**	**2**	**1**	**1**	**1**
Cuba	**5**	**3**	**10**	**16**	**19**	**19**	**14**
Dominican Rep.	20	20	20	20	14*	10	6
Ecuador	12*	7	6	9	12	7	10
El Salvador	14	14	8	13	11	8	8
Guatemala	**11**	**11**	**13**	**12**	**13**	**9**	**9**
Haiti	19	17	14	18	20	20	20
Honduras	17	8	11	14	14*	12	12
Mexico	7	9	5	7	6	6	4
Nicaragua	**15**	**18**	**19**	**17**	**17**	**16**	**17**
Panama	6	10	7	11	9	11	11
Paraguay	18	19	18	19	18	18	19
Peru	8	15*	17	10	8	13	13
Uruguay	1	1	1	1	2*	3	7
Venezuela	**10**	**12**	**10**	**8**	**4**	**4**	**2**

Note: excludes Latin American respondents added to the survey beginning in 1970. The five criteria for the assessment are:
1. free speech
2. free elections
3. free party organization
4. independent judiciary
5. civilian supremacy

(c) Calculated by Wilkie from data in Johnson's Table, cited in source below.

Source: Johnson, "Measuring the Scholarly Image of Latin American Democracy, 1945–1970," tables 3201 and 3204; and Johnson, "Scholarly Images of Latin American Political Democracy in 1975," p. 137. See discussion of the index by James W. Wilkie, *Statistics and National Policy,* Statistical Abstract of Latin America, Supplement 3. Los Angeles: UCLA Latin American Center Publications, University of California, 1974, pp. 480–481.

TABLE 4.4

Bollen Political Democracy Index for 1960 and 1965

	Political Democracy	
	1960	1965
United States	94.6	92.4
Colombia	69.7	71.4
Costa Rica	91.3	90.1
Cuba	13.9	5.2
Guatemala	69.8	39.5
Nicaragua	48.7	55.4
Venezuela	72.5	73.4

Source: Kenneth A. Bollen, "Issues in the Comparative Measurement of Political Democracy," *American Sociological Review,* 45 (June 1980), Appendix 2.

behavioral traits: democratic, peaceful, respectful of civil and political liberty, tolerant, and egalitarian. Negatively, his respondents typified the Costa Rican as conformist, traditionalist, indifferent to public problems, lazy, and prone to emulate foreigners.[5] In many respects this "stereotypical" view fits Gabriel Almond's and Sidney Verba's classical conception of the civic culture, namely a "mixed political culture" which combines participant, subject, and parochial political orientations.

This is in substantial agreement with the literature surveyed for this study which scored the country high on all of the operational variables used to measure the Western Democratic value system. The only features of the Costa Rican political culture that were identified as "Latin American" were tendencies toward informal corporatism, centralism, and utopianism in public policy (on the Thomism scale); and red tape, corruption, and circumvention of the law (on the Machiavellian scale). The existence of opposition ideological parties and periodic strikes (particularly on the banana plantations) are also a feature of its political life.

In 1948 Costa Rica experienced what might be called a "restorative revolution" led by José Figueres. It can be called this in the sense that it "restored" Costa Rica to the path of political evolution it had been on since the creation of the Liberal Synthesis that had been nurtured by both the Liberal and Conservative parties in the period between 1880 and 1930.[6] Launched under the administration of Tomas Guardia (1870–1882), classical Latin American liberalism took firm root in an environment considerably different from the other Central American states. Comprised originally of a sparse population of independent farmers with neither mineral resources nor large numbers of Indians to exploit, the lack of an excessively wealthy elite or a large servant class gave rise to a society marked by greater equality and social trust than in the rest of Latin America. Thus, when President Bernardo Soto, a liberal, turned power over to a conservative in 1890, a tradition of free elections and the peaceful transfer of power began to develop in the country. Furthermore, in setting up the first system of free public education in Costa Rica, President Soto also launched a tradition of social reformism that was perpetuated by both the populist regimes of the 1930s and 1940s, and the Democratic Left regimes brought into power by the revolution of 1948.

The break in 1948 in Costa Rica's political evolution was preceded by a number of developments, beginning with the establishment of the United Fruit Company in the country around 1900. The establishment of the banana industry, manned largely by Jamaican workers, led to the organization of the banana workers' union under communist auspices in 1929 and to a major strike in 1935. In 1936 a populist party, the Partido Republicano Nacional, came to power through the votes of the urban and rural lower classes, particularly those of the banana workers. Retaining power for twelve years, it continued the tradition of social reform legislation by enacting a new labor code, a social security law, and by proposing an income tax. It also permitted the Communists to organize legally.

The alliance between the populists and the communists thoroughly frightened the ruling class, whose tradition of moderation and compromise had held the Liberal Synthesis on course for seventy years. When the Republican party's congressional majority voted to annul the presidential elections of 1948 which had been won by the opposition, coffee planter, José Figueres led a revolt that toppled the government. As the successful leader of the restorative revolution of 1948, Figueres became the personal embodiment of the social democratic synthesis that emerged from that upheaval, and Costa Rica's leading politician for the next twenty-five years.[7]

The synthesis that emerged embraced three fundamental principles: (1) the maintenance of a liberal democratic political system in Costa Rica; (2) the creation of a mixed economy with guarantees for private property; and (3) the expansion of the welfare state. Although the shift of power back and forth for three decades between the Partido de Liberación Nacional PLN and an opposition coalition made up of the conservative Partido de Unificación Nacional and the populist Partido Republicano Nacional caused changes of emphasis in public policy, elite consensus kept the synthesis intact.

The Costa Rican political elite has taken special pains to guarantee constitutional democracy in the country. The Figueres-led junta of the Second Republic permanently dissolved the army, established a totally independent electoral tribunal, and wrote a great many safeguards against the abuse of executive power into the Constitution of 1949. The result has been an orderly democratic decision-making process, a peaceful transfer of power over the past ten elections, and a highly competitive political system—particularly at the presidential level— although the growing dominance of the PLN over the past decade has caused increasing concern.

As a result of these developments, Costa Rica has evolved one of the few participant civic cultures in Latin America. As John Booth writes:

> Although Costa Ricans often characterize themselves as uncoop- erative, individualistic, and difficult to mobilize, they in fact frequently vote, join and take part in organizations, perform electioneering and party activities, engage in communal self-help activities, discuss politics and community affairs, and contact public officials. They do so at levels higher than many other Third World and Latin American nations and only slightly lower—if at all—than levels observed in the United States and Europe. Such participation bespeaks the democratic nature of Costa Rican political culture.[8]

Political participation is balanced by an incremental orientation toward political and social change, particularly on the part of the political elite. In fact, something of a "Tory Democratic" attitude has developed among the upper classes: a willingness to respond to mass demands, on the one hand, and a reluctance to disrupt the social consensus, on the other.[9]

Costa Rican political leaders have also displayed a marked inven- tiveness in institution building and public policy. Not only did they disband the military establishment and dedicate its funding to education in 1948, but they also created a constitutional system designed to offset the worst manifestations of *caudillismo* and executive tyranny.[10] The strong legislative, judicial and electoral institutions which emerged have even caused some interpreters to conclude that the powers of the president are unduly weakened for effective leadership and decision making and that the system is overly subject to immobilism.[11]

Immobilism in decision making at times produces political violence in the form of strikes and confrontations involving limited small arms fire. However, the reaction of the government has usually been moderate, force has been used sparingly, and conciliation is usually employed to contain and defuse violence. Thus, as Booth points out, "while violence is not infrequent, it is rarely extolled even by the leftist parties and is generally regarded as exceptional and warranting special efforts to resolve its causes."[12] Whatever tendencies to anomic behavior that do exist are counterbalanced by empirical studies showing high levels of citizen rationality and tolerance.[13]

In February 1990 Costa Rica conducted its tenth successive democratic election since the political turmoil of 1948. Although the PLN had won the last two elections—and four of the last five—power was peacefully transferred to the opposition party for the sixth time. Of particular interest was the background of the winner, Rafael Calderón Fournier. He is the son of the left-leaning populist Rafael Calderón Guardia, whose election was overturned by the Figueres-led revolution of 1948. In a sense, then, Costa Rica's political history had turned full circle. Rafael Junior, whose Social Christian Unity party (PUSC) is composed of a coalition of opposition groups, has taken a much more anti-statist, market-oriented stand in economic affairs and also supported the Contra insurgency against the Sandinistas. Thus, although the nation has suffered the stresses of debt, inflation, and tension along its border with Nicaragua—issues which apparently motivated the electorate to back a candidate calling for new directions in economic and foreign policy—the democratic consensus that has undergirded Costa Rican political life for the past forty years clearly has remained intact.

Costa Rican Foreign Policy

The major contours of Costa Rican foreign policy have clearly reflected the nation's democratic culture, namely, a reluctance to associate itself with the other nations of the old "Gran Patria de Centro America," a preoccupation with the promotion of democracy outside its borders, and an acceptance of its dependency on the "democratic *caudillo* of the north."

Costa Rican separatism. Costa Rica has always had a sense of its apartness from the rest of Central America. During the colonial period it was an isolated "backwater" in the "Capitanía General de Guatemala." By the end of this period the territory had only achieved the status of a *gobierno* which was below the rank of *intendencia* which had been achieved by El Salvador, Honduras, and Nicaragua. Even after the other provinces of the *capitania* declared their independence from Spain in September 1821, Costa Rica delayed doing so until December of that year. Although it joined the United Provinces in 1823, it was never at the center of its governance; rather, it briefly seceded from the union in 1829 because of its political turbulence. When the United Provinces began disintegrating in 1838, Costa Rica was one of the first to declare its independence.

Since that time the ideal of Central American political reunification has been the topic of many international conferences of the isthmian nations. Costa Rica, however, declined to send representatives to fully two-thirds of those conferences.[14] This desire to maintain its distinctiveness resulted in the country's refusal to join the United States-backed Central American Defense Council (CONDECA) in 1963, and again when it was revived in 1983.[15] Its refusal in 1963 had more to do with the authoritarian complexion of the regimes in the Central American member countries than with the fact that Costa Rica had no standing army and only a small security force to contribute to regional defense. Its refusal in 1983 stemmed from San José's desire to avoid being drawn into the ongoing Central American crisis—the crisis that gave rise to the revival of CONDECA.[16]

Perhaps the most dramatic case of the country's reluctance to become a functional part of Central America is found in Costa Rica's behavior in the formative stages of the movement toward Central American economic integration in the late 1950s and early 1960s.[17] Costa Rica did participate actively in the initial stages of the movement and it co-sponsored the 1951 Economic Commission for Latin America resolution that launched the movement toward regional economic integration. It also took part in the subsequent conferences on Central American economic integration and signed the economic integration agreements drafted in 1958 and 1959. Shortly after doing so, San José became dubious about participation in the integration of the region and, finally, decided against it, refusing to ratify the agreements it had signed.

Officially the decision not to ratify was made on economic grounds. Economics Minister Jorge Borbon, in an important paper, gave as the most salient reasons the concern that the integration protocols would cause Costa Rica to lose control of its economic development policy, that most of the economic benefits would accrue to Guatemala and El Salvador which were closer to the center of the region's population and had lower labor costs, and that the nation would lose control of its customs collections and thus be deprived of the revenue required to fund its more highly developed social welfare programs.[18]

The fact that Cost Rica later joined the integration movement suggests that the alleged economic disadvantages were neither as great nor as real as Borbon had suggested. What appears most likely is that although the government did anticipate some unfavorable economic effects if the country joined the Central American Common Market, there were other reasons—essentially nationalistic ones—for remaining apart. One major concern was Costa Rica's fear of becoming too closely involved with the other authoritarian regimes of Central America. In particular, as Staley noted, "a number of Costa Rican officials have indicated reluctance to become closely associated with a country with such different political and ethnic conditions as Nicaragua."[19]

Costa Rica was also motivated by the sense of its own cultural uniqueness and superiority to the rest of Central America. Thus, in December 1960, it refused to sign the General Treaty of Central American Integration. This contravened its traditional practice of signing but not ratifying controversial international agreements. However, the Costa Rican member on the Central American Cooperation Committee averred that this action

> in no way meant that the ideals of economic co-existence were being finally discarded; on the contrary, those ideals were more vividly present than before, and Costa Rica's sympathies would always lie with those who showed a proud and firm determination to raise the level of industrialization of the underdeveloped countries.[20]

This statement was a way for Costa Rica to keep the door open, and the country's decision to remain apart proved indeed to be a temporary one. In 1963 Costa Rica became a full member of the Central American Common Market, ratifying all Central American economic integration agreements. That prompts the question of why San José changed its position—a position rooted in some of the most deeply felt features of its political culture.

The answer is multifaceted. First, Costa Rican officials had to abandon any notion they may have had that their country did not need to develop its economy through industrialization. However attractive, being a sort of pastoral Switzerland of Central America was recognized as not a real option. Worsening economic conditions, especially the deterioration of international commodity prices, had shown that economic change, which meant diversification and industrialization, was essential. The government concluded, however reluctantly, that regional economic integration was probably the most promising—if not the most attractive—means of achieving those ends.

Second, presidential elections were held in 1962. The incumbent party, which had opposed Costa Rican participation in the integration movement, was defeated and the influential, anti-integration Borbon was replaced as minister of economy. The decision to reverse direction was made by a relatively insulated foreign policy establishment. Third, the agreement establishing the Central American Bank for Economic Integration stipulated that only projects located in countires that had ratified all of the Central American economic integration agreements were eligible for financial assistance from the bank. The bank, generously backed by the United States Agency for International Development, was a source of development funds that Costa Rica could not ignore, even if it meant a close association with countries from which it wanted to remain apart.

The fourth, and perhaps major, reason for the change in Costa Rica's position was a growing belief among the political elite that although Costa Rica might experience some disadvantages as a participant, the disadvantages would be even greater if it remained apart. Although it had not produced any dramatic accomplishments, the economic integration movement had resulted in small gains, and in the Central American context even small economic gains are of significance. Moreover, the other four Central American countries were demonstrating their determination to integrate their economies, with or without Costa Rica. By remaining apart, Costa Rica ran the risk of permanently cutting itself off. Costa Rica thus subordinated nationalistic concerns for pragmatic ones.

Promotion of democracy. After the Revolution of 1948 Costa Rica took some extraordinary steps (for Latin America) to preserve its newly reconstituted democratic order. It not only decided to depend on the "beneficent *caudillo*" to the north to protect its territorial integrity (made vulnerable when it abolished its army), it greatly enhanced the independence of its electoral tribunal and judicial system and reduced the powers of the presidency.

The Costa Rican commitment to democracy and human rights is not confined to its own territory. The country has endeavored, in various ways, to advance these values abroad through its foreign policy and international relations since 1948. One means by which it has demonstrated its commitment to democracy is by serving as a center for refugees from and opponents of oppressive governments, especially located elsewhere in Central America and the Caribbean. This is particularly true of refugees from Nicaragua, both under the Somoza dynasty and the Sandinista regime. More than that, the San José government allowed its border territory near Nicaragua to be used for para-military forays into that country by opponents of the Somozas; in the 1980s it also turned a blind eye to some of the activities of the anti-Sandinistas.

In 1954 Costa Rica refused to attend the 10th Inter-American Conference in Caracas, called to discuss the threat posed by the penetration into the hemisphere of "international communism." Its refusal was not because it was unconcerned with the threat and, more specifically, with the Arbenz regime in Guatemala. It clearly was concerned about both, but it looked to Washington to protect Costa Rica from any destabilization caused by the Guatemalan government. Costa Rica refused to attend the meeting as a way of protesting the holding of a major Organization of American States' meeting in a country ruled by a dictatorship.[21]

During the early 1960s, the country sought to mobilize the Organization of American States to act against Latin American dictatorships. This reflected Costa Rican desire to impose its values on the whole of Latin America and to do so through the OAS. Following the military coup in Peru in July 1962 that overthrew a democratic government, Costa Rica joined several other Latin American countries in requesting an OAS Meeting of Consultation. The topic of the proposed meeting was to consider the policy that OAS members should follow in the event that a democratic government was overthrown by a military coup. Costa Rica and the others who requested the meeting argued that a military overthrow of a democratic government constituted a threat to hemispheric peace and, as well, was a violation of the Charter of the Organization of American States.[22] In 1963, San José sought, unsuccessfully, to mobilize OAS action against the Duvalier dictatorship in Haiti.

The democratic elements in Costa Rican foreign policy account for the country's 1981 break in diplomatic relations with Cuba.[23] It broke with Havana (shortly after having established ties) both to protest and call attention to alleged Cuban mistreatment of political prisoners.

To be sure, these various moves on behalf of democracy and human rights did little to materially advance the cause of either. However, that is not an indictment against Costa Rican endeavors. A much stronger country with many more resources—the United States— has not been able until recently to markedly advance democracy and human rights in Latin America, or elsewhere. What is significant about this aspect of Costa Rican foreign policy is how consistently the country has adhered to an element that is at the very heart of its political culture. Perhaps only very small countries, with few or no international responsibilities, can pursue such a foreign policy orientation.

One of the most significant and tangible of Costa Rica's foreign policy initiatives directed at ending dictatorship and promoting democracy and respect for human rights was the aid it gave to the Sandinistas in ousting the Somoza regime in Nicaragua. Costa Rica, along with Cuba, Panama, and Venezuela, provided various sorts of material support to the anti-Somoza forces.[24] Its aid—given Costa Rica's reputation as an established democracy and economically and socially progressive country—lent the Sandinistas significant legitimacy. However, the tangible resources that Costa Rica could give to the Sandinista forces battling the Somoza regime were limited. At the outset of the struggle, Venezuela was their main financial supporter—a role it could play because of the oil revenues Caracas enjoyed at the time. But in early 1979, the Venezuelan president who had given the Sandinistas financial support was succeeded by a member of the opposition party who was not so inclined. At that point, Costa Rican President Rodrigo Carazo Odio convinced the then oil rich government of Mexico to assume the role of financial supporter of the Sandinistas previously played by Venezuela. Without this Costa Rican initiative, the outcome of the Nicaraguan revolution might have been very different.[25]

The outcome of the Sandinista victory—the drift leftward, the restrictions on civil liberties, and the installation of an increasingly authoritarian government in Nicaragua—disappointed Costa Rica. That disappointment, plus its concern that the Central American crisis might degenerate into a Central America-wide war, prompted Costa Rican president Oscar Arias to put forward a peace plan for Central America. The Arias plan was aimed at creating both a peaceful and democratic Central America. It called for a negotiated cease-fire to internal or civil wars; a grant of amnesty to all political prisoners; denying use of territory by insurgents for military or terrorist action against neighboring governments; cut-off of aid to insurgents against established governments; increasing political freedom and democracy in the Central American countries; and encouragement of the relocation of refuges and political exiles.[26]

Putting forward and actively pushing a peace plan for Central America may seem at odds with Costa Rica's desire to remain apart from the countries of the region. It is not: the plan was designed to construct a democratic Central America that would be compatible with Costa Rica's political culture. Costa Rica's active pursuit of the accord, as well as some of the other foreign policy initiatives noted, appear to be at odds with Hazelton's observation that "leaders of small states are generally reluctant to expand the resources necessary for an active foreign policy."[27] Granted, although Central America has few tangible resources and it has not devoted the ones it has to foreign policy initiatives, the country has been very willing to devote various intangible resources (e.g., the time and energy of its officials, diplomatic skills, reputation, and prestige) to foreign policy concerns, particularly initiatives directed towards protecting its vulnerable democratic system.

Dependence. Costa Rica has been a country economically, politically, and militarily dependent on the United States for most of the twentieth century. In fact, since 1948 it has predicated the very character of its socio-political system on the presumption that the United States would function as its beneficent *caudillo.* Indeed, in terms of indebtedness, it is on a per capita basis the most indebted and dependent of all Latin American countries. It is dependent on both the United States government and its private sector to provide the funds to sustain its social welfare programs and to further its economic development. Like other Central American states, Costa Rica is economically dependent on the export of a few primary products—coffee, sugar, and bananas. The main market for those exports is the United States. Dependent status has certain foreign policy corollaries. One is frequent Costa Rican support for United States foreign policy initiatives, for example, taking a hard-line position on Castro's Cuba in the early and mid-1960s (something that may well have been in its own self-interest as well as in line with United States desires), participating in the Inter-American force in the Dominican Republic in the mid-1960s, allowing some United States-sponsored Contra forces on its territory, and its willingness (albeit reluctant) to accept United States military assistance and expand its own security forces as a result of the Central American crisis. Another corollary of dependence is a Costa Rican tendency to look to the United States to defend it from foreign incursions, as when it called upon the Kennedy administration to pressure Somoza to call off his threatened invasion.

At the same time that it is dependent on the United States and recognizes the fact, Costa Rica has, particularly in the 1970s and 1980s, acted in ways at odds with Washington. It established diplomatic relations with Moscow, an action that the United States sought to discourage among its Latin American clients. It established diplomatic ties with Castro's Cuba, again something the United States did not want to see happen. More recently, the Arias peace plan was at odds with Reagan administration policy toward Sandinista Nicaragua and the rest of Central America. This independent Costa Rican behavior reflects the fact that the nation's rulers realize that dependency is a reciprocal process: while dependent on the United States, America also looks to Costa Rica as a bastion of democracy and political support in an increasingly volatile and uncertain region. These mutual realizations ultimately reflect the classic pattern of clientalism: a dyadic contract between actors of unequal power and status in which each provides mutually understood supports and services to each other.

Venezuelan Political Culture

Although for much of the nineteenth and the first half of the twentieth centuries Venezuela was characterized by tyranny, political conflict and bloodshed, since the overthrow of General Marco Pérez Jiménez in 1958 the country has evolved into one of the most stable and competitive democratic systems in the Americas. As can be seen from table 4.2, there was, with relatively minor exceptions, generally high agreement by the authors consulted on the essentially Western Democratic character of the Venezuelan value system and behavior pattern, although a residue of *caudillaje* behavior is seen as remaining in the culture. These evaluations are also in general agreement with the democratic index presented in tables 4.3 and 4.4.

Two basic ingredients have enabled Venezuela to evolve from the "historically turbulent birthplace of Simon Bolivar into the leading example of intensely competitive, broadly participatory electoral politics in Latin America."[28] One is the development of the oil industry, the second is the institutionalization of a national competitive party system.

Before the systematic exploitation of the nation's oil resources in 1921, Venezuela was predominantly an agricultural society with a decentralized, *caudillo*-dominated political system to match its rural social structure. However, with the tripling of crude oil production between 1927 and 1957, not only did the national income expand rapidly, the nation's economic system was modernized. As Pedro-Pablo Kuczynski wrote in 1976,

Even though oil has been the major source of foreign-exchange earnings for half a century, Venezuela has over the years developed a diversified economy, with substantial agricultural and manufac-turing sectors. Human resources development has moved ahead at a rapid pace, especially in the last two decades. Venezuela's development is thus far at a more advanced stage than most, if not all, of the other major developing oil exporting countries.[29]

Since that time Venezuela has been able to maintain the highest per capita levels of income and gross domestic product (GDP) in all of Latin America.[30]

Even though the oil industry provided direct employment for a very small percentage of the workforce, its revenues provided a sufficient margin of surplus to supply decent incomes for the growing middle and blue-collar classes without having to shift resources away from the industrial and agricultural sectors. Oil income, in other words, enabled Venezuela to substantially repeal the "zero sum game" mentality so characteristic of Latin America's economic and political culture.

While oil money was, in effect, buying social peace, Venezuela's political leadership was working to create a party system that would produce political peace. From 1830, when Venezuela seceded from the Republic of Gran Colombia, until the death of Juan Vicente Gómez in 1935, Venezuelan politics was characterized by localism, *caudillismo*, and internecine political warfare. The half century since Gómez' death has largely (although not entirely) eliminated those features from the nation's political system. Actually, the process began under Gómez when the revenues from oil enabled him to create a national army strong enough to crush the militias of the rival regional *caudillos*.[31] Thus, after his death, the nascent party system found itself operating in a much more nationalized, and in some respects a less militarized, political system. Although the ensuing nine years featured military rule, Generals Eleazar López Contreras and Isaias Medina Angarita permitted political parties and mass organizations to organize themselves and participate in the political process. The emergence of these organizations, which led to the controversial overthrow of the Medina government in 1945, ushered in three years of bitter interparty conflict known as the *trienio*. Daniel H. Levine describes the impact of this period on Venezuela's political elite as follows:

> Politics in the *trienio* was marked by widespread, bitter, and unrelenting conflict, culminating in military intervention and a decade of brutal repression. The experience of those years marked Venezuela's political leaders deeply. They became convinced that their own failure to control and channel political conflict had opened the door to military rule. They learned, in addition, that political leadership involved more than adherence to ideology and program—compromise, conciliation, and negotiation became key political values.[32]

Thus, when democracy was given a second chance in 1958 after the ten-year dictatorial rule of Colonel Marcos Perez Jimenez, Venezuela's political elites had been undergoing a learning process which culminated in the institutionalization of a stable party and constitutional system.

This "learning process," R. Lynn Kelley contends, began with the signing of the *Pacto de Punto Fijo* in October 1958 which committed the three major parties (AD, COPEI, and URD) to holding democratic elections, the inclusion of minority parties in the first post-election government, and the writing of a constitution placing curbs on executive power.[33] Although the URD later withdrew from the coalition, its continued support by COPEI enabled Rómulo Betancourt to complete his term, thereby enhancing the legitimacy of elections as the sole road to power. In addition, the ability of the Acción Democrática (AD) politicians of the moderate left to co-opt the business and commercial elites of the right by consultation and compromise not only neutralized a powerful potential enemy but further legitimized the utility of the democratic system.

Although AD monopolized the presidency for the first decade after 1958, it was the fragmentation of that party that led to the legitimation of extensive party competition. Because of personalistic and ideological divisions within AD, in the elections of 1968 Rafael Caldera of COPEI was able to edge past Gonzalo Barrios of AD by just 31,000 votes.[34] The acceptance of the results by the party that had dominated the executive for ten years represented the first time that power had been transferred from one party to another in a free election in Venezuelan history. At the same time, the fragmentation of the parties and movements on the left and right of AD and COPEI had the effect of producing what amounted to a primarily bipolar competitive system leading to a general convergence of the two parties around what might be called "moderate reformism."[35] This general consensus around the parameters of public policy, which Diego Abente has classified as a consociational system,[36] has enabled both parties to appeal to a broad spectrum of classes and to facilitate the transfer of leadership from one political generation to the next.

How did the economic surplus produced by oil and the political stability largely created by the stabilization of Venezuela's party system affect the nation's political culture? David Eugene Blank, in his discussion of the Venezuelan political culture (published in 1973), states that Venezuelans "have learned to hedge their bets on democracy."[37] This tendency, he argues, is a result of the confusion engendered by the discontinuity in the nation's political history. This judgment is in general agreement with the results of the VENEVOTE study reported by Enrique A. Baloyra.[38] The Venezuelans interviewed in this study appeared to be ambivalent in their assessment of the nation's democratic experiment: they were generally negative in their evaluation of the *performance* of the government, but highly supportive of electoral democracy as a *process*. There exists, in other words, a widespread feeling that parties are important to the nation, that elections are politically efficacious mechanisms for influencing government policy, that elections are important for democracy, and strong opposition to one-party dominance. Yet 48.2 percent of the respondents would not vote if the compulsory voting law were dropped and feel inefficacious in all areas of political activity other than elections.[39] Generally speaking, a positive orientation toward the democratic system increases as respondents ascend the social scale.[40] Venezuela's reputation for an effectively functioning democratic system (as reflected in the Fitzgibbon-Johnson and Bollen index) appears to depend primarily on the cultural attitudes and behavior of the middle classes and the political elites.

The ambivalence toward the Venezuelan political system reflected in the VENEVOTE study is mirrored in our finding that while Western Democratic behavior patterns were seen as predominating in the literature, *caudillaje* behavior patterns were also highly reported. David Eugene Blank argues that Venezuela's value system is a synthesis of traditional Latin American and modern orientations. He explains this by stating that their value system "comprises traditional, nondemocratic values which have been adapted successfully to the demands of urbanization and industrialization."[41] Thus the traditional individual loyalties engendered by personalism and clientalism have been transformed into support for organizational leaders operating in political parties, bureaucracies, and places of employment. By the same token, Blank argues, power seeking, once viewed as an end in itself and free from moral restraints, is now seen as a way to promote economic development and social justice. "Taking and holding power now depends upon popular support. Themes like reconciliation, national unity, and accommodation provide the framework for politics today."[42]

Since the election of Jaime Lusinchi in 1984, the rapid drop in oil prices coupled with Venezuela's $32 billion debt have motivated the government to attempt to reduce its dependency on oil income. The efforts of President Carlos Andrés Pérez, elected for a second time in 1988, to impose austerity in order to obtain the International Monetary Fund (IMF) loans necessary to stabilize the economy led to street demonstrations, student strikes, and the Caracas food riots of 1989. For a population used to seeing its government solve social problems through "subsidies, price controls and swollen state payrolls,"[43] the killing of three hundred people by army units mobilized to back up the Caracas police severely strained the nation's historic national unity and politics of accommodation.

In summary, Venezuela's political culture gives evidence of being in the latter stages of transition from a traditional Latin American Machiavellian/*caudillaje* type to a Western Democratic type. This was largely the work of the political elites led by the Generation of 28 which sought to change the national value system. These value changes, coupled with the economic and social development of the nation driven by oil, have gradually modified, although not fully eradicated, the nation's *caudillaje* behavior patterns.

Venezuelan Foreign Policy

We have noted that Venezuela is an even more recently secured democracy than Costa Rica, having ended dictatorship in 1958. This South American democracy shares certain basic foreign policy traits with its Central American democratic counterpart: commitment to democracy and human rights in its foreign policy and international behavior, and dependence. But as a much larger country with greater resources and one more strategically located, Venezuela pursues a more active international role. In its foreign policy Venezuela has addressed some of the same issues as has Costa Rica and has done so in the same way. In part, this is because the two are well-established democracies in a geographical region where democracy has been notable for its absence. The similarity between Venezuelan and Costa Rican policy in the international arena is attributable to two other factors as well. Before democracy was firmly established in Venezuela, Costa Rica served as a refuge for some of Venezuela's democratic leaders. While in Costa Rica, they absorbed some Costa Rican foriegn policy orientations, including that of endeavoring to advance the cause of democracy internationally as well as domestically. Further, the dominant democratic personages of the two countries—Venezuela's Rómulo Betancourt and Costa Rica's José Figueres—were personal as well as political friends. As a result, there was both explicit and implicit policy coordination between the two.

Promotion of democracy. A prominent element of Venezuelan politics, especially in the decade after the overthrow of the Pérez Jiménez dictatorship in 1958, was the effort to advance the cause of democracy. As Bond observes:

The primary, overriding goal of the Venezuelan leadership since 1958 has been to create a viable democratic polity. Venezuela's political leaders returned from exile convinced that the esablishment of a democratic system capable of controlling and challenging conflict must take priority over all other development goals. Social and economic reforms were not to be abandoned, but their accomplishment was to be subordinated.[44]

The international front was also employed to advance the cause of democracy and to secure the country's emerging political system. As Levine explains, "President Betancourt saw the survival of democracy in Venezuela as dependent on the isolation and defeat of dictatorship throughout the region.[45]

In 1959, while still only a fledgling and embattled democracy, Venezuela's representative to the OAS argued that the root cause of political turbulence in the Caribbean was the presence of dictatorial repressive governments such as the Trujillo and Duvalier dictatorships in the Dominican Republic and Haiti. The Venezuelan spokesman contended that the way to eliminate those tensions was for the members of the organization to apply collective sanctions against such regimes in order to safeguard the values associated with political democracies. He went on to declare that even if OAS members did not adopt collective measures, they should at least not take action against the activities of exiles from repressive regimes; those activities should be tolerated and, from the Venezuelan perspective, encouraged and assisted. Venezuela's representative rejected the proposition that democracy could not be imposed from without. To support his position he pointed to the successful imposition by the United States of democracy in Japan follwing World War II.

Venezuela went even further in its campaign for democracy in the OAS by making a most atypical Latin American argument, namely, that the inter-American doctrine of non-intervention in the affairs of American states was not applicable to countries dominated by dictatorships. The doctrine of non-intervention, the Venezuelan spokesman asserted, applied to and protected only popular, legitimate governments.[46] This "atypical" approach originated in the fact that Venezuela's Betancourt and the Dominican Republic's Trujillo had long been the "closest of enemies." Each was bent on overthrowing the other—Betancourt by way of collective action against the Trujillo regime and Trujillo by more direct actions against Betancourt. In 1960, an attempt was made on the life of the Venezuelan President in which he escaped serious injury. Caracas protested to the OAS, alleging

Dominican involvement in the act, and requested an OAS investigation. The investigation confirmed the Venezuelan charge, and the OAS imposed sanctions on the Dominican Republic that contributed to the subsequent demise of the Trujillo dictatorship.[47]

In the early and mid-1960s, Venezuela actively supported United States-backed efforts in the Organization of American States to isolate the Castro dictatorship from the Western Hemisphere. Caracas voted for the break in communication and transportation links between OAS member countries and Cuba, and it voted for the ouster of the Castro government from participation in both the OAS and the Inter-American Defense Board. Moreover, Venezuela initiated actions that led to OAS sanctions against the Castro regime for conducting subversion against the government of Venezuela and for the presence of some Cuban arms on the Venezuelan coast. The organization dispatched a committee to investigate the charges, which were confirmed. The committee's report laid the groundwork for the final OAS sanction against Cuba, the call for OAS member countries to sever diplomatic ties with Havana.[48]

Without question, the most dramatic evidence of Venezuela's commitment to democracy in foreign policy in the early years of its democratic existence was the Betancourt Doctrine. The doctrine declared that Caracas would not maintain diplomatic relations with governments that gained power through illegal means. To give effect to the doctrine, Venezuela not only broke diplomatic ties with Castro's Cuba but, at one time or another, with Argentina, Brazil, Guatemala, Honduras, and Peru because they had gained power by overturning constitutionally-elected governments.[49]

The doctrine was followed by Betancourt's successor, Raul Leoni. However, the doctrine posed certain practical limitations for a country that aspired to influence in Latin America and beyond. Thus in 1969 Leoni's successor, Rafael Caldera, replaced it with an approach that could be called the acceptance of "ideological pluralism." In announcing his departure from the Betancourt doctrine, Caldera stated:

It seems to me public opinion favors the establishment of relations with countries of political organizations and ideology different from ours, for their presence in the world and their influence on economic relations cannot be ignored.

On the other hand, I consider it advisable to change the policy of discontinuing relations with regimes arising from acts of violence against duly elected authorities on this continent. Venezuela cannot continue without relations with peoples united by brotherly ties.[50]

Caldera's departure from the Betancourt Doctrine did not reflect any lesser commitment to democracy either at home or in foreign affairs, but as Levine states: "As open threat to democratic survival at home began to disappear, foreign policy gradually moved *away* from a primary political concern with the international defense of democracy and toward a broader concern for economic issues (with a concomitant increase in ideological tolerance)".[51]

With or without the Betancourt Doctrine, there is, in the opinion of both Bond and Levine, a strong relationship between Venezuela's domestic political process and the way that Venezuela conducts its foreign relations.[52] As Venezuelan political leaders set about constructing a democratic political system in the late 1950s and early and mid-1960s, emphasis was placed on pragmatism, caution, sensitivity to diversity, and coalition building. According to Levine:

> The style which Venezuelan political leaders developed for hand-ling [domestic] diversity emphasized conciliation and coalition building. This characteristic style of action grew out of a profound learning experience which taught elites the values of pragmatic compromise as opposed to all-out insistence on ideology.[53]

Expressed differently, Venezuelan leaders who succeeded the first generation of democratic presidents found the Betancourt Doctrine an obstacle to realization of several of the country's foreign policy objectives: regional economic cooperation, regional leadership, and global influence in the North/South dialogue.

The country's domestic political style has also carried over into the international arena where Venezuela emphasizes the need for and importance of constructing institutions where issues can be dealt with in collective fashion. Evidence of this orientation to foreign affairs is plentiful. It was a founder, along with Saudi Arabia, of the Organization of Petroleum Exporting Countries.

> Venezuela and OPEC provide two noteworthy examples of the compromise-oriented and institution-building style of Venezuelan foreign policy: (1) Juan Pablo Pérez Alfonso, the prime promoter of OPEC, originally sought to construct an organization which would take account of not only the interests of producers in establishing oil supply and prices, but also the interests of consumers and the oil companies; and (2) Venezuela has consistently been the champion of conciliation and cohesion in the organization.[54]

A second example is its active leadership position in the Conferences on International Economic Cooperation, a North/South negotiating forum. A third example is Venezuela's active role in the formation of the Andean Group: it participated at the presidential level in the formation of this effort at Latin American regional economic integration, believing that the undertaking was a device for promoting economic develoment and also a means of dealing with Andean economic problems. Venezuela was also convinced that the Andean Group represented a democratic bloc, evidenced by all participant countries' commitment to this ideal.[55] Yet another example of Venezuela's support for institution building in the international arena as a means of dealing with international problems is the country's co-sponsorship (along with Mexico) of SELA, the Latin American Economic System. From the Venezuelan perspective, the objectives of that organization were to promote communication among Latin American countries on economic issues and to provide a formal framework for dialogue with the Western developed countries in general and with the United States in particular. To be certain, not all of these efforts at institution building in the international arena have yielded the results Venezuela desired.

In addition to efforts at strengthening formal international institutions, Venezuela has participated in at least two informal efforts, both aimed at finding a democratic solution to international problems of concern to the country. In the fall of 1982, Venezuela joined with Mexico in advancing a peace proposal for Central America that called upon Honduras, Nicaragua, and the United States to negotiate a settlement of their differences rather than rely on military means.[56] In additon, Venezuela joined with Colombia, Mexico, and Panama in forming the Contadora Group whose objective was reaching a peaceful settlement of the turmoil in Central America. According to Hazelton, what motivated Venezuela to take this action was Caracas' fear that the crisis in Central America would escalate into a full-scale war that could threaten the security of Venezuela's democratic political system.[57]

Venezuela's involvement in the Central American crisis reveals another very different aspect of that country's foreign policy behavior— its highly personalistic nature. Grabendorff reports that President Carlos Andres Perez' dislike for and disgust towards "Tachito" Somoza contributed considerably to the Venezuelan decision to give material aid to the Sandinista forces doing battle against him in Nicaragua. But when his successor from another political party (the Christian Democratic COPEI), Luis Herrera Campíns, assumed the Venezuelan presidency, aid to the Sandinistas was diverted to El Salvador to aid José Napoleon Duarte, a fellow Christian Democrat.[58] It was at this point that Costa Rica assumed the broker role to induce Mexico to absorb the financial effects of Venezuela's switch of funding targets.

The previoulsy noted Venezuelan preference for pragmatism and conciliation in politics, be it domestic or international, can be seen in the way it handles the tensions between its political principals and the realities of state behavior. Liss observes that Venezuela's foreign affairs is based on certain theoretical principles such as respect for human rights, national self-determination, nonintervention, full representation of citizens in the political process, peaceful resolution of international disputes, respect for treaties and other international obligations, and support for democratic governments. On a more pragmatic level, Venezuela acts to protect its independence and interests; to enhance its living standards; to secure economic cooperation among countries so as to advance economic well-being in Venezuela and elsewhere; and to maintain the export price of primary products.[59] The first set of principles have their roots in the country's political culture and democratic value system; the second are rooted in the country's economic and social vision of the future.

Given this mix of foreign policy principles, it is not surprising that the country has at times found some of them to be in conflict. The nonintervention principle has been violated on several occasions, for example, when the Caracas government called for collective intervention against nondemocratic regimes and when it backed the Sandinista forces in their campaign against the Somoza government in Nicaragua. The principle of solidarity with democratic gevernments and opposition to regimes that do not recognize and respect basic human rights was violated when Venezuela, after dropping the Betancourt Doctrine, established diplomatic ties with the USSR, Cuba, and other authoritarian governments. The principle of peaceful settlement of disputes through arbitration, adjudication, and mediation has been violated or ignored in the case of the country's border and territorial disputes with its neighbors. These departures from its foreign policy principles do not represent a lack of commitment to them or to the country's democratic values. Rather, the departures reflect the country's previously mentioned pragmatic approach to both foreign and domestic affairs. Further, as Liss notes, Venezuela's foreign policy is subject to various conflicting pressures, influences, and dictates. Some emanate from the international system—foreign governments, international lending agencies, international organizations, and multinational corporations; others stem from domestic needs—the interests of domestic groups, political parties, and elements of the national government bureaucracy.[60]

In an effort to give effect to its commitment to democracy and respect for human righs, Venezuela has extended sanctuary to political oppostion and it has used its embassies in various countries to extend safe conduct passes. In international forums such as the United Nations and its many specialized agencies, and the OAS, Venezuela enjoys what Lott terms "a tremendous psychological advantage" due to its democratic political system.[61] This reputation helped Venezuela obtain various United Nations posts—repeated election to membership on the Economic and Social Council (a body especially important to a developing country), election as a nonpermanent member of the Security Council, and election of its United Nations delgate as president of the General Assembly. With regard to the U.N. General Assembly, Lott observes that "although all states are at least theoretically equal in the General Assembly, it is quite clear that a member's voice is listened to in proportion to the audience's estimate of its capabilities and sense of responsibility to the organization."[62] Venezuela commands respect in the Assembly for its capabilities, although they are very limited compared to those of first- and second-rank powers, and, even more, for its sense of responsibility as an international actor.[63] At the United Nations, the country also serves as a vocal champion of Third World economic concerns.

Dependence. Although it is much larger, stronger militarily, wealthier, and better endowed with valuable natural resources, Venezuela, like Costa Rica, is a dependent country. The degree of its dependence has ebbed and flowed since 1958, largely a function of its perception of threats to its national security (and the security of its democratic system) and the strength of its petroleum-based economy. Under any circumstances, however, dependence has been and is an enduring reality.

In the late 1950s and early 1960s when it was a fledgling democratic regime under attack from Cuban-backed subversives, the Venezuelan government attached itself closely to the United States. In doing so, Caracas looked to Washington to behave as a beneficent *caudillo* providing what Venezuela conceived to be the *bien común*, namely, the economic and military assistance necessary for the fledgling democracy to survive. Indeed that assistance was forthcoming, especially in the early 1960s, when the United States pointed to Venezuela and Costa Rica as model Latin American countries: socially progressive, economically developing, and democratic. However, there were limits to the willingness of Washington to fulfill the beneficent *caudillo* role. The United States could not unreservedly support Venezuela's application of the nonintervention doctrine, and it found the Betancourt

Doctrine objectionable when Venezuela opposed the 1964 military takeover in Brazil that the United States welcomed. However, the United States did ultimately act in accordance with Venezuela's wishes with regard to the Trujillo dictatorship in the Dominican Republic. It was mainly United States enforcement of OAS sanctions against that country following the Dominican-sponsored attempt to assassinate the Venezuelan president that brought an end to the Trujillo dictatorship. And it was United States action later that caused the Trujillo family to leave the Dominican Republic after the dictator's assassination. Venezuela also applauded Washington's efforts in the early and mid-1960s to isolate the Castro regime in Cuba. In fact, it took an active role in the Organization of American States in marshalling support for that policy.

Beginning in the mid-1960s, when its democratic system was secure at home and subject to fewer challenges from abroad, the Venezuelan government began to put distance between itself and the United States. President Leoni condemned the United States military intervention in the revolt in the Dominican Republic in 1965. Leoni also expressed concern with, if not actual opposition to, United States involvement in Vietnam. Futhermore, the country championed various Third World positions that the United States opposed. And Venezuela joined other Latin American countries in the somewhat confrontational Consensus of Viña del Mar, which made a series of economic demands on the United States. Venezuela sided with Argentina in the Falklands/Malvinas dispute (although it did not approve Argentina's use of force to take the islands), and it criticized Washington for siding with its NATO ally Great Britain. Venezuela, as noted, provided material aid to the Sandinistas in their campaign against the Somoza regime, a staunch ally of the United States. As also noted, Venezuela has advocated a settlement of the Central American crisis at odds with the United States approach. Further, Venezuela—like many other Latin American countries—moved during the late 1960s and 1970s to diversify its international relations in order to reduce its dependence on the United States. Funded by oil revenues, it became both more assertive and more autonomous in its international behavior.

Despite all this, dependence on the United States remains the enduring reality. As Hazelton aptly puts it, "while Caracas...may undertake independent initiative, even at Washington's displeasure, there is also a certain convergence of interests and a coincidence of policies between ...[the country] and the United States that is readily apparent over the long run."[64] Further, the process of diversification was substantially halted in the early 1980s as a consequence of the foreign debt crisis.[65] With this crisis, the United States once again became more salient to Venezuela; in fact, Venezuela found itself even more dependent on the United States. Why? United Sates banks hold forty percent or more of the Latin American debt; moreover, the United States has a very influential role in the International Monetary Fund and other international institutions that aid Latin American countries in managing their foreign debt.[66]

There is yet another form of Venezuelan external dependence: its vast petroleum resources. Earlier on, the country was dependent on the major foreign oil companies to exploit and market those resources. Over time the country asserted more control over these resources and even the companies exploiting them.[67] Ultimately, the Venezuelan government displaced the foreign companies by nationalizing them in a generally friendly way, with fair compensation for the oil multinationals. Nationalization provided Venezuela with a tremendous psychological sense of greatly increased independence, as well as greatly increasing national control over its important natural resource. In reality, however, there was no great increase in independence or reduction in dependence coming from the petroleum nationalization. After the nationalization, Venezuela was as oil dependent as before. That dependence is manifested in two ways. One, the country's revenues from petroleum exports are dependent on the machinations of the international petroleum export market over which Venezuela has limited influence but no control. Two, while the country now has formal control of its petroleum industry, it remains dependent on the multinational oil companies for the international sale of its petroleum and for new state-of-the-art petroleum technology.

There is a further example of Venezuela's oil dependence. Despite the country's long-term status as a dependable supplier of petroleum to the United Sates, Venezuela was subjected to sanctions by the U.S. Trade Act of 1974. The act's stringent provisions were in reaction to the substantial petroleum price increase and embargo on oil shipments to the United States by the Arab members of OPEC earlier in the 1970s. The United States legislation targeted all OPEC members, not just the Arab ones. Thus, Venezuela was made a target merely because it was a member of the organization, even though it had not embargoed petroleum shipments to the United States.

Conclusion

This comparative analysis of political culture in Costa Rica and Venezuela has revealed remarkable similarities between the two otherwise different countries. Both have evolved into stable democratic regimes that are models for Latin America and the circum-Caribbean. Just as remarkable is how both states have, for much of the postwar era, proved to be champions of democratic relations between states. Both have made strenuous efforts to "export" democracy to other hemispheric actors. The two countries have traditionally stressed a process of negotiation to resolve disputes and have rarely been guilty of forceful behavior in the international arena that aimed at furthering their influence. The congruence between commitment to democracy at home and to a democratic process in interstate relations has been clearly demonstrated by the evidence presented in this chapter.

Other similarities have also been noted. Although their degree of economic dependence is by no means equal, the disparity in their power relative to the United States has caused them to accept a *caudillo* role for the Colossus of the North. Venezuela's oil wealth has allowed it to play a somewhat more activist role regionally while Costa Rica, because of its lack of sufficient economic or military resources to independently protect its democratic polity, has been much more isolationist in relation to its Central American neighbors (although it did help overthrow the Somoza regime). However, the political crisis on the isthmus over the past decade, which Costa Rica has perceived as a potential threat to its national security and democratic political system, has encouraged it to assume a leadership role in finding an acceptable peace in the region. Thus, although it still looks to the United States for support and protection, it is also concerned that American actions to defend its security interests in Central America could so destabilize the region that its own political system could be affected. Like Venezuela, Costa Rica also seeks to create international institutions to serve as a substitute for the tutelary and interventionist role of the United States.

The question remains whether the Western Democratic ethos found in their respective political cultures is the principal source for their corresponding international politics. Is it mere coincidence that the two so resemble each other? Or is there something inevitable about a democratic political culture carrying over into inter-state behavior? The most cautious and tentative conclusion we can draw from this first pair of case studies—and it may be limited to such ideal-type democracies—is that the domestic and international value systems operationalized by a democratic state cannot be at odds with each other. To see whether this association holds under differing political conditions, let us turn to the political cultures of a less ideal type—mixed ones that oscillate between democratic and authoritarian interludes.

Notes

1. Alejandro Portes and John Walton, *Urban Latin America: The Political Condition from Above and Below.* Austin: University of Texas Press, 1976, p. 141.

2. These ratings represent the judgment of the authors and of one additional knowledgeable collaborator on each of the operational variables. They are based on a secondary analysis of a representative selection of scholarly literature on each country. Appendix A lists the sources used.

3. Harry B. Murkland, "Costa Rica: Fortunate Society," *Current History,* XXII (March 1952), p. 141. Also see Ralph Lee Woodward, Jr., *Central America: A Nation Divided*, 2nd edn. New York: Oxford University Press, 1985, esp. pp. 213–214.

4. Hubert Herring, "Problems Facing Democracy," in A. Curtis Wilgus (ed.), *The Caribbean: Its Political Problems.* Gainesville: University of Florida Press, 1956, p. 154.

5. Gaetano Cerósimo, *Los estereotipos del costarricense.* San José: Editorial Universidad de Costa Rica, n.d., p. 57.

6. For a discussion of the term "Liberal Synthesis" see Roland H. Ebel, "Thomism and Machiavellianism in Central American Political Development." Paper presented at the 44th International Congress of Americanists, Manchester, England, September 5–10, 1982. The ensuing discussion is primarily taken from that paper.

7. A number of contemporary Costa Rican writers would dispute the application of the term "social democracy" to the *liberacion* movement, preferring to call it a modernizing regime (Schifter), a middle class bureaucratic regime (Cerdas), or state capitalism (Gudmanson). However, defined in this work as a regime embracing political democracy, a mixed economy, and a welfare state, the term social democracy is not far off the mark. See Lowell Gudmandson, "Costa Rica and the 1948 Revolution: Rethinking the Social Democratic Paradigm," *Latin American Research Review,* 19, no. 1 (1948).

8. John Booth, "Representative Constitutional Democracy in Costa Rica: Adaption to Crisis in the Turbulent 1980s," in Steve C. Ropp and James A. Morris (eds.), *Central America: Crisis and Adaptation.* Alberquerque: University of New Mexico Press, 1984, p. 165.

9. Charles F. Denton, *Patterns of Costa Rican Politics.* Boston: Allyn and Bacon, Inc., 1971, p. 8.

10. For a discussion of this point in detail see James L. Busey, "Observations on Latin American Constitutionalism," *The Americas,* 24, no. 1 (July 1967).

11. Denton, *Patterns of Costa Rican Politics*. pp. 35–36, 41.

12. Booth, "Representative Constitutional Democracy in Costa Rica," p. 168.

13. See John A, Booth, "Are Latin Americans Politically Rational? Citizen Participation and Democracy in Costa Rica," in Mitchell Seligson and John A. Booth (eds.), *Political Participation in Latin America*, Vol. 1 *Citizen and State*. New York: Holmes and Meier, 1978, p. 110; and Dan Caspi and Mitchell Seligson, "Toward an Empirical Theory of Tolerance: Radical Groups in Israel and Costa Rica," *Comparative Political Studies*, 15, no. 4 (January 1983), pp. 385–404.

14. Thomas L. Karnes, "The Central American Republics," in Harold Eugene Davis, Larman C. Wilson, et al (eds.), *Latin American Foreign Policies: An Analysis*. Baltimore: Johns Hopkins, 1975, p. 148.

15. Richard Millet, "Praetorians or Patriots? The Central American Military," in Robert S. Leiken (ed.), *Central America: Anatomy of Conflict*. New York: Pergamon, 1984, pp. 87–88.

16. Since the onset of the Central American crisis in the late 1970s, Costa Rica has become significantly more militarized, contrary to its wishes. It receives military aid and training from the United States. The security force has about doubled from five thousand to about ten thousand, and the country has formed a militia of about ten thousand. See Richard Fagen, *Forging Peace: The Challenge of Central America*. New York: Basil Blackwell, 1987, p. 115.

17. This discussion draws on James D. Cochrane, *The Politics of Regionalism: The Central American Case*. New Orleans: Tulane Studies in Political Science, 1969.

18. Charles E. Staley, "Costa Rica and the Central American Common Market," *Economia Internazionale*, XV, no. 1 (Febbraio 1962), pp. 118–119.

19. Staley, "Costa Rica and the Central American Common Market," pp. 117–118. For an excellent comparison of Costa Rica and Somoza's Nicaragua, see James L. Busey, "Foundations of Political Contract: Costa Rica and Nicaragua," *Western Political Quarterly*, XI, no. 3 (September 1954), pp. 627–659.

20. United Nations, Economic and Social Council, Economic Commission for Latin America, *Report of the Central American Economic Cooperation Committee, 3 September 1959 to 13 December 1960*. (E/CN. 12/552, E/CN. 12/cce/224), June 1961, p. 6.

21. Gordon Connell-Smith, *The Inter-American System*. New York: Oxford University Press, 1966, p. 161.

22. Connell-Smith, *The Inter-American System*, p. 225.

23. H. Michael Erisman, *Cuba's International Relations: The Anatomy of a Nationalistic Foreign Policy*. Boulder, CO: Westview Press, 1985, p. 136. The break

reveals a not much dicussed aspect of Costa Rican foreign policy: however committed to democracy, Costa Rica would establish diplomatic relations with nondemocratic countries. For example, in the 1970s Costa Rica established diplomatic relations with both Moscow and Havana.

24. See: William M. LeoGrande, "Cuba and Nicaragua: From the Somoza to the Sandinista," in Barry B, Levine (ed.), *The New Cuban Presence in the Caribbean*. Boulder, CO: Westview Press, 1983, pp. 43–58.

25. Mario Ojeda, "Mexican Policy toward Central America in the Context of U.S.-Mexican Relations," in Richard R. Fagen and Olga Pellicer (eds.), *The Future of Central America; Policy Choices for the U.S. and Mexico*. Stanford: Stanford University Press, 1983, pp. 141–142.

26. *The New York Times*, (November 7, 1987), p. 6.

27. William A. Hazelton, "Will There Always be a Uruguay? Interdependence and Independence in the Inter-American System," in Elizabeth G. Ferris and Jennie K. Lincoln (eds.), *Latin American Foreign Politicies: Global and Regional Dimensions*, p. 64.

28. John D. Martz, "The Party System: Towards Institutionalization," in John D Martz and David J. Meyers (eds.), *Venezuela: The Democratic Experience*. New York: Praeger, 1977, p. 93.

29. Pedro-Pablo Kuczynski, "The Economic Development of Venezuela: A Summary View as of 1975-1976," in Robert D. Bond (ed.), *Contemporary Venezuela and Its Role in International Affairs*. New York: New York University Press, 1977, p. 50.

30. The only exceptions to this generalization are some of the countries of the English and Dutch Caribbean in the 1980s. *Economic and Social Progress in Latin America, 1987 Report*. Washington: Inter-American Development Bank, 1987, Statistical Appendix, Table 3. See also Kuczynski, "The Economic Development of Venezuela," p. 51.

31. David Eugene Blank, *Politics in Venezuela*. Boston: Little, Brown and Company, 1973, p. 51.

32. Daniel H. Levine, "Venezuelan Politics: Past and Future," in Bond, *Contemporary Venezuela and Its Role in International Affairs*, p. 11.

33. R. Lynn Kelley, "Venezuelan Constitutional Forms and Realities," in Martz and Myers, *Venezuela: The Democratic Experience*, pp. 27, 37.

34. Martz, "The Party System: Towards Institutionalization," in Martz and Myers, *Venezuela: The Democratic Experience*, pp. 94-97.

35. Martz, "The Party System," p. 105.

36. Abente states that the *Pacto de Punto Fijo* "called for a Calhounian political democracy that would insure the vital interests of all major contenders (the AD, labor and peasant coalition, other political parties, socioeconomic elites, army, church) through the establishment of an implicit concurrent majority rule. It also lowered political tensions through the deliberate toning down of partisan discourse." See Diego Abente, "Politics and Policies: The Limits of the Venezuelan Consociational Regime," in Donald L. Herman (ed.), *Democracy in Latin America; Colombia and Venezuela.* New York: Praeger, 1988, p. 137.

37. Blank, *Politics in Venezuela*, p. 54.

38. Enrique A. Baloyra, "Public Attitudes Toward the Democratic Regime," in Martz and Myers, *Venezuela: The Democratic Experience*, Chapter 3.

39. Baloyra, "Public Attitudes," pp. 50–51.

40. According to Baloyra, "students, the middle class and professional people form a relatively stable cluster in terms of a series of relevant items: they believe the bureaucracy to be capable, think government would not improve without politicians, are most likely to vote null in elections, and have a greater sense of political efficacy. A somewhat more disparate cluster shows peasants and housewives being most critical of the bureaucracy, politicians and national political parties. These two groups are also the least likely to vote null, the least efficacious politically, have no particular preference for any type of economic system, and identify with the Right. Workers are also very bitter and critical, joining the students as the most leftist groups." Baloyra, "Public Attitudes," p. 58.

41. Blank, *Politics in Venezuela*, p. 54.

42. Blank, *Politics in Venezuela*, p. 58.

43. Joseph Mason, "Venezuela Caught in the IMF Crunch," *The Times of the Americas*, (January 24, 1990).

44. Robert D. Bond, "Venezuela's Role in International Affairs," in Robert D. Bond (ed.), *Contemporary Venezuela and Its Role in International Affairs.* New York: New York University Press for the Council on Foreign Relations, 1977, p. 231.

45. Daniel H. Levine, "Venezuelan Politics: Past and Future," in Bond, *Contemporary Venezuela and Its Role in International Affairs*, p. 20.

46. Jerome Slater, *The OAS and the United States Foreign Policy.* Columbus, OH: Ohio State University Press, 1967, pp. 93–95.

47. See Slater, *The OAS and United States Foreign Policy*, Chapters 5 and 6.

48. Franklin Tugwell, "The United States and Venezuela: Prospects for Accomodations," in Bond, *Contemporary Venezuela and Its Role in International Affairs*, p. 202.

49. Leo B. Lott, *Venezuela and Paraguay: Political Modernity and Tradition in Conflict*. New York: Holt, Rinehart and Winston, 1972, pp. 346–347.

50. *Venezuela-up-to-date*, 12 (Spring 1969), p. 5.

51. Levine, "Venezuela's Role in International Affairs," in Bond, *Contemporary Venezuela and Its Role in International Affairs*, p. 234–235; and Levine, "Venezuelan Politics; Past and Future," in Bond, *Contemporary Venezuela and Its Role in International Affairs*, p. 22.

53. Levine, "Venezuelan Politics: Past and Future," p. 22.

54. Bond, "Venezuela's Role in International Affairs," p. 235.

55. William P. Avery and James D, Cochrane, "Innovation in Latin American Regionalism: The Andean Common Market," *International Organization*, 27, no. 2 (Spring 1973), pp. 181–223.

56. Bruce M. Bagley, "The Politics of Asymmetrical Interdependence: U.S.-Mexican Relations in the 1980s," in H. Michael Erisman (ed.), *The Caribbean Challenge: U.S. Policy in a Volatile Region*. Boulder, CO: Westview Press, 1984, pp. 153–154.

57. William A. Hazelton, "The Foreign Policies of Venezuela and Colombia: Collaboration, Competition, and Conflict," in Lincoln and Ferris (eds.), *Latin American Foreign Policies: Global and Regional Dimensions*, p. 165.

58. Wolf Grabendorf, "The Role of Regional Powers in Central America: Mexico, Venezuela, Cuba, and Colombia," in Munoz and Tulchin (eds.) *Latin American Nations in World Affairs*, pp. 88–89.

59. Sheldon B. Liss, "Venezuela," in Harold Eugene Davis, Larman C. Wilson, et al. (eds.), *Latin American Foreign Policies: An Analysis*. Baltimore, MD: Johns Hopkins University Press, 1975, p. 435.

60. Liss, "Venezuela," p. 435. Venezuela is not the only Latin American country, of course, to profess to have a foreign policy based on deep-seated principles and international behavior that sometimes departs from those principles. Mexico furnishes another example: nonintervention in the affairs of another country is a cornerstone principle of Mexican foreign policy, but the principle did not prevent Mexico from withdrawing diplomatic recognition of Somoza's Nicaragua and supporting the effort to overturn his government. Another Mexican foreign policy principle, enunciated in the Estrada Doctrine, calls for automatic recognition of new governments, yet Mexico refused to recognize the Franco government in Spain.

61. Lott, *Venezuela and Paraguay*, p. 363.

62. Lott, *Venezuela and Paraguay*, p. 361.

63. Tugwell, "The United States and Venezuela," p. 200.

64. Hazelton, "The Foreign Policies of Venezuela and Colombia," p. 156.

65. Laurence Whitehead, "Debt, Diversification, and Dependency: Latin America's International Political Relations," in Kevin J. Middlebrook and Carlos Rico (eds.), *The United States and Latin America in the 1980s: Contending Perspectives on a Decade of Crisis*. Pittsburgh: University of Pittsburg Press, 1986, p.102.

66. Kevin J. Middlebrook and Carlos Rico, "The United States and Latin America in the 1980s: Change, Complexity, and Contending Perspectives," in Middlebrook and Rico (eds.), *The United States and Latin America in the 1980s*, p. 22.

67. See Franklin Tugwell, *The Politics of Oil in Venezuela*. Stanford: Stanford University Press, 1975; and Paul E. Sigmund, *Multinationals in Latin America: The Politics of Nationalization*. Madison, WI: University of Wisconsin Press, 1980, Chapters 7–8.

5

Alternating Monistic Systems and Foreign Policy: Colombia and Guatemala

In this chapter, we examine two circum-Caribbean states whose political histories suggest regular alternation between monistic or authoritarian rule and democratic interludes. Both Colombia and Guatemala have been selected as case studies so as to represent a type of Latin American political culture that, in the best Thomistic and Machiavellian traditions, contains the roots of both monistic and pluralist rule. In fact, the explanation for this alternating regime type may be found, in part at least, in the respective political cultures of the countries. It is difficult to dispute the classification of both states as alternating monisms, for even in recent decades the pattern of alternation has been clearly manifested. In the case of Colombia, *La Violencia* of 1948 was followed by military rule (1953–1957), then after 1958, coalition politics between Liberals and Conservatives. In the case of Guatemala, the latest transition from authoritarian to democratic rule is even more recent, dating to the mid-1980s. Do these otherwise different countries, sharing this one characteristic of alternating regimes in common, have foreign policies that resemble each other? This is the subject of this chapter.

Colombian Political Culture

The checkered political history of Colombia presents anyone attempting to understand the underlying patterns of the nation's political culture with a paradox. On the one hand, one can identify such continuing cultural characteristics as the nation's political elitism and endemic violence. On the other hand, the nation has gone through relatively long periods (for Latin America) of regime stability, competitive elections, and peaceful transfers of power. For purposes of this chapter, the past one hundred years of Colombian political history can be divided into four general periods: an era of alternating, yet fairly long periods of one-party hegemony, lasting from 1880 to 1948; a second period of intense conflict known as *La Violencia* which lasted roughly from 1948 to 1958; the period of the National Front Agreement under which the Liberal and Conservative parties shared the offices and power of government (1958–1974); and a post-National Front period during which power has alternated relatively peacefully between the two major parties (1974–1988). Political violence, however, has been an ever-present feature of Colombia's political system throughout these 108 years, rising in intensity between 1948 and 1958, subsiding somewhat during the National Front, gradually escalating in the post-Front years, exacerbated now by the Medellin drug cartel.

The cultural traits of political elitism and political violence historically have had a symbiotic relationship with each other. From independence forward Colombia's elites have cooperated in maintaining the clientalist structure of the society while at the same time using their followers to fight the often intense battles resulting from their political rivalries. As one important study put it in 1956, Colombian society seemed to be more a " 'society of castes' than a 'society of classes.' "[1] Unlike much of the rest of Latin America, the political and economic elites continued to dominate the nation's political life well after the formation of the urban middle classes; in fact, they have been quite successful in adding the leadership elements of the upper bourgeoisie to their dominance of the peasant masses.[2]

The political parties of the Colombian elites generated intense conflict during much of the nineteenth century. Divided into intensely hostile "political families" flying the banner of either Liberalism or Conservativism, these *caudillo*-led aggregations fought over the spoils of government using their private armies of peasants who worked on the *haciendas* of their followers. As the Colombian intellectual, Fernando Guillén Martínez, has written: "The history of Colombia since 1928 has been this: a mass of public employees arms in hand faces a mass of armed aspirants to public office."[3] While, theoretically, the two parties were democratic bodies, James Henderson writes,

> They were closer in spirit and function to the feudal principality of medieval western Europe....The Conservative and Liberal parties constituted militant, hierarchical, corporate states within the nineteenth century Colombian state. Throughout the remainder of the nineteenth century they provided the Colombian common man a value-laden body of myth that replaced the Hispanic moral unity destroyed after 1810.[4]

Because of the often religious nature of the conflict ("atheist" Liberals vs. "Catholic" Conservatives), peasants were socialized into "two closed worlds—one Liberal and the other Conservative"—each with its flag, its heroes, and its martyrs.[5] Thus, the Colombian peasantry, as John Booth writes, inherited a "tragic legacy," namely, "a violent political tradition, families scarred by partisan revanchism, and deadly hatreds between individuals and between adjoining communities of different party affiliation."[6]

The problem of political violence, however, has had the paradoxical effect of stimulating the Colombian political elites to take a creative approach to their political institutions. Harvey Kline notes that although between 1886 and 1930 the country was wracked by a number of civil wars, the party elites often formed electoral or governing coalitions with each other which produced periods of relative stability.[7] The period of Conservative dominance following the War of the Thousand Days in 1902 to the Great Depression of 1930 was one such period. The intense partisan competition generated by the relative electoral parity between the two parties after 1930, exacerbated by the demand of younger urban voters for greater participation in the political system, led to increasing conflict culminating in the famous urban riots known as the *bogotazo* following the assassination of the Liberal populist, Jorge Gaitán, in 1948. Thus, when the *bogotazo* sparked a new round of political killings, the elites were forced to mediate their differences through the institutional mechanism of the National Front Agreement, the result of which has been thirty years of relatively stable pluralist (if not always competitive) government.

The first sixteen years (1958–1974) saw power shared between the Liberal and Conservative parties according to an agreed-upon "consociational" formula embracing *alternación* and *paridad*.[8] The period from 1974 to 1990 saw each party win the presidency twice in competitive elections and peacefully transfer power to the other. In addition, three of the four presidents continued to maintain at least some of the features of parity in office holding even though not required to do so by law. These mechanisms, which have produced conciliation and compromise among the party elites, however, have been offset by continued civilian lawlessness and an ongoing guerilla struggle which reignited in November 1985 with the attack on the Colombian Palace of Justice by the M-19 guerillas and the murder of Liberal party presidential candidate, Luis Carlos Galán, by the drug lords in August 1989.[9] Gary Hoskin seeks to explain the continued and escalating violence, in spite of thirty years of elite cooperation, by arguing that coalition government, while producing a form of political peace, has not given adequate incentives to the Colombian leadership to modernize their political structure so as to enable them to meet the society's problems. The past thirty years have seen sectarian conflict transformed into social conflict.[10] However, the traditional party elites have sought to solve social problems by the traditional political mechanisms of guaranteeing safety and participation to previously excluded groups— amnesty and cease-fire agreements with guerilla groups, a national dialogue with opposition groups, and the newly established election of local mayors. This so-called "peace process" initiated by Conservative party president Belisario Betancur in 1982 was effectively brought to an end in 1985 with the attack on the Palace of Justice. President Virgilio Barco Vargas had responded by returning the polity to a system of *gobierno de partido* or partisan government.[11]

The ambiguities and paradoxes of Colombian political history are reflected in the ratings presented in table 4.2. In terms of its national value system, the period from 1948 to 1974 was marked, not surprisingly, by an almost equal mixture of Thomistic and Machiavellian values. That is, the Machiavellian traits of violence, political combat, and disobedience to law were counterbalanced by an orientation toward such monistic devices as creating inter-party agreements (the National Front), the sharing of governmental office (*paridad*), and elite domination. During that same period the nation's behavior patterns were clearly *caudillaje* in character. This is reflected in the number of analysts citing such things as the existence of personalistic factions and parties, the degree of patronage in the bureaucracy, and the levels of clientalism and corruption in political and governmental institutions.

Since the termination of the National Front Agreement in 1974 with its "monistic" emphasis on *alternación* and *paridad*, the essentially democratic and competitive character of the political system—at least at the elite level—has had the effect of reducing the Thomistic content of Colombia's political culture. However, such Machiavellian features as political fragmentation, guerrilla activity, corruption, disobedience to law, and the perpetuation of anti-system ideological groups have not noticeably declined. In fact, the bombings and assassinations of the so-called "extradictables" is simply a manifestation of traditional Colombian political behavior under new auspices—the Medellin drug cartel. Thus, both in its value system and political behavior patterns the Machiavellian/*caudillaje* character of the culture continues to predominate.

Certain features of Colombia's democratic life, however, have injected a Western Democratic admixture into its political culture, particularly since 1974. Elite commitment to maintaining the viability of the nation's two major political parties, their willingness to compromise so as to obviate the possibility of a military coup, their generally high respect for civil and human rights (although President Barco is taking a more militant stand against the guerillas), and their willingness to engage in community service are important in this regard.

The Colombian political culture seems to function on two planes. At the elite level a tradition of compromise and bargaining has been engendered by the realization that any serious failure to do so would open up the political system to either another period of uncontrolled political violence or possibly the dismantling of the elitist social and political system by a guerilla-led mass movement. This fear led the political elites to create the National Front as a means of dampening down the fires of partisan passion that produced the *violencia* that nearly destroyed the political system in the decade following the *bogotazo* of 1948. It also caused them to maintain many of the elements of the parity agreement after 1974 as well as the practice of peacefully transferring power.

It is at the sub-elite level of the masses that the political culture seems to be more resistent to change. Guerilla warfare, political violence, mass action, and the machinations of the drug cartel have kept Colombia's "democratic" polity under the threat of serious disruption for a decade and a half and pose the question as to whether it is sustainable over the long pull.

Colombian Foreign Policy

Historically, Colombia has not played an activist role in the region's international politics. A mountainous country with its capital at Santa Fe de Bogota, Colombia retained a greater degree of insularity during the Colonial and independence periods than many of the other countries of the Spanish Main, including Panama. One exception to this generalization was the city of Cartagena which was both an important port city on the official Spanish trade routes and a center for the contraband trade with England. As a result, Colombian foreign policy historically has tended to focus on economic issues.

Colombia was also involved in a flurry of international activity when, as the capital of the Viceroyalty of Nueva Granada, it became involved in both the formation and breakup of the nation of Gran Colombia (1819–1830). However, with the growing instability and violence of the nineteenth century, Colombia turned inward. It was not until the turn of the century when the issues of the construction of a canal across the state of Panama and its demand for independence arose that Colombia once again was forced into intense international activity—largely in confrontation with the United States.

The embittered relationships that resulted from the Panama affair created in Colombia an ambivalent attitude to the United States. On the one hand, as an exporter of agricultural products, Colombia became increasingly dependent on the United States market. On the other hand, the loss of Panama embittered United States-Colombian relations for a number of decades. Either way, the United States had become its international *caudillo*—at times viewed as beneficent, at other times considered malevolent.

In January 1903, Colombia signed the Hay-Herrán Treaty with the United States. The treaty called for the leasing of a canal zone in Panama to the United States, but it was not ratified by the Colombian Congress. As a result, what began as an apparently cordial act ended in causing strained relations between the two countries. The disagreement that followed was the result of two factors that resulted from the failure of the treaty to get through the United States Congress. First and most important, within the *departamento* of Panama a movement to secede from Colombia had been developing, and it—not altogether uncoincidentally—erupted shortly after Colombia's disapproval of the treaty. The second factor was United States military support for the Panamanian revolutionary movement once armed conflict broke out. The deployment of force in the area, justified by the United States as a way of protecting the railroad across the isthmus, effectively prevented the Colombian government from restoring its authority in the area. By November 1903 Panama had seceded and the United States had recognized it as an independent nation. A schism in diplomatic relations between the United States and Colombia followed, not fully repaired until 1924 through the Urrutia-Thompson Treaty. Clearly, Colombia rejected the United States' self-ascribed role of *libertador* and *caudillo* in what had been a Colombian province.

Between 1903 and 1924 Colombia once again removed itself from the international arena and demonstrated its isolationist policy by opting for neutrality during World War I. It withstood pressure from some of its Latin American counterparts such as Brazil, Costa Rica, Guatemala, Haiti, Honduras, and Nicaragua to align itself on the American side so as to uphold the Monroe Doctrine. The reasoning of these nations was that since their North American ally provided them with protection, alignment was the least they could do to reciprocate and so maintain traditional United States-Latin American relations.

Colombia's neutrality during World War I ws located in the dissatisfaction that had built up within the government towards United

States actions in Panama in 1903. Its reasoning was that it would not align itself with the United States until reparations had been paid to compensate for the loss of its province. Why Colombia did not take sides with Germany in retaliation for the alleged injustice committed by the United States can only be understood in terms of fear. Colombia was afraid that if it did not break economic and diplomatic ties with Germany, the United States would in turn deploy troops into the area in the name of "national security".[12]

Only after the war did Colombia come out of its isolationism and begin to take a more active role in foreign affairs. Under Conservative president Marco Fidel Suárez (1918–1921), the "Doctrine of the Polar Star" was elaborated by which explicit recognition was given to Colombia's "natural" ties with the United States. As Harvey Kline describes this doctrine, Colombia

> should look northward, to the powerful United States, both as an example of social and political democracy and as a partner, with whom Colombia's destinies were inextricably linked for reasons of geographic proximity and complementary economies. Despite some of the contretemps. . . , this doctrine (although not in the same rhetorical terms) has guided Colombian foreign policy ever since.[13]

Colombia, in effect, accepted America's *caudillo* role in the hemisphere.

One catalytic event in 1924 influenced Colombia to take a more active part in the international community: the restoration of diplomatic relations with the United States as a result of the Urrutia-Thompson Treaty. The treaty called for Colombia to be compensated for the loss of Panama with a $25 million indemnity in economic aid.[14] The sudden injection of this large sum into the Colombian economy produced a boom which, in turn, made the country attractive for foreign investors. Evidence of this may be noted in the investment by American companies of $310 million between 1924 and 1929 in its oil industry, and in the expansion of bank credit for Colombian utilities. This period of prosperity is known as the "Dance of the Millions."[15]

This newfound prosperity propelled more active Colombian participation in Western hemispheric affairs. Thus in 1924 Colombia reached agreement with Panama on their mutual border and thereafter entered into diplomatic relations with Panama. In 1928 Colombia faced a new territorial dispute, this time with Nicaragua over the archipelago of San Andres and Providencia. The conflict was resolved peacefully with the help of Colombia's newly reacquired North American ally.

The United States role took the form of military aid to secure the archipelago, an action that accelerated the actual resolution of the dispute at the negotiating table between Nicaragua and Colombia. The agreement called for Colombia to drop its claim to "la Costa de mosquitos" and to the Mangles Islands. In return, Nicaragua would recognize Colombia's sovereignty over San Andres and Providencia.[16] The way both disputes were settled exemplified Colombia's commitment to use peaceful means and its capacity to use its relations with other states to further its own objectives. In other words, the United States was welcome to play a *caudillo* role in the securing of San Andres and Providencia.

In the 1930s Colombia's growing regional activism was manifested in two new areas. In 1932 a conflict arose with Peru when the latter annexed the Leticia territory in the Amazon valley. A decade earlier, during the Leguia regime (the President of Peru from 1919 to 1930), Colombia had reimbursed the Peruvian government for the acquisition of Leticia. In 1932 a group of Peruvian irregulars retook the territory. Colombia denounced the Peruvian annexation and took the issue to the League of Nations. In 1934, the League proposed a solution that returned Leticia to Colombia. The affair was an important event in Colombia's diplomatic history in that it represented an early instance of the recourse to an international organization in order both to promote its position and to resolve external confrontations peacefully. This second area of Colombia's international activity in the 1930s became even more conspicuous when the country became a member of the League's Committee of Investigation and Conciliation in 1932. Through its membership, Colombia's prestige and influence were enhanced, especially after it attempted (without success, however) to arbitrate territorial disputes between Bolivia and Paraguay that resulted in the Chaco War.[17]

Colombia's regional activity in the 1930s paved the way for undertaking a broader role as economic and political actor in the world community during the 1940s and 1950s. As such it applied the "good neighbor" policy itself: it sided with the Allies during World War II in order to promote a sense of "hemispheric solidarity." This was based on a perception of the United States as beneficent *caudillo*. For example, in 1939 the Colombian foreign minister stated his conviction that "the government of the North" wished to stimulate the economies of the Latin peoples, and that it was thus in the interest of Colombia to support the United States defense system.[18] As a result, Colombia signed a trade agreement with the United States in 1940 and joined Mexico and Venezuela in sponsoring a regional resolution at the Rio Conference in 1942 calling for all Latin American states to break off diplomatic ties with the Axis powers. The result of these two decisions was the strengthening of the economic and political partnership between Colombia and the United States.

In 1948 Bogota played host to the founding conference of the OAS and, as a result of its close ties with the United States which had been the prime mover in creating the organization, Colombia provided the first General Secretary, Carlos Lleras Camargo. According to Drekonja: "Through the OAS a partnership was institutionalized at the regional level."[19] Colombia thus entered a new phase in foreign affairs which primarily revolved around United States policy on the one hand, and Colombian economic interests on the other. Examples of how Colombian policy became linked with United States preferences at this time abound: Colombia became one of the first members of the United Nations; as such it was the only South American state to send troops to aid the U.N. forces in the Korean conflict. During the "Alliance for Progress" years of the 1960s, the country became a "showcase" of how to utilize United States aid effectively and follow United States promptings by attempting to promote a dynamic private sector, limited land reform, and enlightened elite rule.

Further evidence of Colombia's quintessentially economistic foreign policy can be seen in 1958 when it played an important role in inter-American efforts to strengthen development programs through foreign aid and trade, which produced the Declaration of Bogota. The declaration expressed Colombia's, Venezuela's, and Ecuador's concern for peaceful regulation of international relations, their interest in creating a common market, and their greater attention to domestic problems.

In the 1960s economic interests almost exclusively drove Colombian foreign policy. Apart from the Alliance for Progress, we may note the country's decision in 1961 to comply with the Montevideo Treaty. The 1960 treaty, designed to promote free trade among signatories through average annual tariff reductions of eight percent for a period of twelve years, created the Latin American Free Trade Association (LAFTA). It was through LAFTA that Colombia was able to promote greater regional integration of trade, but it ran into trouble when it found itself incurring a high imbalance of payments. As a result, in 1962 Colombia changed its strategy. The new plan was designed to set off an intensive export drive based around oil, coffee, fruit, and cotton. Accordingly, Colombia concluded a number of agreements at the regional level, for example, with Venezuela in 1964 for the coordinated development of industry and agriculture, and with Ecuador for a $102 million joint exploration of the Orito oil field along the border of the two countries. Its plan to expand its external economy also entailed introduction of a system of "mini-devaluations" of its currency.[20]

The next step towards economic development was membership in the General Agreement on Tariffs and Trade (GATT) in 1968, which further stimulated trade. One year later, Colombia supported the creation of the Andean Common Market to aid in regional integration and, through the market's less restrictive policies, to make investment from abroad more attractive in Colombia.[21] Not surprisingly, Colombia during this period came to be less dependent on United States aid. This policy, implemented by a conservative regime, was intended to promote more exports to Western Europe, especially Britain and West Germany. Further diversification of economic relations was the reestablishing of commercial and diplomatic ties, ruptured in 1948, with several Eastern Europe countries in 1966 and with the Soviet Union in 1968. Even so, by the end of the 1960s the United States remained the largest single source of investment in the country.

In the 1970s Colombian governments continued to be preoccupied with boosting the external sector of the economy. Two new export-oriented *institutos decentralizados*—Pro-Expo (Export Promotion Fund) and INCOMEX (Foreign Trade Institute)—began to play an important part in the making of foreign policy. As a consequence, Colombia gradually moved away from its close relations with the United States so as to gain more influence in the rest of the region. An example of this trend was the decision of Alfonso López Michelsen's administration in 1975 to decline United States financial aid. As a result, "Between 1974 and 1978 Colombia acquired much prestige with its multilateral foreign policy. . .and international diversification, which linked it more than ever with the movement of the Non-Aligned."[22]

Colombia's new role incorporated it into a group of Andean nations known as the Contadora Four (the others were Mexico, Venezuela, and Panama) which sought to make the region less influenced by United States interests. The group first became active in the late 1970s when it tried to isolate the Somoza regime at an international level. In fact, this coalition of Latin American states even aided the Sandinistas in their struggle to take power. It was not until the early 1980s, though, that the group took on official status and received the full support of the Colombian government under Liberal president Belisario Betancur. As such, it searched for a diplomatic alternative to the violence in Nicaragua and in other Central American states. At a press conference in 1983 when the Contadora concept was presented to the United Nations, Betancur argued that United States military exercises in the region were only adding to the problem: "I respect the rights of the states to work through their madness, but let them not seek Central America as the area for their conflict."[23] Colombia's own commitment to mediation and peace keeping was further exemplified by its role in restoring diplomatic relations between Guatemala and Spain in 1984, which had been broken three years earlier after a Guatemalan attack on the Spanish embassy. Clearly Colombia aimed at gaining international prestige and influence through diplomatic activities of this kind.

President Betancur's policies also estranged Colombia from the United States on a set of issues going beyond the Central American conflict. Colombia applied for membership in the Non-Aligned Movement, then called "for the reconstructing of the OAS so as to exclude the U.S. and include Cuba."[24] Soon after this declaration in 1985, President Ronald Reagan announced a peace initiative for Central America. Initially Betancur "endorsed the plan," but retracted it several days later when the United States continued to support the Contras and included them in the peace initiative. On the other hand, successive Colombian and United States administrations have agreed on one major international issue, namely, that the country has been a victim of regular Cuban aggression through ties between Havana and the M-19 leftist insurgents. In 1981 Colombia broke off relations with Cuba that had been restored only six years earlier. Thus, if the United States and Colombia disagreed on Central American policy, they concurred on perhaps a more important "litmus test" of alliance strength—perceptions of the Cuban-Communist threat in the hemisphere. A second test, the Falklands/Malvinas war of 1982, also found Colombia as one of only three Latin American states supporting the pro-British/United States position. Clearly, on security issues of vital concern to the United States, Colombia's record of support is stronger than most other countries in the region.

No analysis of Colombian foreign policy would be complete without a brief look at its relations with neighboring Venezuela. We have already seen that border disputes between Colombia and its neighbors were common into the twentieth century. At present, the line of demarcation between Colombia and Venezuela in and off the Gulf of Venezuela remains unsettled, with important consequences for both sides. The gulf waters may contain oil deposits, producing revenues which Colombia would like to have. Moreover, in addition to the off-shore border, the on-shore boundary separating Colombia's Guajira department and Venezuela's Zulia state is largely arbitrary (a state line). In this area known coal deposits are coveted by both sides.

When one factors in a history of cultural animosities between the two nations, the oftentimes confusing guerrilla activities which pose a threat to each government and spill over both sides of the border, the existence of a significant number of Colombian migrant workers in prosperous Venezuela, and the powerful modern air force constructed by Venezuela, the potential for conflict between the neighbors should not be underestimated. In this respect, Colombia especially looks to the United States to serve in the contradictory roles of both regional arbitrator and protector of Colombian interests.

In the 1986 elections, a new leader, Liberal Virgilio Barco, took power and, as expected, Colombian foreign policy shifted back towards a closer alignment with the United States. Colombia's disagreement with the Reagan administration over a Central American peace plan was placed on the back burner, and the issues of Colombian "narco-export" cartels and the appropriate roles that the Colombian Ministry of Justice and the U.S. Drug Enforcement Agency should play became paramount in bilateral relations. The Febraury 1990 Cartagena summit on drug enforcement, hosted by Barco and attended by President Bush and Bolivian and Peruvian leaders, symbolized an effort aimed at greater cooperation among the countries involved in coca production and coca consumption. But whether the meeting could reverse what John Martz described as "Colombia's already sagging international reputation" on the question of drugs and human rights seemed doubtful.[25]

From this analysis of Colombian foreign policy we may conclude that in many areas the country has achieved its foreign policy goals and has developed a distinctive approach to international relations. It has generally put economics over politics, has made use of international organizations to promote its position abroad, and has attempted to resolve conflict through diplomatic means. At the same time, Colombia has largely failed to construct a foreign policy that would be immune to United States influence. Since 1924, in spite of intermittent attempts to distance itself from the United States, the exigencies of economic development have required it to accept the United States as regional *caudillo* when it served American interests. As a result, as German Cavelier has stressed in *La Política Internacional de Colombia*: "Colombia falls clearly within its sphere of influence, with the result that its international politics loses independence each day."[26]

Guatemalan Political Culture

As can be seen from table 4.2, Guatemala is the most *caudillaje* of the six countries in our study. Personalistic parties rent with factionalism, personal dictatorships, political violence and mass action, clientalistic behavior, and patronage relationships in the bureaucracy and the military are commonly cited in the literature.[27] With respect to its national value system, the country manifests a mixture of Thomistic and Machiavellian values. This is not surprising given the fact that the country has oscillated between periods of military rule and rambunctious populism during which time either authoritarianism or a tenuous democracy has coexisted with insurrection and state-sponsored terrorism.

As the capital of the *Capitanía del Reino de Guatemala* under the Viceroyalty of New Spain, Guatemala City became one of the important administrative and commercial centers of the Spanish Empire. As such, it early on also became a center of Hispanic Thomistic culture—particularly in contrast to the more rural settlements in the rest of Central America and much of Southern Mexico. A fairly elaborate administrative structure was established there as well as an evolving set of corporative institutions such as the church, the university, the corporate Indian community, artisans' guilds, and the *Consulado de Commercio*. Although relatively small in comparison to Mexico City or Lima, the political and economic elite created a hierarchic society in the Spanish mold. Writing of its first capital, Santiago de los Caballeros, Ralph Lee Woodward states:

> There was sufficient affluence, however, to permit considerable beautification of Santiago de Guatemala. Magnificent homes and large commercial houses filled with imported goods lined the principal streets near the center of the city, but the grandeur of the metropolis was most reflected in the opulence of the ecclesiastical establishment, as great churches, monasteries, convents and seminaries abounded.[28]

Guatemala also contained one of the densest concentrations of sedentary Indians in the Empire, who were utilized for both tribute and labor. As a result, the territory quickly evolved a very stratified and exploitive social system. The fact that it was the administrative and commercial center of a region stretching from Chiapas to Panama simply reinforced the hierarchic and aristocratic character of its culture. Guatemala, thus, evolved a Thomistic value system that laid great stress on hierarchy, bureaucracy, corporativism, and political unity.

At the same time, the province was also part of an imperial system that was politically and socially very fragmented. Clashing interests between landowners and merchants, rural ladinos and Indians, provincial *cabildos* and the capital, and professionals and provincials, ultimately created a situation in which independence, Woodward states, was seen as "an alternative to possible civil war."[29] As things turned out, independence did not prevent civil war, it just postponed it.

Although independence came peacefully to Guatemala on September 15, 1821, the struggle between Liberal and Conservative *caudillos*, each representing a rival "Thomastic vision" launched Guatemala into 150 years of oscillation between despotism and anarchy.[30] An attempt to create a Liberal Synthesis under Mariano Gálvez (1831–1838) was overturned in December 1838 by Rafael Carrera whose supporters sought to reimpose "a disciplined state with restored Hispanic institutions."[31] Through the judicious use of concession and compromise, force and guile, Carrera managed to hold onto power for twenty-six years (1839–1865), and his successor for another six. However, by 1871 the Liberals under General Justo Rufino Barrios had managed to fight their way back into power.

In summary, political developments in Guatemala during the half century following independence reflected the competing Thomistic and Machiavellian patterns of the colonial political culture.[32] First, there was the search for a political "synthesis" by both the Liberals and Conservatives. However, these rival visions, untempered by any tradition of compromise or consensus, produce intense conflict and ultimately tyranny. Second, there was the search for a "monarchical substitute," a leader capable of articulating and implementing the principles and programs that it was hoped would create the *bien común*. But without an institutionalized leadership recruitment process to replace hereditary succession coupled with the tradition of a patrimonial power structure, the Guatemalan political system was left with the *caudillo* as the only source of authority. Finally, there was an abstract ideological commitment to political unification and democracy, but the provincialism and economic, ethnic, and religious rivalry endemic in the social structure of the nation worked against all attempts to implement these values.

The Liberal regimes that came to power in Central America in 1871 represented a true "Thomistic synthesis." In many respects the Liberals were the *desarrollistas* or "developmentalists" of their day. They believed that economic progress could best be achieved by tying their economies to the world system of division of labor. The trading of primary products for manufactured goods was seen as the natural outworking of the law of comparative advantage. To achieve this, a domestic and social system had to be built that would encourage and support the productive sectors of the society, namely, the producers of agricultural products for export.

Thus, the improvement of the economic infrastructure with the aid of foreign capital was stressed; empty lands were opened up to settlement and cultivation; Indian *ejidos* were put on the open market with the expectation that private ownership would create a more efficient agricultural production system; public education and laws designed to modify the Indian culture were put forward as a means of achieving social modernization; and legislation designed to insure a cheap and dependable labor supply for commercial agriculture and public works—the labor draft and debt peonage—was enacted.

Important to the success of Liberalism in Central America was the emergence of a number of strong-willed *caudillos* such as Tomás Guardia of Costa Rica, José Santos Zelaya of Nicaragua, and Jorge Meléndez of El Savador. Probably the most important was Justo Rufino Barrios of Guatemala whose long political shadow was also cast over El Salvador and Honduras until his death on the field of battle in 1885 while attempting to reestablish the United Provinces by force. The Liberal program in Guatemala had wide support among the groups that counted: intellectuals, the export-oriented economic elites, the new commercial and professional middle classes and foreign investors. However, the social and economic system that was created—a system that produced material progress and economic growth for the nation and the upper and nascent middle sectors—was achieved at the cost of social disruption and deprivation for the masses. After Barrios' death, the system gradually hardened into a series of *caudillistic* dictatorships which ruled in the name of Liberal principles, particularly economic modernization and development, but with essentially Machiavellian methods. Probably the most clearly painted image of the Central American *caudillistic* dictator has been done by the Guatemalan nobel laureate, Miguel Angel Asturias, in his novel, *El Señor Presidente*. In it, the dictator, rumored to be based on the career of Manuel Estrada Cabrera (1898–1920), is quixotic, ruthless, capricious, narcissistic and tyrannical.

When the "depression dictator," Jorge Ubico, was overthrown in June 1944, there was great hope, particularly among the Guatemalan middle classes, that the *caudillistic* political leader would be replaced by a more institutionalized type of political leadership based on democratic and constitutional norms. To this end, the idealistic students, intellectuals, and teachers rallied around a relatively unknown quantity in the person of the "spiritual socialist," Dr. Juan José Arévalo. Although imbued with abstract democratic aspirations, his lack of experience in government as well as that of his followers soon converted him into a "party *caudillo*." Eduardo Taracena de la Cerda, one of the founders of the *Frente Popular Libertador*, an *arevalista* party, has described his shock and disillusionment in the months following his hero's election to the presidency.[33] He recounts the physical attacks on dissident members of the *arevalista* movement, the protests, the charges of electoral fraud in 1947, the censorship of the press (*la ley mordaza*), the many decrees suspending constitutional guarantees, culminating in the assassination of opposition presidential candidate, Colonel Francisco Javier Arana, on July 18, 1949.

Although the murder of Arana and the persecution of other candidates who sought to take his place enabled Colonel Jacobo Arbenz to win an overwhelming electoral victory in November 1950, the Machiavellian methods used to achieve power deprived him of any deeply rooted legitimacy. And his attempt to implement what was viewed by both large and small landowners as a radical and dangerous agrarian law undermined it further. By the time he was overthrown in June 1954, he had alienated both the large and the small (particularly Indian) landowners, the military, the university students, and much of the once pro-populist middle class. The United States simply used these disaffected sectors to help rid itself of an unwanted regime in the Caribbean.[34]

The revolutionary decade in Guatemala ultimately produced what Samuel Huntington has termed the "praetorian society,"[35] namely, a Machiavellian political system in which: (1) no institutions or political leaders are seen as fully legitimate; (2) no single "political currency" exists, but rather, all roads to power are considered to be equally legitimate—election, military force, a strike, a boycott, etc.; (3) powerful interest groups exist, each with its own power potential—electoral strength, economic resources, moral suasion, disruption, military force, etc.; (4) no equally powerful political institutions (parties, courts, legislatures, etc.) exist capable of arbitrating disputes between the power contenders. In such polities political decisions are often tentative, always subject to veto by a stike, a riot, or a boycott. The chief executive is often unable to function as a national leader or political decision-maker because he is "reigning" rather than "ruling."[36] Because of the instability and immobilism of such systems the military often assumes the role of political arbiter or takes over as the official governing authority. Military governments, however, are themselves often weak because of their lack of electoral legitimacy. Thus, a "praetorianized" polity often suffers from oscillations between periods of immobilsm under civilian governments and periods of military caesarism. Under these conditions the effective political leaders, both those in power and those in the opposition, are those with *caudillaje* personalities. Machiavellian values and *caudillaje* cultural traits are the ones that have survival value.

Since the overthrow of President Jacobo Arbenz in 1954, Guatemalan politics has been dominated by *caudillaje* personalities, both in power and in opposition, each seeking to impose his personal conception of the *bien común* on the society. Castillo Armas (1954–1957) governed in the name of anti-communism; Ydígoras Fuentes (1958–1963) in the name of economic development and Central American unification; the generals, from 1963 to 1985, sought political stability and national security (as well as personal enrichment); the guerilla leaders of the URNG seek to impose some form of egalitarianism. Vinicio Cerezo, after surviving innumerable attempts on his life, has managed to achieve power by a Machiavellian combination of a vaguely populist platform coupled with a set of tacit agreements with the military. Since his inauguration in January 1986, the army high command has rescued him from attempted military coups in 1988 and 1989 and supported him in a number of massive strikes by many of the groups that originally elected him to office. Thus, whether he could continue to negotiate the heavily mined Guatemalan political landscape to complete his term in 1991 would depend on his possessing all of the skills that Machiavelli expected in a prince.

Guatemalan Foreign Policy

Historically, Guatemala's foreign policy behavior has largely been driven by its relationships with the two "Colossi of the North:" the United States and Mexico. In the early colonial period, the Kingdom of Guatemala was formally under the jurisdiction of the Viceroyalty of New Spain. This arrangement effectively provided for Mexican rule over Central America, but even in the sixteenth century the province of Guatemala disputed this claim. Woodward states that vice regal intervention from Mexico caused the Central Americans early on to develop feelings of antagonism towards that country.[37]

The location in Guatemala of the *Audiencia*—the Spanish institution which combined legislative and judicial authority in the colony—ensured that province's preeminent status when Spanish rule came to an end in the nineteeth century. Thus, before the seventeenth century had ended, the principal axes of Guatemala's international relations had been defined: a distrustful attitude towards Spain, animosity towards Mexico, and rivalry for preeminence in the Central American isthmus with the other provinces—El Salvador, Nicaragua, Honduras, and Costa Rica. The colonial period also developed in Guatemalan authorities a deep concern for whether other countries politically involved in the region—above all, Mexico—demonstrated in their actions both legitimate interests and policies contributing to the *bien comun*.

Elizabeth Ferris has pointed to the essential symmetry between Mexico's attitude towards Guatemala and that of the United States to Mexico:

> Mexican diplomatic relations with Guatemala in particular show a surprising replication of Mexican-U.S. relations in the nineteenth century. While Mexico refused to acknowledge Texas independence in the 1830s, . . . Mexico acquired the Soconusco region—long disputed with Guatemala—by arguing that the region's residents had the right to make the ultimate decision. Mexico intervened in Guatemalan politics on several occasions though such actions never reached the degree of U.S. intervention in Mexico.[38]

Similarly, other Central American states (especially El Salvador) feared domination by Guatemala since it had served as the seat of Spanish colonial authority and had more experience in administering the region than anyone else. These states did not want to see United States-Mexican and Mexican-Guatemalan symmetry applied in Guatemalan-Central American relations. But in subsequent decades efforts—often including military ones—were undertaken by Guatemalan leaders (especially Carrera and Barrios) aimed at policing the region, propping up like-minded rulers, and eventually restoring Central American unity. These objectives were viewed by the other states as Guatemalan expansionist designs.

In the 1870s anticlerical etatist Liberal factions triumphed throughout most of Central America. An overriding concern of Liberal regimes was developmentalism, which posited in turn abandonment of an isolationist foreign policy and the progressive integration of the region into the international economy. Foreign investment was actively sought, concessions were granted to foreign enterprises, and export crops and industries were given priority. Expansion of the coffee crop— and to a lesser extent cochineal—which had been promoted in Guatemala as early as 1845, was especially important: the value of coffee among Guatemalan exports shot up from one percent in 1860 to forty-four percent in 1870. And though a high proportion of the coffee crop was cultivated by German settlers to Guatemala, it was the emergence of the banana industry under Liberal rule that turned Guatemala and other isthmus states into distinctively new republics controlled by foreign interests.[39] Best known of the foreign companies operating in the isthmus at this time were the United Fruit Company, its railroad subsidiary, International Railways of Central America, and its shipping concern, the Great White Fleet. At the most general level, as Woodward has pointed out, "The banana trade brought the Caribbean coast of Central America much closer to the United States." More specifically, "The banana industry accomplished many of the Liberals' objectives, albeit at the price of national sovereignty and economic independence."[40]

The corollary of greater American economic involvement in the isthmus was a "watchdog" role in the international relations of the region. Whether due to its alleged emergent semi-colonial status or its genuine admiration for the American political system, the Guatemalan government supported such a role by the United States. As a Guatemalan ambassador to the United States in the 1880s put it, the United States "is the natural protector of the integrity of the Central American territory."[41] At times such protection favored Guatemala, as when Mexico threatened to invade at the beginning of the 1880s, until the long border between the countries was fixed in 1882. But at other times it worked against the country, as when Guatemala invaded El Salvador in 1885.

Increasingly the United States and all of Central America were locked in an action-response model of foreign relations; the more activist foreign policy of Theodore Roosevelt in the first decade of the twentieth century included efforts to increase inter-American cooperation. Together with the Porfirio Diaz regime of Mexico, the United States sought to diminish centrifugal forces, political instability, and civil disorder in the isthmus, all which threatened foreign economic interests. The United States again sought to resurrect the goal of Central American unification, and as a first step a series of arbitration procedures designed to resolve disputes among the five Central American states was established, culminating in the Washington conference of 1923. These accords sought to regulate international relations in the area by enforcing the principles of noninterference in a country's internal affairs and support for constitutional rule. Because these mechanisms proved largely ineffective, the United States felt compelled to intervene directly in the region (most often in Nicaragua). While the other four states often resented United States military involvement, the government of Guatemala, at this time headed by Estrada Cabrera, consistently accepted United States leadership. For example, the 1916 Bryan-Chamorro Treaty which formalized the protectorate status of Nicaragua was opposed by Costa Rica, El Salvador, and Honduras, and the recently established Central American Court of Justice supported their position. Estrada, however, took the United States side. Part of the explanation for this pro-Americanist tradition lay in threats posed to Guatemala by its own "Colossus of the North," Mexico, especially after that nation's revolution began to move it to the left.

Perhaps the litmus test of Guatemala's foreign policy took place when World War II broke out. Under the presidency of Ubico (1931–1944), American commercial interests continued to enjoy special favor, but as a result of the size and influence of the German community in the country (By 1939 Germans controlled about one-third of the most productive plantations and two-thirds of the country's exports.) a pro-German course was simultaneously pursued. Before the United States entered World War II, Ubico even granted German submarines refuelling rights at Puerto Barrios. After Pearl Harbor, however, the Guatemalan government acquiesced to United States demands that German influence be curtailed. Accordingly, some Germans were taken from the country to internment camps in Texas, many others had their property expropriated, the Guatemalan government permitted American military bases and intelligence operations in the country, and it went so far in its pro-American policy as to purchase United States war bonds.

A reversal of the policy supporting the United States as *caudillo* in the region took place during the ten-year period of social revolution under Arévalo (1944–1950) and Arbenz (1951–1954). On taking power Arbenz made known the objectives of his administration: "First, to convert our country from a dependent nation with a semi-colonial economy into an economically independent country; second, to transform our nation from a backward past with a predominantly feudal economy into a modern capitalist country."[42] Both objectives collided with United States vested interests in the country.

It is important to note, however, that Guatemala's foreign policy in this decade was never as radical as the social and economic policies pursued at home—largely inspired, incidentally, by programs originating in the ideas of Franklin D. Roosevelt's New Deal in the United States, Lazaro Cárdenas' social reforms in Mexico between 1934 and 1940, and Juan Perón's populist "third way" policies in Argentina after his 1946 election.[43] In foreign policy, Guatemala continued to maintain correct, if not as cordial, relations with the United States. Thus when the Korean war erupted Arevalo quickly declared his support for American policy and even promised to curtail Communist activity in the country. Conversely, in 1945 Guatemala officially recognized the Soviet government, but did not immediately move to establish official relations. Nevertheless, scholars have come to very different conclusions concerning the extent to which Arbenz moved the country into the

Soviet orbit. According to LaFeber, "the Arbenz government had supported Washington in the United Nations on major issues, including those that required choosing sides in the Cold War."[44] By contrast, Woodward concluded: "the position of the Guatemalan delegation to the United Nations as well as official statements of the Guatemalan government suggested that, insofar as foreign policy was concerned, Guatemala had become a virtual Soviet satellite by 1954."[45] However, according to Cole Blasier,

> While the USSR provided political and moral support to the Guatemalan revolution of 1944 to 1954, Soviet leaders knew little about it, had little contact with it, and provided no known material assistance except possibly for an arms shipment that arrived late.[46]

In this confused international picture, what appears clearer is that the threat posed to long-standing United States economic interests in Guatemala by agrarian reform legislation and controls on foreign investment was primarily responsible for motivating Truman, then Eisenhower and his Secretary of State, John Foster Dulles, to attack the leftist regime as pro-Communist.

They had numerous grounds for doing so. Most important was the 1951 legalization and reorganization of the Communist party (PGT), its takeover of the country's main labor union, and its subsequent participation in key posts in all three branches of government. Inadvertently, or perhaps inevitably, Arbenz accepted policies favored by Communist party members which ranged from symbolic politics (eulogizing Stalin after his death in 1953 and inviting foreign Communist leaders to Guatemala on a regular basis) to national security issues (cutting military spending by forty percent, then purchasing arms from Czechoslovakia in May 1954). The Communist image of the Arbenz regime was clearly, therefore, not just a fanciful fabrication of the U.S. State Department. Just as clear was the fact that the Arbenz regime had charted a foreign policy course out of line with the traditional Guatemalan position. Aside from ideological considerations, Guatemala was, in the view of U.S. Secretary of State Dulles, "already the heaviest armed of all Central American states" and would soon be in a position "to dominate the Central American area."[47] Its military might would have exceeded that of the rest of Central America combined (a point invoked against the Sandinista buildup in the 1980s).

The relative ease with which Castillo Armas seized power was at least due in part to the fact that the United States-Guatemalan confrontation of the past ten years had contributed to the erosion of popular support for Arbenz. It is improbable that the Honduras-based invasion would have succeeded without CIA support; in turn, however, the Guatemalan army never rallied round Arbenz.[48]

From 1954 until 1977 successive Guatemalan presidents maintained close ideological ties with the United States and largely accepted America's *caudillo* role. For one thing they backed United States-sponsored efforts to unify the isthmus economically and militarily. Pro forma support was also given to Alliance for Progress reforms—particularly as the quid pro quo for American economic aid. One particularly important example of Guatemala's client status was President Miguel Ydigoras Fuentes' support for the United States-sponsored Bay of Pigs invasion in 1961, even allowing a CIA training base for Cuban exiles to be established in the country. Fidel Castro and other Latin American Communist leaders responded by continuing to sponsor, finance, and organize guerrilla movements in Guatemala, thereby precluding any possibility of conducting normal relations with the Guatemalan government.

It is not surprising, therefore, that throughout this period Guatemala received substantial military and economic assistance from Washington. Perhaps more than any other country on the isthmus, Guatemala was intended to be the bastion, or "garrison,"[49] against Communist infiltration, largely because it was ranked first by the U.S. State Department among Latin American countries threatened by revolution.

The year 1977 marked a watershed in Guatemala's international relations. First, the issue of Belize's independence served to isolate Guatemala from other Latin American states. Other countries in the hemisphere recognized the right of the British colony to independence, causing the Guatemalan government often to cut diplomatic relations. An even more significant foreign policy development in 1977 was the deterioration in bilateral relations with the United States. Jimmy Carter's election to the White House marked a turning point in bilateral relations by bringing human rights issues to the fore. He promptly commissioned a State Department human rights report which concluded that Guatemala's record was dismal. The next three Guatemalan presidents (Laugerud, Lucas García, and Ríos Montt) viewed such American interference in internal affairs as harmful and decided that the United States was now acting as a nonbeneficent *caudillo*. LaFeber was not far from the truth when he concluded: "By 1980, the guerrillas and the military had only one point of agreement: both despised the United States."[50] Guatemalan leaders thereupon refused to accept American military assistance and began to look to Western Europe and, above all, Israel, for arms transfers.

The disproportionate importance of Guatemala's relations with the United States until this time is most clearly underscored when we note that even in the 1980s this Central American nation had forged diplomatic relations with fewer than fifty other countries in the world. Of the ten directorates within the Guatemalan government's Ministry of Foreign Relations, only two are area-specific: one on Central American Affairs, the other on Belize Affairs.[51] Guatemala's activity in the global economy has also been modest and restrained, leaving the country with one of the lowest external debts and debt service ratios in Latin America. In large measure, therefore, Guatemala's insular political culture has been replicated in its relatively isolationist foreign policy.

Guatemala has been active, by contrast, in a number of key international organizations. It was a founding member of the United Nations and has participated extensively in the Group of 77, a bloc of Third World nations formed within the United Nations Conference on Trade and Development. Generally, it has rejected the militant Third Worldism characteristic of regional actors such as Cuba and Nicaragua. Similarly, Guatemala joined the Organization of American States when it was formed in 1948 and has consistently supported the revitalization of Inter-American System and Central American integration. But it has not wavered from the view that the United States must remain an important cog in this Inter-American System and has opposed efforts to exclude or weaken United States participation.

Beginning in 1981, after Reagan's inauguration, an attempt was made to restore traditional relations between Guatemala and the United States. Apart from its trade aspects, Reagan's Caribbean Basin Initiative promised new aid to conservative governments such as that of Guatemala. While the freeze on arms sales was officially rescinded, Reagan's request for a resumption of military as well as economic assistance in November 1983 was turned down by Congress. Instead, Congress approved a $53 million development aid and support fund package and, coupled with credits from the International Monetary Fund and World Bank funds, Guatemala was able to finance development projects.

Improved relations were also assisted by Ríos Montt's views on the guerrilla insurgency in Guatemala. It was seen as part of a broader Communist conspiracy designed to destabilize the region, given vivid proof through the Sandinista revolution in Nicaragua in 1979. By the mid-1980s the Guatemalan military had substantially crushed internal resistance, thereby making the security of the regime no longer contingent on United States assistance. Nevertheless the August 1983 coup by which General Oscar Mejía overthrew Ríos Montt appeared to be sanctioned by the United States: two days earlier Mejía had met with U.S. Southern Command (SOUTHCOM, based in Panama) Commander General Paul Gorman. Mejía welcomed the renewal in October 1983 of the CONDECA pact under United States auspices, concluded in the aftermath of the United States invasion of Grenada which Guatemala also endorsed. But even Mejía was wary of United States policy in the region. His minister of Foreign Affairs, Andrade Díaz-Durán, asserted that "Guatemala will stay in CONDECA, but it will not carry forward any policy that could be used to threaten any other country in the region." He added that Guatemala would maintain "a correct and respectful relationship with Nicaragua."[52] Accordingly, Guatemala decided not to participate in joint military maneuvers with CONDECA members during Granadero I and Ahuas Tara II held in 1984.

Another obstacle in normalizing United States-Guatemalan relations was the peace process being formulated for Central America. In October 1984 Guatemala abstained from voting on a United States-backed peace plan for the region that was to serve as a counterdraft to Contadora, thereby assuming a posture of greater neutrality towards Sandinista Nicaragua. This new tack was primarily grounded in economic considerations: with about forty percent of the country's exports going to CACM and with a very favorable trade balance with Central American countries, any regional conflict was likely to affect Guatemala's economy severely.

Relations with Mexico remained proper in the 1980s in spite of outstanding issues, such as Guatemala's reservations about the Contadora peace process (in which Mexico was a leading actor) and Mexico's support for revolutionary movements in areas of Central America (most notably, the Frente Farabundo Martí in El Salvador). But under President Miguel de la Madrid, it did not encourage revolutionary activity in neighboring Guatemala itself and, to the contrary, Mexico has even engaged in joint military maneuvers with the Guatemalan forces.[53] Mexico's rich oil fields are centered in the states of Chiapas and Tabasco, on the Guatemalan border, largely accounting for this prudential policy. In fact, according to Steven Sanderson, "Some of Mexico's recent concern with building up its military strength comes from fears of Guatemalan military superiority."[54]

From Guatemala's perspective, an even less desirable *caudillo* in the region would be Cuba or Nicaragua. Guatemala has always jealously guarded its preeminence in the region's affairs, and compounded by ideological differences with both countries, a Cuban or Nicaraguan claim to a regional leadership role would be doubly unacceptable. Cuba has always been viewed as an external force to the isthmus, and Castro's open acknowledgement for the past two decades of support for Guatemalan guerrilla groups makes Cuba's claims particularly illegitimate. Guatemala also rejects outright any claim by the Soviet Union to have a legitimate role to play in the international relations of the region. In fact, neither country has been enthusiastic about exchanging ambassadors, and in 1988 the TASS news agency closed its Guatemala City office after the host government claimed it could not ensure the Soviet representative's security.

In late 1985 congressional and presidential elections were held in Guatemala in an effort to improve the country's international image. The military felt confident that such elections would not undermine its power, and the result was a victory by the Christian Democratic candidate, Vinicio Cerezo Arevalo. The new President had no illusions about his role: "They need a president who can obtain money for the country."[55] At the same time, he was critical of United States support for the Contras. The Cerezo government thus embarked on a foreign policy that it termed "active neutrality." At a press conference in September 1986, Cerezo described this policy "as a serious attempt to avoid armed conflicts and a decision to contribute to any political mechanism that may establish bases for a permanent peace, for the development of democracy and ideological pluralism."[56] With this pronouncement, Cerezo once again distanced Guatemala from the patron-client relationship that characterized its historic relations with the United States.

Active neutrality has served as the cornerstone for an improvement of relations with a number of countries. First, Guatemalan-Mexican relations improved markedly when Mexican President Miguel de la Madrid paid a visist to Guatemala in April 1987—the first state visit by a Mexican leader to its southern neighbor in twelve years. Cerezo was accordingly praised as Contadora's staunchest supporter in Central America.[57] Second, the Belize issue was deflated when Cerezo reestablished trade relations with the disputed country in the fall of 1986. Third, Guatemala sought to reclaim its leadership role on the isthmus through a number of initiatives. Cerezo proposed the concept of a Central American Parliament as a forum for the discussion and resolution of regional problems. He then played host to both Esquipulas I (May 1986) and II (August 1987), which led to the drafting and signing of the Arias peace plan—known also as the Guatemala Plan. Fourth, President Cerezo visited Western Europe in the fall of 1986 to revitalize ties and diversify benefactors for economic assistance to the country.

Other achievements of Cerezo's European interest included France's promise to offer $20 million in non-lethal military assistance to Guatemala and the restoration of full diplomatic relations with the United Kingdom in December 1986.

In short, Cerezo went a long way toward restoring Guatemala's image in the international community. Paradoxically, the catalyst for diversification of foreign policy was the breakdown of the United States *caudillo* role following attacks by Carter and the U.S. Congress on Guatemala. While Cerezo undertook efforts to remove the principal issue of contention between the two countries—the country's human rights record—by early 1990 this record was again being questioned by political leaders in Washington. In short, for a decade the United States has been unable to recapture fully its traditional preeminent role in Guatemala.

Conclusion

This chapter has concerned two circum-Caribbean states whose history is replete with shifts between democratic and authoritarian regimes. Guatemala was more obviously an example of a *caudillaje*-type society, but in recent years it has made the perilous shift to elected civilian government. Colombia was able to institutionalize a pattern of alternation between political parties, but we should not overlook the earlier authoritarianism and political violence that shaped its political culture.

From our survey of their respective foreign policies, it becomes clear that United States influence in both countries remains substantial. In Guatemala it has weakened since the Carter human rights campaign, and Guatemala's recent status as a fledging social democracy had led to diversification of its international relations. We should not lose sight of the fact, however, that up to 1977 Guatemala's foreign relations were essentially unidimensional: the United States was accepted to be the "patron," or as Bailey called it, the *caudillo*, and Guatemala readily embraced its role as client, with the notable exception of the Arbenz period. In Colombia there have been more frequent periods in which the government quarreled with the United States, and support for the United States as *caudillo* has been more limited compared to Guatemala. The Betancur administration and, at present, the Barco Vargas government, have expressed misgivings about various aspects of United States policy. On the other hand, the United States is still viewed as ultimate protector in any potential conflict situation Colombia might face.

The role of the *caudillo* was to exhibit both strength and beneficence in dealings with the client-state. The first attribute involved sponsoring regional defense pacts, maintaining order and stability, and generally protecting the interests of the client from encroachment by other regional actors. In the case of Guatemalan elites, it also involved intervention to rescue them from unacceptable regimes. The overthrow of Arbenz is the most obvious example, but the United States was also implicated in the ouster of Ydigoras Fuentes in 1963, the election of Méndez Montenegro in 1966, and the overthrow of Rios Montt in 1983. The second attribute, beneficence, was to consist of understanding and tolerance for the internal politics of the client and generosity expressed in the form of military and development assistance. In these respects the United States was indeed a beneficent *caudillo* for Guatemala up to the time Carter became President. Carter's attack on Guatemala's human rights record signalled a new development. The United States was continuing to assert what it conceived as a historic right, as *caudillo*, to take an active part in shaping the country's internal affairs. For Guatemalan leaders, *caudillismo* did not include the right to push for social and political policies that would significantly change the nation's class structure. Thus, intolerance for aspects of Guatemala's counter-insurgency strategy was incompatible with benevolence. Compounded by such domestic circumstances as a U.S. Congress controlled by Democrats, compounded by the emotional issue of the slaying of U.S. AID officials in Guatemala, President Reagan possessed neither the internal nor external resources to reassert America's *caudillo* role in the country.

Similarly, with respect to Colombia, United States *caudillismo* in the Panamanian war of independence in 1903 was perceived by the Colombian government as out of line. At present, Colombian authorities are sensitive to what they consider undue United States involvement in policing drug traffickers in the country.

We have described the behavioral dimension of the political cultures of Guatemala and Colombia as *caudillaje*—the pursuit of political power through largely manipulative means. To what extent does this characterization manifest itself in their international behavior?

Clearly Guatemala has played an interventionist and manipulative role in Central America and the Caribbean since its independence. The success of the Conservative *caudillo* Rafael Carrera in overturning the United Provinces in 1839, the attempt of the great Liberal *caudillo* Justo Rufino Barrios to forcibly reunite the Central American Union in 1885 (a military undertaking that cost him his life), General Jorge Ubico's flirtation with the Third Reich and his switch to the side of the Allies in December 1941, the connivance of portions of the military and the elite to overthrow Arbenz, the provision of a secret base by President Ydígoras Fuentes to train Cuban exiles for the Bay of Pigs invasion, and the incursion into Belize in 1961 are just some of the examples of *caudillaje* behavior in international relations.

Colombia, on the other hand, has been moving towards a more Western Democratic pattern during the past three decades and has displayed considerably less *caudillaje*-type behavior in international relations. However, it was also less interventionist even during periods when its internal politics were much more violent and *caudillaje* in character.

Thus, Guatemala best fits the predicted congruence between a *caudillaje* culture and *caudillaje* international behavior. This can be explained as the interaction between its historic culture and its geopolitical position. That is, the fact that Guatemala has for centuries been caught up in the maelstrom of isthmian and Caribbean rivalries and thrown into direct proximity to the *two* "Colossi of the North" has exacerbated and reinforced the natural *caudillaje* traits of its culture. For Guatemalan foreign policy, *caudillaje* behavior has had survival value.

Colombia, on the other hand, has been more geographically and politically isolated. Furthermore, the intensity of its internecine struggles had made it less willing historically to play an activist regional role.

With the emergence of democracy in both countries (albeit fragile and tenuous), both are participating more actively in regional stabilization plans, and both are seeking to distance themselves from the United States orbit. The seeds for civilian President Cerezo's policy of active neutrality—a response to the United States acting as nonbeneficent regional actor—were planted under Guatemala's earlier military strongmen, who challenged the United States on a number of issues ranging from anti-Sandinista rhetoric to economic sanctions. Cerezo has more stringently asserted, however, that Guatemala would not submit to being utilized as an instrument of United States policy in the region. Instead he has emphasized a "general policy toward all the countries in the world," especially democratic ones, rather than a "specific international policy toward specific countries."[58] This more multidimensional foreign policy has produced a diversification of Guatemala's international relations while enhancing its regional role, evidenced in the 1987 Arias peace plan. But when we recall the quintessentially *caudillaje* nature of Guatemalan political culture, we should exercise caution when predicting that patron-client relations of a previous era will never be restored. For as a consequence of a constellation of factors—economic, political, historic, and political cultural—the axis the Guatemalan elite values most deeply (though not necessarily always acknowledging it) is that with Washington. Corresponding to this, at some future date Guatemala may wish to re-assert its preeminence on the isthmus. Thus Guatemala has had a propensity—in large part due to its political culture, we argue—to serve as both object and subject of *caudillismo*.

Colombia's method of escaping American influence when the United States was perceived as having overstepped its *caudillo* role was introversion into economic pragmatism at home, combined with recourse to intergovernmental organizations in the international arena. Indeed, Colombia's institutionalized activity internationally is remarkable and may reflect the concern with institutional arrangements in domestic politics. Further, Colombia's less-*caudillistic* political culture is doubly reflected in its foreign policy: the country's relative reticence about unjustified United States activism is matched by its own reluctance to undertake a regional *caudillo* role itself. Instead, Colombia has set as a foreign policy objective the carrying out of a mediatory role in regional disputes, which it has undertaken successfully, especially on border disputes.

We may conclude, therefore, that alternating monistic regimes such as those of Colombia and Guatemala tend to act ambiguously, often even inconsistently, in international relations. In the case of Colombia, the drive to establish a permanent but precarious political equilibrium at home has signified a tendency to search for procedures and institutional arrangements guaranteeing negotiated settlements of international problems. In the case of Guatemala, authoritarianism at home has meant, more often than not, support for strong-handed methods in the international arena. While exceptions can be found to these patterns, the evidence presented indicates that congruence does indeed occur between political cultures that have a mix of democratic and authoritarian values and the foreign policy approaches pursued by the alternating governments in such states.

Notes

1. Mision, "Economia y Humanismo," (Louis J. Lebret, O.P., Director), *Estudio sobre las Condiciones del Desarrollo en Colombia.* Bogota, Colombia: Aedita, 1958, p. 109. Quoted in Robert H. Dix, *Colombia: The Political Dimensions of Change.* New Haven: Yale University Press, 1967, p. 44.

2. Dix, *Colombia*, p. 58.

3. Cited in Harvey F. Kline, "From Rural to Urban Society: The Transformation of Colombian Democracy," in Donald L. Herman (ed.), *Democracy in Latin America: Colombia and Venezuela*. New York: Praeger, 1988, p. 19.

4. Roland H. Ebel and James Henderson, "Patterns of Continuity in Latin American Society: Political and Historical Perspectives," *Annals of the Southeastern Conference on Latin American Studies* (March 1974), p. 112.

5. Harvey F. Kline, "Colombia: Modified Two-Party and Elitist Politics," in Howard J. Wiarda and Harvey F. Kline (eds.), *Latin American Politics and Development*. 2nd edn. Boulder, CO: Westview Press, 1985, p. 255.

6. John A. Booth, "Comparing Political Violence in Colombia and Guatemala," in Mitchell A. Seligson and John A. Booth (eds.), *Political Participation in Latin America. Volume II, Politics and the Poor*. New York: Holmes and Meier, 1979, p. 99.

7. Kline, "Colombia," pp. 255–256.

8. According to the political formula worked out under the National Front Agreement, there would be *alternacion* and *paridad* between the two parties, namely, the Liberals and Conservatives would alternate the presidency every four years and divide equally the offices of government from the cabinet to the municipal councils regardless of the electoral outcome within a given jurisdiction. See Kline, "Colombia," p. 258.

9. *Movimiento 19 de Abril* (M-19) is the military branch of the National Popular Alliance (ANAPO), formed originally as the personal political party of ex-military populist dictator, Gustavo Rojas Pinilla, who died in 1979.

10. Gary Hoskin, "Colombia's Political Crisis," *Current History*, 87 (January 1988), p. 10.

11. Hoskin, "Colombia's Political Crisis," pp. 10–12.

12. German Cavelier, *La Política Internacional de Colombia*. Tomo III. Bogota, Colombia: Editorial Iqueina, 1960, p. 82.

13. Harvey F. Kline, *Colombia: Portrait of Unity and Diversity*. Boulder, CO.: Westview Press, 1983, p. 124.

14. Gerhard K. Drekonja, *Retos de la Política Exterior Colombia*. Bogota, Colombia: Fondo Editorial CEREC, 1983, p. 71.

15. Paul Oquist, *Violence, Conflict, and Politics in Colombia*. New York: Academic Press, 1980, p. 93.

16. Cavelier, *La Política Internacional de Colombia*, tomo III, p. 119.

17. David S. McMorris, et al., *Area Handbook for Colombia*. Washington, DC: Foreign Area Studies, The American University, 1970, p. 300.

18. Janet Hohmann De Tobon, "Factors Influencing the Conduct of Colombia Foreign Relations." Bogota, Colombia [s.n.], 1966, p. 12. Based on an unpublished Masters thesis, "Colombia and the United Nations: The Role of the Small American Nation in the World Organization." Minneapolis: University of Minnesota, 1950.

19. Drekonja, *Retos de la Political Exterior Colombia*, p. 74.

20. David R. Decker and Ignacio Duran, *The Political, Economic, and Labor Climate in Colombia*. Philadelphia: The Warton School, Vance Hall/CS, 1982, p. 39.

21. For details on the Andean Pact, see Kline, *Colombia*, pp. 128–131.

22. Drekonja, *Retos de la Política Exterior Colombia*, p. 83.

23. Harvey F. Kline, "New Direction in Colombia," *Current History*, 84 (February 1985), p. 66.

24. Susan Kaufman Purcell, "Demystifying Contadora," *Foreign Affairs*, 64 (Fall 1985), p. 84.

25. John D. Martz, "Colombia's Search for Peace," *Current History*, 88 (March 1989), p. 127.

26. Cavelier, *La Política Internacional de Colombia*, tomo III, p. 103.

27. The writers surveyed for this study are Robert Trudeau and Lars Schoultz (1986), Shelton H. Davis (1983), Roger Plant (1978), George Black (1984), Julio Castellanos Cambranes (1984), Edelberto Torres-Rivas (1981), Susanne Jonas (1974), and Jerry Weaver (1969).

28. Ralph Lee Woodward, *Central America: A Nation Divided*. New York: Oxford University Press, 1976, p. 50.

29. Woodward, *Central America*, p. 89.

30. Guatemala declared its annexation to Augustin Iturbide's Mexican empire on January 5, 1802. It broke away from that union on July 1, 1823, three months after Iturbide was overthrown. The United Provinces of Central America was formed on that date and its constitution was completed on November 22, 1824. Franklin D. Parker, *The Central American Republics*. New York: Oxford University Press, 1964, pp. 75–78.

31. Woodward, *Central America*, p. 113.

32. For a more extensive discussion of the following interpretation, see Roland H. Ebel, "Thomism and Machiavellianism in Central American Political Development." Paper presented at the 44th Internal Congress of Americanists, Manchester, England, September 5–10, 1982.

33. Eduardo Taracena do la Cerda, "El rol de los partidos politicos: Testimonio II," in *I Seminario: El rol de los partidos politicos en Guatemala*. Guatemala: Asociacion de Investigacion y Estudios Sociales, Julio 1985, p. 52.

34. See Roland H. Ebel, "Populist Opposition to Populism: Middle Class Opposition to the Arevalo and Arbenz Regimes in Guatemala." Paper presented at the Southwestern Political Science Association Meetings, Houston, Texas, March 25, 1968.

35. Samuel Huntington, *Political Order in Changing Societies*. New Haven: Yale University Press, 1968, Chapter 4.

36. Eldon Kenworthy, "Coalitions in the Political Develoment of Latin America," in Sven Goennings et al. (eds.), *The Study of Coalition Behavior: Theoretical Perspectives and Cases from Four Continents*. New York: Holt, Rinehart and Winston, 1970, p. 129.

37. Woodward, *Central America*, p. 39.

38. Elizabeth G. Ferris, "Mexico's Foreign Policies: A Study in Contradictions," in Jennie K. Lincoln and Elizabeth G. Ferris (eds.), *The Dynamics of Latin American Foreign Policies*. Boulder, CO: Westview Press, 1984, p. 215.

39. See Woodward, *Central America*, p. 181.

40. Woodward, *Central America*, pp. 180, 182.

41. Cited by Walter LaFeber, *Inevitable Revolutions: The United States in Central America*. New York: W.W. Norton 1984, p. 33.

42. Tom Barry and Deb Preusch, *The Central America Fact Book*. New York: Grove Press, 1986, p. 227.

43. See Robert Trudeau and Lars Schoultz, "Guatemala," in Morris J. Blachman, William M. LeoGrande, and Kenneth Sharpe (eds.), *Confronting Revolution: Security through Diplomacy in Central America*. New York: Pantheon Books, 1986, p. 25. Also see L. Francis Bouchey and Albert M. Piedra, *Guatemala: A Promise in Peril*. Washington, D.C.: Council for Inter-American Security, 1980, pp. 10–11.

44. LaFeber, *Inevitable Revolutions*, p. 119.

45. Woodward, *Central America*, pp. 237–238.

46. Cole Blasier, " The Soviet Union," in Blachman, LeoGrande, and Sharpe (eds.), *Confronting Revolution*, p. 406n.

47. Quoted in Daniel James, *Red Design for the Americas: Guatemalan Prelude*. New York: John Day Company, 1954, p. 305.

48. For a full account of the 1954 counter-coup, see Stephen Schlesinger and Stephen Kinzer, *Bitter Fruit: The Untold Story of the American Coup in Guatemala*. Garden City, NJ: Doubleday, 1982. See also Richard H. Immerman, *The CIA in Guatemala*. Austin, TX: University of Texas Press, 1985.

49. See George Black, *Garrison Guatemala*. New York: Monthly Review Press, 1984.

50. LaFeber, *Inevitable Revolutions*, p. 261.

51. Much of this discussion is taken from Richard F. Nyrop (ed.), *Guatemala: A Country Study*, 2nd edn. Washington, D.C.: American University, 1984, pp. 168–176.

52. Quoted in Robert L. Peterson, "Guatemala," in Jack W. Hopkins (ed.), *Latin America and Caribbean Contemporary Record, Volume IV, 1984–1985*. New York: Holmes and Meier, 1986, p. 514.

53. Ferris, "Mexico's Foreign Policies," p. 217.

54. Steven E. Sanderson, "A Profile of United-States-Mexican Relations," in *Latin America and Caribbean Contemporary Record, Volume I, 1981–1982*. Jack W. Hopkins (ed.). New York: Holmes and Meier, 1983, p. 132.

55. Cited in Trudeau and Schoultz, *Confronting Revolution*, p. 43.

56. Foreign Broadcasting Information Service, "Guatemala" (September 17, 1986), pp. 10–11.

57. *Washington Post* (April 9, 1987), p. A42a.

58. Foreign Broadcasting Information Service, "Guatemala" (January 13 and 21, 1986).

6

Political Culture and Foreign Policy in Monistic Regimes: The Cases of Cuba and Nicaragua

In this chapter we examine the relationship between political culture and foreign policy in two monistic circum-Caribbean states. While few scholars on Latin America would challenge our classification of Costa Rica and Venezuela as democratic systems, and while enough historical evidence can be brought to bear to support the claim that Guatemala and Colombia have experienced both democratic and authoritarian periods, the assertion that generally Cuba and Nicaragua have not broken away from an authoritarian pattern—despite undergoing the most thorough political transformations of all our case studies—may not go unchallenged. While the transition from the Batista dictatorship to the Castroite regime is more likely to be viewed as the replacement of one monism by another (though we make qualifications to this), what of the case of Nicaragua under the Somozas, then under the Sandinistas, and most recently under Chamorro? Did Nicaragua's political culture become less monistic under the FSLN, only to shift toward liberal democratic values after the February 1990 elections? In addition to drawing the linkage between political culture and international politics, then, this chapter addresses the issue of the monistic nature of Cuban and Nicaraguan societies.

Cuban Political Culture

Based on the survey of the literature undertaken in this study, Cuba's political culture has been undergoing a number of interesting changes. Three distinct patterns or developments are reflected in the scores presented in figure 4.1. The period from the overthrow of Gerardo Machado (August 12, 1933) to the taking of power by the 26th of July Movement on January 1, 1959 was marked by a decidedly Machiavellian national value system and by *caudillaje* patterns of behavior. With the advent of Castro, the national value system retained its essentially Latin American character, but shifted from a Machiavellian to a Thomistic direction. At the same time Cuba's behavior patterns edged in a more Western Democratic direction. What follows is an attempt to explain these changes.

The Machiavellian and *caudillaje* values and behavior patterns characteristic of our first period (1933–1959) had been rooted in Cuban political culture for well over a hundred years. Beginning with the conspiracy against the Spanish crown of Joaquin Infante in 1809, Cuban political life was marked by rebellion and civil war which only increased in intensity after 1868. Because of the interminable civil wars before independence was achieved, Cuban politics, writes Harvey Klein, was more violent than in most other Latin American countries. The radical tradition was also older and stronger.[1] Cuban political history was also marked by political generations that banded together to fight the great struggles of the nation's history, often, in the process, discrediting the previous generation and its institutions.[2] The net result of this history was a very amorphous political system composed of personalistic, generational, and organizational rivalries operating outside of any semblence of national consensus on either public policy or the way such policy should be made. Political conflict was usually settled either in the streets or the U.S. embassy, and the nation oscillated between tyranny, anarchy, and an American-imposed settlement.

These tendencies were simply exacerbated after the American-mediated "retirement" of Gerardo Machado in 1933. Describing Cuban political behavior in the period just before Machado's removal from office, Juan M. del Aguila states that the nation's politics took on an increasingly violent character.

> Opposition forces employed terrorism, shootings, and political assassinations, as well as street protests, mass rallies, and strikes, as a means of expressing widespread discontent. The government responded with repression and counterviolence, deepening the rift between popular forces and established—although illegitimate—authority. As a result, a classic prerevolutionary situation emerged as social forces nakedly confronted one another.[3]

The regime that followed was overturned the following month by the "sargeants' revolt" headed by Sargeant Fulgencio Batista, which in turn was forced to give way to the first Grau San Martín government five days later. Strongly opposed by the U.S. State Department for its populism, the civilian, Ramon Grau San Martín, was forced out of office by pressure from the U.S. embassy and the Cuban army in January 1934. During the next ten years no fewer than seven presidents were installed in the national palace, each largely following a populist political program. Even the now General Fulgencio Batista, who was popularly elected in 1940 and peacefully gave up power in 1944, presided over a reformist, although not entirely incorrupt, government. When Grau San Martín was elected once again in 1944 under the banner of the Autentico party, both Cubans and Americans hoped that Cuba was about to settle into a pattern of stable democratic rule. However, the patronage, nepotism, and embezzlement which was rife during the Grau government, and in the Prío Socarrás administration that followed, undermined the fragile legitimacy of the Cuban political system.[4]

The 1947 split in the Autentico party led by the vitriolic personalistic *caudillo* Eduardo Chibás greatly undermined the hope that a democratic reformist party had either the moral authority or the political support to significantly change the historic patterns of Cuban political life. As del Aguila writes, the Autenticos failed to end the tradition of political violence in Cuba.

> Driven by a rampant disregard for public order, often protected and encouraged by government officials, devoid of ideology, and ridden with personal vendettas and internecine political quarrels, the *pistolerismo* (gang warfare) of the action groups further discredited the democratic regime. Not surprisingly, low levels of public ethics and the breakdown of law and order contributed to the emergence of a new type of 'revolutionary.' This new breed was willing to exchange loyalty for pay, while carrying out threats and intimidation in the name of lofty principles.[5]

The suicide of Eduardo Chibas in 1951 and the military coup by Fulgencio Batista in 1952 caused the Cuban people to turn to a young follower of Chibas to restore their dashed hopes for democracy and honesty in government—Fidel Castro. The next thirty years would see a concerted attempt to change the political and social culture of Cuba. The result was that under the Machiavellian tutelage of Cuba's *caudillo máximo*, the country's national value system would indeed shift in a Thomistic direction while its political behavior, paradoxically, would also edge slightly in a Western Democratic direction.

These changes are clearly reflected in the national value and behavioral operational variable scores presented in table 4.1. The party and interest group fragmentation, the prevalence of open political conflict and mass action, and the excessive bureaucratic inefficiency and corruption characteristic of a Machiavellian value system is replaced by a centralized, monistic regime run by a small elite governing in the name of "higher principles" (the traditional Hispanic concept of *derecho*)—in this case Marxist principle—in order to create a new *bien común.*[6] Castroite Cuba, in other words, has produced a neo-Thomistic system that is hierarchical, idealistic, patrimonial (the Castro brothers and Raúl's wife, for example, sit on almost all of the major bodies of the government and the PCC, Cuban Communist Party), and corporative (e.g., the state-run mass organizations).

At the same time, the authoritarian political system imposed after 1959 has produced some interesting behavioral changes. Table 4.2 shows a distinct drop in *caudillaje* behavior after 1959 and a marked increase in what we have called Western Democratic behavior. How do we account for this behavioral shift in a country that still retains its overwhelming Latin American value system? One part of the answer is to notice that with the shift from a predominantly Machiavellian value system to a Thomistic one, there also occurred an increase in the incidence of what we have called Western Democratic values, primarily in the area of a more rational and less corrupt bureaucracy. Marxist Thomism, in other words, carries with it the seeds of a legal-rational administrative system. Also in terms of behavior, Cuba's authoritarian political system has greatly reduced political fragmentation, mass action, and governmental corruption on the one hand, and increased political stability and administrative coherence on the other. In other words, the shift in Cuba's political culture since 1959 has been in the direction of "Westernization" rather than "democracy."

This shift in the direction of a political culture marked by a Thomistic value system coupled with a more Western behavior pattern is understandable in terms of what might be called a more generalized "combat culture" found in contemporary Communism.[7] A combat culture engages in ongoing clashes with all the elements of its social environment: institutions, personalities, organizations, and competing value systems. Such a culture develops through four stages. The first stage is the forging of a committed leadership cadre by subjecting them to incessant political combat with actual or potential rival organizations, institutions, and groups. This process, which led to the imposition of a monistic political system in Cuba, embraced roughly the period beginning with the attack on the Moncada Barracks on July 26, 1953 to the collapse of Fulgencio Batista during the waning hours of 1958.

The second stage is one of intra-party struggle during which the various factions of the victorious party or movement contest each other for supremacy. This period lasted from the take-over on January 1, 1959 to the creation of the PCC in 1965. During that period Castro not only eliminated his opponents in the 26th of July Movement and the Popular Socialist Party (PSP), but had succeeded in imposing "unity candidates" on the University Student Federation (FEU) and the Cuban Confederation of Workers (CTC). In addition, the United States and its counter-revolutionary allies were also eliminated from the political system through both emigration and defeat in battle. As the Cuban revolution moved toward the end of its first decade in power, the environment for a monistic political system had been established.

The third phase in the evolution of a combat culture involves "supracultural struggle," namely, a struggle among the leadership to determine the direction of the revolution. In Cuba this period did not involve so much a struggle among the top leaders as such (Fidel and his brother Raúl were clearly in command), but rather uncertainty and differences among the secondary echelons over the precise direction the revolution should take. During this phase, which overlapped somewhat with the second, Cuba experimented with industrialization (1961–1963) and then returned to intensive sugar production (1963–1970), only to be followed by a stress on the diversification of agriculture.[8] Material incentives gave way to moral ones, only to be replaced after 1970 by *cálculo económico* or managed economic efficiency.[9]

Although the period was marked by policy instability and numerous changes in direction, what resulted was an effort to move the culture in a more legal-rational direction.

> The new system stressed centralized economic planning, cost accounting and enterprise profitability, material rewards. . . . Managerial expertise on the administrative level began to take precedence over revolutionary zeal.[10]

Such an orientation is totally at odds with *caudillaje* behavior.

This period also saw the institutionalization of the Cuban political system. Throughout the first two decades of Castro's rule, the political system operated under his personalistic charismatic authority. Relatively little attention was given to the creation of an institutional structure that could either function without him or survive him. Since 1975 Castro has put in place a highly interrelated political structure which rests on five pillars: the Cuban Communist party, the National Assembly, the Council of Ministers and its bureaucracy, the mass organizations, and the army. The system is marked by the two Communist organizational principles of interlocking membership and democratic centralism along with some popular participation. The communist style of organization, in other words, is almost completely compatible with the creation of a monistic system in the traditional Hispanic mold. The principle of interlocking membership, by which Fidel and Raúl each sit on the party Politburo, Secretariat, and Central Committee as well as the Council of State and the Council of Ministers, and, in Raul's case, the army as well, is totally congruent with Hispanic patrimonialism. Raul's wife, Vilma Espin, is now an alternate member of the Politburo, a member of the Central Committee and the Council of State, and Director of the Cuban Federation of Women, one of the mass organizations. The principle of democratic centralism obviously reinforces the traditions of hierarchy and centralism endemic to Hispanic political culture.

The fourth stage in the evolution of a Communist combat culture, namely, the fomenting of tension with other states, is dealt with in the next section and in the conclusion to this chapter.

In summary, the consolidation of a Communist regime in Cuba has created a political system that is made up of a mixture of Leninist and Hispanic characteristics—both sets of which are congruent with each other. Democratic centralism reinforces the Hispanic tradition of centralism while interlocking membership has perpetuated the patrimonialism of the Castros and their revolutionary followers. Similarly, the creation of party-led mass organizations is not incompatible with the Hispanic tradition of corporatism and the Latin American practice of creating *intereses creados* with *personería jurídica*. At the same time Fidel continued to be the national *caudillo* in political communion with the masses; and his younger brother, Raúl, waits in the wings to succeed him.

While we have detected change in Cuba's political culture over time, let us not overlook the continuing *personalismo* that exists. As Domínguez has written of Fidel's behavior in the late 1980s:

> Instead of delegating authority to powerful subordinates, as he had done since the early 1970s, he has recentralized it. Instead of liberalizing the economy, he has reversed several market-reliant policies of the past decade. And instead of stressing pragmatic policy goals, he has again been emphasizing the need to follow the 'correct' ideological route in building socialism.[11]

At the same time, in an ongoing process of *rectificación*, party members were called upon at a September 1989 meeting to make a "special effort to deal with and overcome organizational deficiencies and the still prevailing lack of a consistently rational practice in our economy."

Further, heroic efforts were to be made to combat "incompetence and flaws in government..., indolence and negligent attitudes..., and manifestations of labor and social indiscipline." Invoking traditional Spartan Communist values, Fidel argues that "austerity must characterize life in our society, particularly the life of our cadres."[12]

The failure of the regime to achieve its economic goals through its original ideological postulates has forced it to adopt certain legal-rational and managerial modes of operation and behavior. One of the ongoing causes of political instability in Latin America has been the incompatibility between the Thomistic and Machiavellian strains in its political culture. It is possible that by creating an amalgam of Hispanic, Marxist, and Western values and behavior patterns, the Cubans may have constructed a more stable political system than might have initially been predicted. But whether it can survive the apparent demise of Communism elsewhere in the world, the distintegration of the Soviet empire, and its own economic failures is more questionable today than a decade ago.

Cuban Foreign Policy

As suggested in the foregoing section, Cuba before 1959 had a political system that reflected its Machiavellian value system and *caudillaje* culture. In addition, as Francis Lambert wrote, "Pre-Castro Cuba had most of the features of instability common to the rest of Latin America and very few of the features of stability." Given its comparatively late securing of independence, weak Roman Catholic church, volatile political parties, fragmented class system, foreign (primarily North American) economic domination, and even unstable army, it became highly probable that "Cuban political culture was unstable and fluctuating to a degree only paralleled in the smaller republics round the Caribbean."[13]

By contrast, there was less evidence that Cuba's instability stemmed from economic underdevelopment. Compared to other Latin American countries, Cuba on the eve of Castro's revolution ranked high in most important socio-economic development indexes: fourth in gross national product per capita, fifth in literacy, third in number of physicians, fourth in daily newspaper circulation, and seventh in students in higher education per capita.[14] Moreover, according to Fagen, "Batista's Cuba exhibited a greater degree of national integration than did Mexico after fifty years of 'integrative revolution.' " Too, the country "was among the most culturally homogeneous nations in Latin America, Asia, or Africa."[15] What Cuba shared with much of Latin

America at this time was a distorted dependence on the United States and its internal consequences: vast inequalities in the distribution of wealth, goods, services, and opportunities—a necessary, if insufficient, condition for political revolution.

The importance of *personalismo* in Cuba's political culture doubtless helped shape the form of rule after the revolution and the crusading nature of its new foreign policy. The most notable personality cult surrounded the poet and revolutionary José Martí (1853–1895) and was based on the juxtaposition of the ideal, "moral fundamentalist" republic he struggled for with the corruption and venality of Cuban governments between 1902 and 1959. If Lambert is correct in asserting that "a consistent feature of Cuban political experience has been a feeling that the revolution [as Martí symbolized] has been betrayed," then it is not surprising that Castro has adopted policies lying at the other extreme— to demonstrate that his revolution has not been betrayed and remains morally upright. These are now permanent features of *fidelismo*. But the continued commitment to revolutionary élan and to principles of "high" morality also has direct consequences for the assertive foreign policy the Castro government has pursued.

As in virtually all countries of the region, nationalism is a potent— perhaps dominant—political force:

> Ever since the nineteenth century Cuban nationalism had (inevitably) been directed against the United States. Cuba's wars of independence had created a tradition of armed struggle of which the heroes were the common people—the *guajiro* or peasant and the *mambi* or negro. . . .The heroic struggle is emphasized for two reasons. It establishes Castro as a gallant and successful *caudillo*, and it lays stress on the idea of continuous struggle, which is a notable feature of the Cuban version of Communism.[16]

Since combat is the pervasive ethos of ideal-type Communist political culture, as we noted above, Cuban revolutionary leaders have successfully fused the prescriptions of both Communist and indigenous cultures. They have, as a result, emphasized struggle more than any other contemporary Communist state (Albania excepted). The reinforcement of the Communist combat ethic by the national culture helps explain why Cuba seeks a leading role in the international anti-imperialist struggle. Foreign military operations reinforces the ethos of militant revolutionary struggle.

Anti-Americanism is the obverse side of the nationalist coin. Fagen has shown that the essential groundwork for Castro's revolution was "the tangled and passionate history of Cuban-American relations in the first six decades of the twentieth century."[17] Benjamin has described the hegemony and dependent development that charcterized United States policy towards Cuba between 1880 and 1934:

> The ability of the United States to maintain its hegemony over Cuban society, despite the rise of nationalist and anticapitalist doctrines and movements on the island in the 1930s, resulted from the ties of structural dependency which had been woven into the fabric of the Cuban economy and into the mind-sets of the island's elite during more than three decades of political tutelage and massive economic presence. This state of dependency led native leaders to accept U.S. social values and models of economic development, and caused a realignment of their economic pursuits so as to conform to the needs of the U.S. economy.[18]

Morris Morley has sought to explain the unequal relations between the United States and Cuba in terms of "the notion of the imperial state—a state with boundaries for capital accumulation located far beyond its geographic limits." In this respect, Castro's revolution represented, among other things, a fundamental challenge to United States capital accumulation. Thus,

> The process of large-scale structural transformation in Cuba raised, from Washington's perspective, the possibility of an economic development model that might take hold in other parts of the Third World. The initial U.S. response was to seek to destabilize and overthrow the revolutionary regime. But the speed with which Castro constructed a new state structure, largely socialized the means of production, and the ease with which he disenfranchised bourgeois political institutions and neutralized non-working-class opposition created insurmountable obstacles to the internal subversion goal.[19]

According to Morley, after a period of incremental decline in the imperial state, United States policy under the Reagan administration brought about the "revival of vendetta politics," part of which involved maintaining a regional diplomatic quarantine around Cuba.

Finally, as Rafael Hernández writes, in the face of "The persistence of U.S. destabilization plans and of the U.S. blockade against Cuba, the continued U.S. occupation of the Guatanamo naval base, U.S. military intelligence flights over Cuba—along with other U.S. policies now reduced or cancelled," a paradox emerges that "U.S. policy, against its own interests, contributes to strengthening the Cuban perception that Cuba is a besieged fortress, with its corresponding results of mobilization and internal cohesion."[20] Action taken by the Bush administration to overthrow Panamanian dictator Manuel Noriega in late 1989 probably enhanced Castro's sense of insecurity.

For a variety of reasons, therefore, not all of them rational or justified, anti-*Yanquismo* has developed into a potent force in Cuba and in other parts of Latin America (in the same way anti-Russianism exists in Eastern Europe). In the Cuban case, a mixture of real grievances (the Platt Amendment, United States military interventions and economic warfare) and psychological grievances (relative deprivation, humiliation, inferiority complex) combined to give anti-Americanism an institutional form in the Autentico party as early as the 1930s. Rather than having at his disposal a purely amorphous and inarticulate force, Castro was able to invoke a specific political legacy to which he could tie the aims of his revolution. Since the revolution, however, the indispensability of anti-Americanism to Cuban nationalism may be fading as Cuba can point to some achievements recorded in its own right: expanded health care and widespread literacy at home, gold medal bonanzas in international sporting events, and a decisive role played by the Cuban army in two African wars.

Ironically, the one area in which a more traditional diplomatic approach is employed is in Latin America. To be sure, there was an early "adventurist" period in Cuban foreign policy, marked by the Havana meetings of the Latin American Communist parties in 1964, the Tricontinental conference in 1966, and the Cuban-controlled, rural-oriented Latin American Solidarity Organization (OLAS) conference in 1967, all of which exhorted revolutionaries in Latin America and elsewhere to engage in armed struggle (despite Soviet pressures urging greater restraint).[21] Certain Latin American countries were deemed ripe for revolution. This aggressive foreign policy, Ratliff has argued, had its origins in cultural factors—from our point of view, Cuba's *caudillaje* culture:

The outstanding characteristics of the castroite line as it came from Cuba during the 1960s, and as it was to a considerable extent reflected by the Latin American guerrillas, were impatience, elitism, and intolerance. These qualities were born of youthful exuberance, feelings of depression and frustration, perhaps some inclinations toward 'gangsterism,' and conviction that political, economic, and social conditions could not be changed gradually—

that the complete and sudden uprooting of the existing order was essential.[22]

By the mid-1970s, however, especially in the aftermath of the overthrow of the Allende government in Chile, Cuba's foreign policy in Latin America had matured and had become more flexible at the same time that, not coincidentally, new security commitments were being made to embryonic Marxist states in Africa. At the end of the 1960s only Mexico maintained diplomatic relations with Cuba; however, by 1977 eleven Latin American and Caribbean states had reestablished relations, and by the late 1980s only four had not (Honduras, El Salvador, Chile, and Paraguay).

In previous chapters we discussed the activism of selected circum-Caribbean states in regional organizations; since the mid-1970s Cuba, too, has become a leading regional economic actor. According to Steven Reed,

> The magnitude of the transformation in Cuban-Latin American relations is perhaps most dramatically demonstrated by Cuba's new and active role in Latin American regional organizations. Cuba has been an active supporter of the Latin American Economic System (SELA), the Caribbean Committee of Development and Cooperation (CCDC), the Latin American Energy Organization (OLADE), the Latin American and Caribbean Sugar Exporting Group (GEPLACEA), and the Caribbean Multinational Shipping Company (NAMACUR).[23]

In addition, Pamela Falk has pointed to Cuban activism since the 1970s in international organizations such as the United Nations and its various agencies (UNESCO, UNCTAD, UNDP) and the Economic Commission for Latin America (ECLA).[24] The increasing internationalization of economic activity may, thus, be producing a "convergence" in the international behavior of the circum-Caribbean states in our study. Interestingly, this has been going on coterminously with the institutionalization and bureaucratization of Cuba's *fidelista* political system.

Nowhere is traditional diplomacy used more as the chief instrument of furthering Cuban influence than in relations with the Southern Cone nations following the installation of democratic regimes in the mid-1980s. A primary reason for this is the search for prestige—as opposed to an earlier strategic-military orientation—in the hemisphere. Clearly there are limits—spatially and temporally—to the influence of a combat culture. Thus, the regular exchange of visits in recent years by government leaders from Cuba, Uruguay, Brazil, Argentina and, of course, Mexico demonstrates the maturing of foreign policy positions in line with the detectable shift to Western Democratic values at home.

Other factors, such as *fidelismo*, must be evaluated in seeking to identify the domestic roots of Cuban foreign policy. This may necessitate sketching a psychological portrait of Cuba's long-serving leader.[25] While insights are inevitably gained from such studies, the sociological counterargument can be advanced that a ruler of a given psychological profile is the logical product of a society with a particular socio-psychological makeup, as we noted Thucydides concluded in chapter 1. Moreover, to accept the *fidelismo* explanation fully is to adopt a "Cuba-as-autonomous-actor" perspective. In the contemporary global order, few states can be said to be fully in control of their own destinies. Even fewer leaders exclusively determine their nation's foreign policies. Again, the world system is undoubtedly having a cultural convergence effect.

Conversely, a further argument running contrary to the *personalismo* thesis can be made from evidence that suggests Fidel has not enjoyed a monopoly over foreign policy. Some time ago Edward González claimed to have identified three tendencies in foreign policy making: a pragmatic economic tendency whose spokesman was Carlos Rafael Rodríguez; a revolutionary political tendency headed by Fidel Himself; and a military tendency led by Raúl Castro and the Ministry of the Revolutionary Armed Forces.[26] More recently, Julia Preston made the case that the trial and execution of General Ochoa Sanchez in July 1989 represented "a crisis in Castro's regime, and not merely a noisy scandal." In particular, she suggested that Ochoa and others had decided that a "Gorbachev-style opening in Cuban politics" was required to address growing complaints against the regime."[27] If such accounts are accurate, then Fidel may not be the unchallenged ruler he is often depicted as, and *personalismo* in Cuban politics may involve a number of prominent military and political leaders.

Finally, even if some of Cuba's foreign policy decisions are primarily voluntaristic, owing more to *personalismo* than to other variables, they should be viewed in the broader context of a nationalist, anti-American, inherently insurgent, political culture. In this way, Cuba's distinctive political culture serves, directly or indirectly, as a critical explanatory variable for foreign policy.

What are some of the specific manifestations of Cuban political culture in the international arena? Most obvious to the "colossus" across the strait is Cuba's acknowledged political and military presence (approximately fifty thousand personnel) in thirty-five countries throughout the world. Such globalism involves extralegal military involvement seeking to overthrow established governments; one such alleged target is El Salvador, a more incontestable one is support given to the Polisario Front fighting for the independence of the Sahaouri people. It also includes legal military assistance to prop up established, if unstable and increasingly less socialist, regimes; Angola, Mozambique, Ethiopia, and Nicaragua have been cases in point. In the latter case, while some observers noted the limited presence of three thousand Cuban military advisors and an equal number of technical advisors, there was a more intangible, insidious dimension. According to Antonio Jorge, "a noticeable convergence in ideological persuasion, structures, modus operandi, and even in intangibles such as political and revolutionary style" ensured that an "intense political-ideology affinity and shared *Weltanschauung* will finally impose itself" on the relationship.[28] This possible ideological convergence may have contributed to the ouster of the Sandinista government in 1990.

A further instrument of Cuban globalist policy is foreign assistance programs; important recipients in the hemisphere have been Nicaragua, and Grenada until the 1983 United States invasion. We should stress, therefore, that the exact mix of methods employed to promote Cuba's foreign policy has altered over time. According to Enrique Baloyra, "The *modus operandi* has changed: from guerrilla outbreaks to army units, from subversive incursions to formal agreements with one of the parties to different local conflicts."[29]

That a small island nation can undertake international commitments on such a scale has aroused the suspicions of statesmen and scholars alike. According to the "surrogate" thesis, Cuba was simply fulfilling the expansionist strategy of the Soviet Union.[30] Even where Cuba champions hemispherically popular causes, for example, greater degrees of non-alignment for regional states, exhortations for Latin America to "renege on the foreign debt," or support for Argentina in the 1982 Malvinas war, such critics argue that Cuba is merely spearheading the Soviet's "hidden agenda." For a variety of reasons—some having more to do with Soviet foreign policy objectives than with Cuban ones (and therefore inappropriate for consideration here)—this thesis remains unconvincing. The crucial argument in favor of the counterthesis that Havana in large measure decides its own foreign policy is Cuban nationalism.

Many of the sources for Cuba's foreign policy drive the international relations of all nations, while some are specific to a Communist Third World country. Jorge Domínguez emphasizes the latter and identifies, in rank order, Cuba's major foreign policy goals:

survival of the revolutionary government, economic development, influence in other states, input in the international socialist movement, and support for other revolutions.[31] H. Michael Erisman adopts a more traditional perspective:

> The main factors that have influenced Havana's foreign policy from 1959 to the present are its quest for military and economic security; ideological considerations; its aspirations for Third World leadership; its sense of mission; and nationalism.[32]

For Erisman nationalism is the "neglected dimension" behind Cuba's globalism: "It is, granted, a restrained nationalism—restrained not only by the imperatives of small-state survival in the face of great power animosity, but also by the Fidelistas' ideological convictions."[33] But it lies at the root of Cuban global assertion, which in turn is an over-compensatory mechanism for past humiliation. Baloyra has called attention to one specific aspect of this nationalism that is rarely identified. He writes, in the context of United States-Cuban relations:

> [I]t is easier for the Cuban regime to deal with a confrontation than with a process of detente whose outcome is not easily predictable. In short, Cuba entered the 1980s on a war footing *against a lifestyle* to which Cuba has sought an alternative for twenty-three years. Herein lies the Cuban regime's radicalism—something much deeper than mere ideology.[34]

From this account we can observe the historical roots of Cuba's foreign policy today. As Falk has argued, "Any interpretation of Cuban foreign policy that focuses solely on Cuba's post-1959 ideological commitments to Marxism fails to understand the complex and subtle interplay of the currents that feed both this foreign policy and Cuba's ideological commitment to Communism."[35] Cuban international behavior has reflected a mix of cultural factors: its traditional *caudillaje* political culture, the admixture of a Communist combat ethos after 1959, Fidel's anti-American *caudillismo* and, until the rectification campaign, the bureaucratization of the regime. What we have found particularly striking is the way in which these changes in political culture, political structure, and foreign policy have occurred in tandem over the past thirty years. This pattern is all the more remarkable given that we may have expected Cuba's foreign policy to be an offshoot of seemingly indominable and uncontrollable external influences—sparring between the two superpowers in this period.

Nicaraguan Political Culture

It is clear from table 4.1 that Nicaragua manifests a classic Latin American national value system composed of a mixture of Thomistic and Machiavellian elements. *Caudillaje* behavior patterns are also strong, particularly during the Somoza dynasty—1934 to 1979. Centralization of authority, rule by a single political group, limitations on political competition, and dissent are characteristic of both of the Latin American cultural strains. The clientalism and informal corporativism during the Somoza era and the formal corporativism that was evident in the Council of State during the first five years of the Sandinista period give the Nicaraguan political culture its Thomistic flavor, while the incessant guerilla wars and insurrections introduce a strong Machiavellian element. With the introduction of a Marxist orientation by the Sandinistas, this insurrectionary tradition was transformed into a "combat culture" analagous (in type if not degree) to that of Cuba. As James L. Busey wrote thirty years ago, Nicaraguan politics since it left the United Provinces in 1838 had been marked "by chaos alternating with dictatorship, foreign intervention, violence and extreme tumult."[36] David Close put it more starkly: "Pre-revolutionary Nicaragua knew neither liberal democracy nor even constitutional government."[37] These judgments, for the Somoza period at least, are in agreement with the Fitzgibbon-Johnson and Bollen indexes presented in table 4.2.

The one aspect of Nicaraguan political culture that changed noticeably since the victory by the Sandinistas was the steep decline in *caudillaje* behavior. This was due to some apparent lessening of *personalismo* in the contemporary political process. Power shifted from a family dynasty to a stable junta of revolutionary leaders (*Los Comandantes*). Seen in this light, the holding of free elections in February 1990, which led to the Sandinista defeat, fits an already-established pattern of linear development away from monolithic rule.

In many respects Nicaragua is a prime example of the "nucleated 'city-state'" which Richard Morse sees as providing fertile ground for the emergence of Machiavellianism.[38] The nation's topography has always impeded its social and political integration. Eastern Nicaragua, the Mosquito Coast, separated from the rest of the country by swamps and jungles, nurtured a distinct Indian Culture. By the same token, throughout much of the nineteenth century there was a distinct cultural cleavage between the subsistence-based peasants living in the hill country east of Lakes Managua and Nicaragua and the more Europeanized population living west of the lakes. However, the major political chasm, which has had a profound effect on the nation's political culture, was the rivalry between Granada and Leon.

Located approximately fifty miles from each other (Granada to the south and Leon to the North of Lake Managua), Granada became the locus of the landowning elite and the stronghold of the Conservative party, especially during the quasi-constitutional *treintino* period of Conservative rule (1857–1893). Leon, on the other hand, became the administrative center of the old *intendencia*, a predominantly commercial center, and the heart of the Liberal party.[39] Until 1926 when General Augusto Cesar Sandino mobilized the peasants in the hill country, Nicaragua could be divided politically into four segments: one was the Miskito people, who did not want to be a part of Nicaragua at all; a second, the peasants in the hills, who were largely passive; and finally, Granada and Leon which fought bitterly to control the state.

Such conditions were tailor-made for the emergence of "opportunistic *caudillos*,"[40] and *caudillistic* warfare opens the door to outside intervention. Thus, Nicaraguan politics from 1838 to 1931 was marked by a constant struggle for power between Liberal and Conservative *caudillos*, punctuated by periodic interventions by their American allies. William Walker and his band of mercenaries first entered Nicaragua at the behest of the Liberals in 1855 to help them unseat the Conservatives (who were being assisted by the British). After capturing Granada, legalizing slavery and declaring English to be the new national language, he was thrown out of the country by an army made up of Nicaraguans of both parties.[41] From 1909 to 1933 United States troops intervened on three different occasions, this time on the side of the Conservatives.[42] The chaos of these years produced *caudillos* of both the left and the right, the most notable being the Liberal dictator José Santos Zelaya (1893–1909), the nationalist *guerillero*, Augusto César Sandino, the American-trained *militar*, President Anastasio Somoza (1937–1956), and his son, Tachito (1967–1972, 1974–1979).[43] The Somoza dynasty was finally brought down by an insurrectionary coalition of Social Christian and Marxist *comandantes* such as Eden Pastora ("Comandante Zero"), Tomás Borge, and the Ortega brothers allied with such middle class *caudillaje* personalities as the fiery newspaper editor Pedro Joaquin Chamorro, cooking oil tycoon Alfonso Robelo, and businessman Jorge Salazar.

Obviously, a regime that maintained itself in power by force and fraud could only be brought down by a coalition capable of using the same tactics; and after the Sandinista victory in 1979 those groups who felt themselves squeezed out of power used insurrectionary tactics to attempt to overthrow the Sandinista leaders whom they also perceived to be coercive and deceptive in their attempts to consolidate power. The Machiavellian character of both sides is captured by Shirley Christian, who writes that after Humberto Ortega stated on August 23, 1980 that the Sandinista elections would be "very distinct from the elections that are wanted by the oligarchs and traitors," Jorge Salazar "began to lead two very different lives—one that was public and law-abiding, another that was private and conspiratorial."[44] The Contras were simply a continuation of the insurrectionary tradition of the political left by the political right.

Although political infighting, foreign intervention, and insurrection produced a variety of Machiavellian leaders—left, right, and center—there have been a number of attempts to stabilize the Nicaraguan city-state through various corporative and monistic devices. This is the Thomistic side of the nation's political culture. In many respects the political system that Anastasio Somoza succeeded in putting together in the 1930s and 1940s might be called a patrimonial-corporatist regime. As such it was composed of both formal and informal elements. The most evident manifestation of formal corporativism under the Somozas was the guaranteed representation of the Conservative party in both houses of the Nicaraguan legislature. Formal corporativism was also reflected in the *reglamento* governing the internal organization and activities of union organizations, employers' associations, and cooperatives.[45] In addition, new unions under government sponsorship were created in the 1940s and 1950s: the Organized Workers of Nicaragua and the Somoza Popular Front.[46]

Another political structure that had a quasi-formal corporative position in the *somocista* political system was the Nicaraguan National Guard. Operating under the command of various family members, *LaGuardia* became an umbrella organization for a great many state functions, including the national radio, the postal service, the natonal health service, and the railroad.[47]

Patrimonial corporativism manifested itself primarily in the clientalistic relationship between the Somoza family and the agro-industrial bourgeoisie. In addition to building up its own economic empire composed of both legal and illegal enterprises, the Somoza family allocated a certain amount of "economic space" to rival segments of the traditional elites. These arrangements had their genesis in the political pacts signed between the Liberal and Conservtive parties in 1948 setting up the power-sharing arrangements. Included was an agreement guaranteeing free commercial activity and respect for the traditional bourgeoisie's economic interests.[48] These groupings were centered around the *Banco Nicaraguense* (BANIC) which was the financial arm of the cotton and industrial concerns associated with the Central American Common Market; and the *Banco de America* (BANAMERICA) which financed the more traditional agro-exports such as sugar and livestock.[49] It was the near monopolization of economic activity after the earthquake of 1972 that motivated many of these businessmen to make common cause with the Sandinistas against "Tachito" Somoza.

In summary, the *somocista* polity was a gigantic family "patrimonial state" in which the military, business, the bureaucracy, organized labor, and the major opposition political parties were integrated into the system in either a corporative or clientalistic manner. Anastasio Somoza and his son, Luis, amassed enormous power and wealth by adroitly manipulating the system in a clearly Machiavellian manner. The excessive *caudillaje* behavior of Tachito finally brought the system down.

The corporativism of the Somoza years was clearly continued by the Sandinistas. The Sandinista Council of State was formally corporative between 1979 and 1984 with seats arbitrarily assigned to a variety of parties, interest groups, and social segments. In addition, the creation of such mass organizations attached to the *Frente Sandinista* as the neighborhood defense committees (CDS), youth and women's organizations, labor and rural workers' organizations, and the Sandinista military represented forms of "popular revolutionary corporativism" found in Cuba and other socialist states.

The ability of the Sandinistas to use this sytem to control behavior largely helps to explain the drop in the incidence of *caudillaje* behavior evident in table 4.1 The Sandinistas made the Nicaraguan political system more bureaucratic and less clientalistic compared to the Somoza era. While many critics would condemn the *comandantes* for their Machiavellianism, the core of Machiavellian values and *caudillaje* behavior has, for a number of years, been largely centered in the internal and external opposition. A clear victory by the Contras probably would have done little to change the historic political culture of Nicaragua.

The willingness of both the internal opposition and the Sandinistas to submit their dispute to an electoral verdict—coupled with the neutralization of the external Contra opposition by the Tela Agreement—has set in motion a process that may, over the long term, bring about further cultural changes. Forced by the electoral campaign to change his leadership style, Daniel Ortega came to resemble the sterotypical "party caudillo," complete with designer jeans and rock musicians. His surprising concession speech on February 26, 1990 was, too, a result of the democratic aspirations of the Nicaraguan population.

The transition from a Sandinista to a UNO government poses a number of questions. Would the *comandantes* give up control of the army, police, and secret service? Would they use their mass organizations (Sandinista women, trade unions, and neighborhood organizations, for example) to harass and obstruct the government of Violeta Chamorro? If the historic political culture of Nicaragua is to be our guide, we would expect that traditional *caudillaje* behavior patterns would dominate the period of the Chamorro presidency. That is, the Sandinistas would indeed attempt, as Daniel Ortega put it, to rule from below as well as from above; that they would struggle to retain control of the coercive institutions of the state; and that they would use their mass organizations to disrupt the new government.

On the other hand, Francis Fukuyama may be correct in contending that a worldwide Liberal movement is sweeping everything before it.[50] If that is so, we may be witnessing the remaking of national political cultures everywhere by global cultural trends. The Nicaraguan elections, and the political behavior induced by them, were largely the result of external political forces. Long-term cultural change in that country may also be produced by those same forces.

Nicaraguan Foreign Policy

Nicaragua's international behavior can best be understood as a symbiotic interaction between two facets of its political culture—the *caudillaje*, combat strain and a recognition of its dependency. As noted above, practically from the day Leon declared its independence from Spain on September 28, 1821, Nicaragua has suffered intervention from other states: from Mexico between 1821 and 1823, from the British along the Mosquito Coast, from American filibusters led by William Walker, from continuous United States direct armed intervention between 1912 and 1933, and from indirect American intervention by way of the Somoza family from 1933 until the Sandinistas took power in 1979. This constant foreign intervention in its national life helped to produce the two cultural patterns mentioned above—a *caudillaje*, combat strain oriented toward repelling foreign enemies and, at the same time, a conciliatory strain which recognizes the limits of its national power.

The latter orientation can be seen in the international stance taken by the Liberal dictator Jose Santos Zelaya (1893–1909). Zelaya preferred to settle boundary disputes with his country's neighbors through arbitration rather than violence, even when it adversely affected Nicaragua's interests. His government signed the Corinto Treaty of 1902 setting up arbitration proceedings for Central American disputes and the 1906 agreement drawn up on the USS Marblehead designed to end the hostilities surrounding the attempt to overthrow Guatemalan dictator Manuel Estrada Cabrera. He was also willing some months later to submit a Nicaraguan-Honduran dispute to the arbitration procedures of the Corinto Treaty.

A further example of this peaceful, even subservient, approach was the 1928 treaty which gave up Nicaraguan lands to Columbia. The historical legacy of generally peaceful resolutions of inter-state conflicts is one Nicaragua appears to share with Colombia. The largely defensive, "regional reactivist" foreign policy of the Sandinista regime can also be understood in terms of this nonbellicose tradition.

Although it shares with Cuba elements of a combat culture, Nicaragua has not aspired to the international role that the latter nation has. A number of reasons may be advanced for the more pragmatic, less ideological international politics of Nicaragua compared to Cuba. For one thing, it is fairly evident that anti-Yanquismo among the population at large did not approach the level of intensity in Nicaragua as in Cuba, though it certainly was an important and not altogether unjustifiable undercurrent. Being more remote from the United States and with fewer American business and cultural organizations physically located in Nicaragua, the acute sense of relative deprivation that overcame Cubans was not as profound there. Within Nicaraguan society, however, relative deprivation was a catalyst of the 1979 revolution.[51] As noted earlier, the intense combat culture that pervades Leninist parties has been largely absent in Nicaragua because the FSLN has not yet developed into the strictly regimented and hierarchical organization characteristic of a traditional Communist party.

Certain geopolitical and economic constraints also came into play. According to Thomas Walker,

> The Soviet Union had made it clear that it was not willing to underwrite a 'second Cuba.' Hard currency would not be forthcoming from that source, nor would military support in the event of a U.S. invasion. Furthermore, unlike Cuba, Nicaragua was not an island. Its long borders were highly vulnerable to paramilitary penetration, and any attempt to impose a dogmatic Marxist-Leninist system would certainly have generated a mass exodus of population. Finally, the Catholic Church in Nicaragua was so important and Catholics had played such a crucial role in the War of Liberation that the Sandinistas were neither inclined nor well situated to attack the Catholic traditions of their country.[52]

The Soviet assessment of Nicaragua's revolutionaries was, therefore, a very skeptical one. As Vernon Aspaturian colorfully put it, "the Soviet view of the Sandinista movement before its advent to power was that of an exotic bloom in Castro's strange revolutionary garden in which flowers were not clearly distinguishable from weeds in the eyes of Moscow."[53]

Another moderating influence, mentioned by Walker, was the part played in the country's political culture by the Catholic church. The ecclesiastical hierarchy and clergy enjoyed a social status that had no parallel in Cuba. They sought to shield the faithful and disadvantaged groups from the worst excesses of *somozismo* even before the rank-and-file clergy discovered liberation theology in the 1970s. Priests subsequently helped erode the familial Somoza dynasty but, at the same time, they were instrumental in blocking hardline Marxist forces within the FSLN from exerting a totally dominant influence. Key clerical actors in the Sandinista movement included Ernesto Cardenal (minister of culture), Miguel d'Escoto (foreign minister), Fernando Cardenal (a director of the Sandinista Youth), and Edgardo Parrales (minister of social services and ambassador to the OAS). None were leftists by Sandinista standards, but all were nonetheless suspended from their pastoral duties by the church hierarchy in 1985.

Finally, let us note that Nicaragua's conversion into a socialist state was a relative "surprise": before the late 1970s other Central American states (Guatemala and El Salvador) had more militant labor movements and seemed "riper" for socialism. As Woodward writes,

> That Nicaragua would move sharply toward socialism ahead of the rest of Central America, after lagging behind it for so many years, is historically a result of the Somozas' Liberal Party failing to allow more moderate but progressive forces to develop and share in the political process during the last half-century.[54]

The byproduct of a movement less steeped in socialist thought and practice (we recall the FSLN was only founded in 1961) was the less strident policies of the Sandinistas both at home and abroad when they first seized power, and their inability to hold on to power in 1990.

The existence of a wide gamut of moderating influences on the Nicaraguan revolution produced—by *revolutionary* regime standards—a cautious foreign policy that could best be described as "nonrevolutionary anti-imperialism." The "anti-imperialist" side of the equation was reflected by the Sandinista leadership's decision to take Nicaragua into the Non-Aligned Movement. Diplomatic ties were established with Second World (the Soviet bloc, China, and Vietnam) and Third World countries (Algeria, India, Tanzania, Zambia, and Zimbabwe) largely on the basis of a shared anti-imperialist world outlook. Furthermore, as Max Azicri has written, "Nicaragua's anti-imperialism is not a passing political fad, but rather a central component of a new revolutionary identity which engulfs the nation and defines its emerging political culture.[55] Confrontational relations in Central America were produced partly by Nicaraguan efforts at exporting revolution (Sandinista support for the FMLN in El Salvador was destabilizing but not decisive, as seen in the FMLN's 1989 full-scale offensive that fell short of taking power), partly by the suspicions and fears of its neighbors.

The "nonrevolutionary" side of Sandinista foreign policy was reflected in a pursuit of diversified international relations. Within the region, the Sandinistas initiated a series of peace proposals preceding Esquipulas I and II (the Arias plan). Some were based on the Contadora peace process, begun in 1983; others represented Nicaraguan initiatives, such as the draft treaties seeking normalization of regional intra-state relations in 1983. When President Oscar Arias Sánchez of Costa Rica put forward his peace program, Daniel Ortega Saavedra accepted it, and by 1988 the Sandinistas were negotiating directly with Contra leaders. Carlos Tunnermann, Nicaraguan ambassador to the United States, listed his country's primary objectives in the peace process:

> Nicaragua is prepared to sign treaties that would assure compliance with a halt to importation of arms, removal of all foreign military advisers and a prohibition on foreign bases in Central American countries. The accords must also include suspension of all threatening military exercises in the region and the end of all assistance to the contras.[56]

In her exhaustive examination of Sandinista foreign policy, Mary Vanderlaan identified some of the immediate objectives, longer term goals, and expected international behavior of Nicaragua. We list these in table 6.1. She cites Foreign Minister Miguel d'Escoto's explanation for the origins of this set of precepts and behavior: democracy, Christian values, social justice, and nationalism. The overriding direction of Sandinista foreign policy was to be of a "principled but pragmatic disposition."[57] While we must approach official discourse with some skepticism, let us note that the non-aligned world shared with Nicaragua similar foreign policy principles and international behavior. By contrast, the Sandinistas' operational goals resembled those of Cuba on some points (formation of a popular militia, membership in the Non-Aligned Movement), but were different on others (support for peace, diversified diplomatic and financial contacts), especially when contrasted with Castro's regime at a comparable stage of development.

Relations with many Latin American states improved significantly following the installation of the Sandinista regime. Nicaragua was

TABLE 6.1

Sandinista Foreign Policy Objectives

Principles:
1. Sovereignty
2. Self-determination
3. National Defense
4. Non-alignment

Operational Goals:
1. Formation of Sandinista People's Army, Police, Popular Militia
2. Membership in the Non-Aligned Movement
3. Systematic support for peace in international forums
4. Membership as observer in the Socialist International
5. Maintenance of diplomatic relations with a broad spectrum of states
6. Stability in international commercial relations
7. Diversification of financial dependence and maintenance of varied bilateral and multilateral financial aid sources

International Behavior:
1. Non-aligned voting pattern in the United Nations
2. Support for national liberation struggles in the Third World
3. Support for a New International Economic Order
4. Maintenance of established diplomatic relations

Source: Adapted from Mary B. Vanderlaan, *Revolution and Foreign Policy in Nicaragua.* Boulder, CO: Westview Press, 1986 p. 26.

particularly well disposed towards the Contadora group (Mexico, Colombia, Venezuela, and Panama), then later to emergent democratic regimes in the Southern Cone (Argentina, Brazil, and Uruguay). The series of improvements in Nicaragua's foreign relations following the revolution stood in sharp contrast to the history of Cuba's international political setbacks after Castro took power. Nonrevolutionary anti-imperialism appeared, therefore, to have a broader appeal in Latin America than Castro's revolutionary-mindedness, and it allowed Nicaragua to escape the ostracization from the regional community that the Reagan administration had sought. In fact, a number of Latin American leaders openly identified with the "third way" that the Sandinistas claimed to be pursuing.

By contrast, the Reagan administration continued to perceive the Sandinistas' international politics in a very different light. They claimed that Managua's foreign policy was driven by the desire to export revolution to its neighbors. Some contended that under the National Directorate Nicaragua shifted from regionalist to globalist policies. A few observers even claimed that the regime's foreign policy was globalist revolutionary. For instance, summarizing the country's international contacts in 1985, the *1986 Yearbook on International Communist Affairs* noted:

> The FSLN's foreign policy during the year attempted to retain if not expand ties with Western Europe and Japan economically and to strengthen links to the Soviet bloc, Cuba, radical Third World regimes, and a number of revolutionary and terrorist organizations from Latin America, Western Europe, and the Middle East.[58]

In the same vein Mark Falcoff has written of the "rising totalitarianism" in Nicaragua that had " an uncommon need for instruments of force and violence." Even disregarding Defense Minister Humberto Ortega's assertion that "without sandinismo we cannot be Marxist-Leninist, and *sandinismo* without Marxism-Leninism cannot be revolutionary," purely internal security concerns would have driven Nicaragua under the FSLN into the Soviet camp. Social control of an unwilling population, Falcoff argued,

> explains why, among other things, the Sandinistas have raised an army larger than that of all other Central American nations combined. It accounts for the need for massive foreign assistance from countries like Cuba, the Soviet Union, East Germany, and Bulgaria, whose major, perhaps only, real contribution to the armature of modern life is the art of domestic surveillance. It also explains the steady pattern of Soviet deliveries of military materiel to Nicaragua...."[59]

This interpretation of the threat posed by Nicaragua is noteworthy in that it did not place direct blame on the country's Marxism nor on its expansionist foreign policy per se for destabilization in Central America. Rather, the functional imperative to police a recalcitrant citizenry accounted for the Sandinista's choice of Soviet bloc support. Falcoff concluded: "thus what at first glance appears to be an exclusively internal affair of the Nicaraguans—how to organize their own society—becomes a matter of legitimate security concern to their neighbors and to the United States."

Former Sandinista official Arturo Cruz defined Nicaragua's security interests more broadly, depicting them as inevitably at odds with the security of other Central American states:

According to the National Directorate, a region as small as Central America allowed for only one of two options: a revolutionary solution for the entire region, given the 'ripple effect' of the Sandinista Revolution, or the eventual defeat of Nicaragua.[60]

But let us look at this same Sandinista foreign policy from another perspective. In a perceptive study, Lars Schoultz argued that "Once the possibility of nonalignment had been eliminated in the minds of Washington policy makers, every step away from the United States was inevitably perceived as a step toward Moscow." In the end, "the simplifying assumption of bipolarity had asserted its control over United States policy toward Nicaragua."[61] Here, too, we observe that Nicaragua had become the stakes in a much larger game between the superpowers. The origins or direction of the Sandinistas' international politics were almost irrelevant once the rival political blocs defined differing security stakes in the country. By contrast, improved superpower relations and a joint search for solutions to regional conflicts by Presidents Bush and Gorbachev made Nicaragua a less important pawn in international politics.

Diversifying relations and seeking less traditional trading partners also produced fewer dividends than the Sandinistas had hoped. Ortega's 1988 trip to Europe resulted in $50 million worth of economic assistance compared to the $250 million he had expected to obtain. At about the same time, Japan made clear it was not interested in building a canal through the country.[62] Coupled with the overthrow of Panamanian dictator Noriega, who had been well disposed toward the Sandinistas, and strain in relations with both the USSR (on economic aid) and Cuba (on the Ochoa affair), foreign policy diversification had reached a cul-de-sac by the time of the Sandinista electoral defeat in early 1990.

Conclusion

For Alfred Meyer, "Communist revolutions entail, among other things, clashes of culture." Because of the desire of revolutionary elites to impose a universal way of life, "communist revolutions aim for the replacement of one *culture* by another. Communist revolutions thus are wars between cultures." The main dynamic between Communist and indigenous cultures is, therefore, a struggle between them to exert dominant influence. Accordingly, Meyer concludes: "communist regimes can be understood only if we recognize the extent to which ancient national cultures have shaped them."[63]

The irreconcilability and inevitable clash of cultures stems not just from the stated objective of new elites to effect a revolutionary transformation of society. As we have seen in this chapter, Communist culture is, sui generis, a combat culture engaging in clashes with all types of institutions, personalities, and value systems around it. The evolution of this combat culture, we recall, passes through three separate phases of Leninist party development. First, the forging of a revolutionary party depends on training sufficient cadres in the process of power struggles; Philip Selznick describes a Leninist party as a hierarchy of leaders tested in and trained for political combat.[64] Lacking the popular support and membership numbers, Leninist-type parties seek to compensate by aggressiveness. The very existence of such parties may be contingent upon engaging in continuous struggle with all manner of perceived opposition. An incidental consequence of such an ethos is, according to Robert C. Tucker, the emergence of a paranoid personality at the top of the combat organization.[65]

The second phase involves intra-party struggle. Here factions struggle against each other for party supremacy. As Jeremy Paltiel has written, "Bolshevism was founded in the course of inner party struggle, and Lenin's cry of 'split, split and split again' typifies the polemical atmosphere of party politics."[66] Especially when the combat culture has lost its salience to the socio-political environment, combat culture must be sustained artificially by identifying class enemies within the movement.

The third phase is intra-elite struggle. Party rank-and-file members and activists play little part (except, perhaps, as victims) in this phase of the struggle. Rather, it is confined to the leadership core itself and involves struggle for power between rival personalities. Again, the winner of such conflicts is likely to be the most ruthless (and therefore, perhaps, most paranoid) of the contestants, and upon emerging triumphant is likely to establish a cult of personality whose chief characteristic is exclusionist. Applying this process to our two case studies, ten years into the revolution *fidelismo* was an all-too-clear cult in Cuba. By contrast, in Nicaragua a collective "cult of the *commandantes*" existed, but it is not as readily identifiable nor as developed as *fidelismo* was.

Does this combat culture affect the relations of a country taken over by a revolutionary elite with other states? That is, can we identify a fourth phase in the evolution of Communist combat culture that is "outer-directed" and involves fomenting tension with other states in a region?

Whether a fourth stage is introduced depends, we would argue, on the indigenous political culture, which can exacerbate or moderate Communist combativeness. To provoke inter-state rivalries, a government requires a supportive population, effective use of resources, and an ideological rationale for reassessing traditional international politics and identifying new potential adversaries. A Marxist government further requires general congruence between the Communist political ethos and the modal national political culture. By this stage in a Communist revolution, external struggle is seldom a fundamental imperative or even a political need of the ruling Leninist party, since the training of cadres and leaders through fire was achieved in earlier phases.

To what extent have Marxist-oriented Cuba and Nicaragua been able to project a combat culture to their external relations? In the case of Cuba, the second and third phases of combat were largely completed in the 1960s with, first, Castro's subordination of the Cuban Socialist Party (PSP) to the 26th of July movement; then, second, with his liquidation of the party "microfaction" in 1968. As a result, Cuba was sufficiently "mature" for a fourth, "external struggle" stage by the 1970s.

The case of Nicaragua is different in a number of respects. The first phase—training of leadership cadres—included the corporativism traditional in Nicaraguan political culture—the formal and informal cooptation of groups outside the inner leadership. It led to the Sandinista doctrine of "political co-responsibility" by a variety of social groups for the fate of the revolution. Even the second phase of struggle (factionalism) had not been completed by 1988: the Sandinista Directorate continued to be precariously balanced among the three major FSLN tendencies—rural *foco*, proletarian, and *terceristas*. Furthermore the FSLN's institutional arrangements did not resemble traditional Leninist organizational structures, and they became ineffective when put to an electoral test.

The ease with which Cuban indigenous culture (and perhaps Fidel's conflictual worldview) blended with the combat culture of Communist movements has made Cuba a revolutionary regime thirty years after the revolution. A different constellation of forces—including political cultural factors—engendered a more cautious, less revolutionary, Nicaraguan foreign policy a decade after its revolution. Its mix of Machiavellian and Thomistic values had produced a less combative, if nonetheless *caudillaje*, political culture. The Frente was more cautious in its efforts to graft a combat ethos onto the country. Cuban nationalism and Nicaraguan nationalism have, therefore, taken on different forms in the international arena.

Notes

1. Harvey F. Kline, "Cuba: The Politics of Socialist Revolution," in Howard J. Wiarda and Harvey F. Kline (eds.), *Latin American Politics and Development*. 2nd edn. Boulder, CO: Westview Press, 1985, p. 451.

2. Klein, "Cuba," p. 451.

3. Juan M. del Aguila, *Cuba: Dilemmas of a Revolution*. Boulder, CO: Westview Press, 1984, p. 18.

4. del Aguila, *Cuba*, pp. 28–30.

5. del Aguila, *Cuba*, p. 29.

6. Moreno writes that the "Spanish monarch acted within a system of *derecho* but without, in practice, being subject to the *ley.*" *Derecho* constituted the higher law (or *Ius*) with its ethical, theological and ideological content; *ley* was the enacted or positive law. See Francisco Jose Moreno, *Legitimacy and Stability in Latin America: A Study of Chilean Political Culture*. New York: New York University Press, 1969, pp. 3–29. For a discussion of the *bien comun* see Glen Dealy, "The Tradition of Monistic Democracy in Latin America," in Howard J. Wiarda (ed.), *Politics and Social Change in Latin America: The Distinct Tradition*. 2nd edn. Amherst, MA: The University of Massachusetts Press, 1982.

7. This discussion is based on Raymond Taras, "Communist and Non-Communist Political Cultures as Determinants of Foreign Policy: Cuba and Central America." Paper delivered at the annual meeting of SECOLAS, Merida, Mexico, April 1987. See also Lowell Dittmer, Comparative Communist Political Culture," *Studies in Comparative Communism*, XVI, nos. 1–2 (Spring/Summer 1983), p. 23.

8. Nelson P. Valdes, "The Cuban Revolution," in Jan Knippers Black (ed.), *Latin America: Its Problems and Its Promise*. Boulder, CO: Westview Press, 1984, pp. 355–357.

9. Valdés, "The Cuban Revolution," pp. 357–358.

10. Valdés, "The Cuban Revolution," p. 357.

11. Jorge I. Domínguez, "Cuba in the 1980s," *Foreign Affairs*, 65, no. 1 (Fall 1986), p. 118.

12. George Volsky, "Cuba," in Richard F. Staar (ed.), *Yearbook on International Communist Affairs 1989*. Stanford: Hoover Institution Press, 1989, p. 74.

13. Francis Lambert, "Cuba: Communist State or Personal Dictatorship?" in Archie Brown and Jack Gray (eds.), *Political Culture and Political Change in Communist States*. London: Macmillan, 1979, p. 233.

14. Data are taken from Bruce M. Russett et al., *World Handbook of Political and Social Indicators*. New Haven: Yale University Press, 1964. Cited by Richard R. Fagen, *The Transformation of Political Culture in Cuba*. Stanford: Stanford University Press, 1969, p. 23.

15. Fagen, *The Transformation of Political Culture in Cuba*, p. 22.

16. Lambert, "Cuba: Communist State or Personal Dictatorship?" p. 237.

17. Fagen, *The Transformation of Political Culture in Cuba*, p. 29.

18. Jules R. Benjamin, *The United States and Cuba*. Pittsburgh: University of Pittsburgh Press, 1977, p. 183.

19. Morris H. Morley, *Imperial State and Revolution: The United States and Cuba, 1952–1986*. Cambridge: Cambridge University Press, 1987, pp. 1, 175.

20. Rafael Hernández, "Cuba and the United States: Political Values and Interests in a Changing International System," in Jorge I. Domínguez and Rafael Hernandez (eds.), *U.S.-Cuban Relations in the 1990s*. Boulder, CO: Westview Press, p. 40.

21. For discussions of this period, see Andres Suarez, *Cuba: Castroism and Communism, 1959–1966*. Cambridge, MA: The M.I.T. Press, 1967. Also, William E. Ratliff, *Castroism and Communism in Latin America, 1959–1976*. Washington: American Enterprise Institute for Public Policy Research, Hoover Institution, 1976.

22. Ratliff, *Castroism and Communism in Latin America*, p. 132.

23. Steven L. Reed, "Participation in Multinational Organizations and Programs in the Hemisphere," in Cole Blasier and Carmelo Mesa-Lago (eds.), *Cuba in the World*. Pittsburgh: University of Pittsburgh Press, 1979, p. 297.

24. Pamela Falk, *Cuban Foreign Policy*. Lexington, MA: Lexington Books, 1986, p. 114.

25. For a biography written by a psychiatrist emphasizing the effects of illegitimacy and his father's *macho* qualities on Castro's conflictual view of the world, see Peter G. Bourne, *Fidel: A Biography of Fidel Castro*. New York: Dodd, Mead, 1986. For a personal portrait of the Cuban leader based on interviews, see Tad Szulc, *Fidel: A Critical Portrait*. New York: Avon Books, 1987.

26. Edward González, "Institutionalizaton, Political Elites, and Foreign Policies," in Cole Blasier and Carmelo Mesa-Lago (eds.), *Cuba in the World*. Pittsburgh: University of Pittsburgh Press, 1979, pp. 3–36. Few scholars, including González himself, believe this distinction remains valid today.

27. Julia Preston, "The Trial That Shook Cuba," *New York Review of Books*, XXXVI, no. 19 (December 7, 1989), pp. 25, 27.

28. Antonio Jorge, "How Exportable is the Cuban Model? Culture Contact in a Modern Context," in Barry B. Levine (ed.), *The New Cuban Presence in the Caribbean*. Boulder, CO: Westview Press, 1983, p. 211.

29. Enrique Baloyra Herp, "Internationalism and the Limits of Autonomy: Cuba's Foreign Relations," in Muñoz and Tulchin (eds.), *Latin American Nations in World Politics*. Boulder, CO: Westview Press, 1984, p. 172.

30. For an introduction to Cuban-Soviet relations, see Peter Shearman, *The Soviet Union and Cuba*. London: Routledge and Kegan Paul, 1987.

31. Jorge Domínguez, "Cuban Foreign Policy," *Foreign Affairs*, 57, (Fall 1978), p. 88.

32. H. Michael Erisman, *Cuba's International Relations: The Anatomy of a Nationalistic Foreign Policy*. Boulder, CO: Westview Press, 1985, p. 7.

33. Erisman, *Cuba's International Relations*, p. 152.

34. Baloyra, "Internationalism and the Limits of Autonomy," p. 169.

35. Falk, *Cuban Foreign Policy*, p. 151.

36. James L. Busey, "Foundations of Political Contrast: Costa Rica and Nicaragua," *The Western Political Quarterly*, 11, no. 3 (September 1958), p. 631.

37. David Close, *Nicaragua: Politics, Economics and Society*. London: Pinter Publishers, 1988, p. 107.

38. Richard Morse, "Toward a Theory of Spanish American Government," in Howard J. Wiarda (ed.), *Politics and Social Change in Latin America: The Distinct Tradition*. Amherst, MA: University of Massachusetts Press, 1974, pp. 112–114.

39. The rivalry began during the colonial period when Granada, the older of the two cities, expected to become the colonial capital only to have that status go to Leon. It was exacerbated in 1811 when Leon, after deposing the Spanish governor, concurred in the sack of Granada by Spanish forces. Franklin W. Parker, *The Central American Republics*. New York: Oxford University Press, 1964, p. 223.

40. Morse, "Toward a Theory of Spanish American Government," p. 113.

41. Thomas W. Walker, *Nicaragua: The Land of Sandino*. Boulder, CO: Westview Press, 1981, pp. 13–14.

42. The periods of United States occupation in some form were 1909–1910, 1912–1925, and 1926–1933.

43. Anastasio Somoza's eldest son, Luis, much more moderate in both temperament and ideology than his brother, Tachito, held the presidency from 1956 to 1963 followed by his political lieutenant, Rene Schick Gutierrez (1963–1967).

44. Shirley Christian, *Nicaragua: Revolution in the Family*. New York: Vintage Books, 1986, pp. 198, 203.

45. John B. Ryan et al., *Area Handbook for Nicaragua*. Washington: U.S. Government Printing Office, July 1970, p. 261.

46. Ryan, *Area Handbook for Nicaragua*, pp. 175–176.

47. John A. Booth, *The End and the Beginning: The Nicaraguan Revolution*. 2nd edn. Boulder, CO: Westview Press, 1985, p. 55.

48. George Black, *Triumph of the People: The Sandinista Revolution in Nicaragua*. London: Zed Press, 1981, p. 32.

49. Black, *Triumph of the People*, pp. 37–38.

50. Francis Fukuyama, "The End of History," *The National Interest* (Summer 1989).

51. Booth, *The End and the Beginning*, p. 218.

52. Walker, *Nicaragua: The Land of Sandino*, p. 43.

53. Vernon V. Aspaturian, "Nicaragua between East and West: The Soviet Perspective," in Jiri Valenta and Esperanza Durán (eds.), *Conflict in Nicaragua*. Boston: Allen and Unwin, 1987, p. 212.

54. Woodward, *Central America*, p. 263.

55. Max Azicri, "Nicaragua's Foreign Relations: The Struggle for Survival," in Lincoln and Ferris (eds.), *The Dynamics of Latin American Foreign Policies: Challenges for the 1980s*, p. 230.

56. Carlos Tunnermann, "Nicaragua's Peace Aims," *New York Times* (March 19, 1987), p. 23.

57. Mary B. Vanderlaan, Revolution and Foreign Policy in Nicaragua. Boulder, CO: Westview Press, 1986, p. 26.

58. Michael S. Radu, "Nicaragua," in *Yearbook on International Communist Affairs 1986*. Stanford: Hoover Institution Press, 1986, p. 126.

59. Mark Falcoff, "Nicaraguan Harvest," in Howard J. Wiarda and Mark Falcoff (eds.), *The Communist Challenge in the Caribbean and Central America*. Washington: American Enterprise Institute for Public Policy Research, 1987, p. 231.

60. Arturo Cruz Sequeira, "The Origins of Sandinista Foreign Policy," in Robert S. Leiken (ed.), *Central America: Anatomy of Conflict*. New York: Pergamon Press, 1984, p. 104.

61. Lars Schoultz, *National Security and United States Foreign Policy toward Latin America*. Princeton: Princeton University Press, 1987, p. 296.

62. Richard L. Millett, "Nicaragua: A Glimmer of Hope?" *Current History*, 89 (January 1990), p. 24.

63. Alfred G. Meyer, "Cultural Revolutions: The Uses of the Concept of Culture in the Comparative Study of Communist Systems," *Studies in Comparative Communism*, XVI, nos. 1–2 (Spring/Summer 1983), pp. 5–6.

64. Philip Selznick, *The Organizational Weapon*. Glencoe, IL: Free Press, 1960, p. 11.

65. Robert C. Tucker, "The Dictator and Totalitarianism," *World Politics*, XVII, no. 4 (July 1964), p. 577.

66. Jeremy T. Paltiel, "The Cult of Personality: Some Comparative Reflections on Political Culture in Leninist Regimes," *Studies in Comparative Communism*, XVI, nos. 1–2 (Spring/Summer 1983), p. 58.

7

Conclusions

Writing in 1988, a leading specialist on United States strategic affairs, Colin Gray, deplored how "Social science has developed no exact methodology for identifying distinctive national cultures and styles." Literature on the "academically unfashionable subject of national character" was anecdotal at best, yet learning about character, culture, and style, and about the "cultural thoughtways" of a nation was crucial to understanding a country's political behavior and its role in the international political system.[1]

Gray listed six methodological weaknesses in studying "the American way": 1) determining which of the many threads found in American history was the typical one; 2) imputing a cultural style to a derivative culture that had been formed by a nation of immigrants; 3) measuring the "culture-neutral" nature of the international arena that confronts all nations; 4) explaining deviant political leaders and deviant behavior that are unrepresentative of the body politic; 5) factoring out characteristics, circumstances, and roots that many nations share in common; and 6) being "alert to the fact that industrious and competent scholars generally are able to find what they seek."[2]

In undertaking our study we were conscious of both the methodological pitfalls that challenge political culture studies *and* the inherent urgency of providing data on the topic. We were especially sensitive to the problem of the "self-fulfilling fallacy": the often elusive nature of the political culture concept lends itself to data selection that can readily confirm the initial hypotheses formulated. Graeme Gill identified

a major weakness in much of the political culture literature: a tendency to pick out from a more or less arbitrarily defined traditional political culture those elements which seem best to suit the argument being advanced, and then to assert their continued validity without any explanation or justification for the choice of those elements in the first place or of their continued salience over time.[3]

Especially when the research design includes only one country and seeks to explain the existence of one specific regime type, the political culture approach—if it is to have any heuristic value at all—must establish an association among a nation's political history, its system of political norms, and the institutional superstructure that is said to result from the first two.

In this concluding chapter, we begin by reviewing nonpolitical cultural factors that make up the domestic and international contexts of a country's foreign policy making. With this background we then present our findings concerning the linkage between political culture and international behavior in our six country studies. We offer explanations for the linkage in political cultural terms and, when our data suggest a weak association, in terms of nonpolitical cultural factors as well. Finally we put forward an agenda for future research on the relationship between the Latin American states' political cultures and their international relations.

Nonpolitical Cultural Influences on International Relations

This study has sought to probe the impact of a nation's political culture on its international behavior. In chapter 1 we referred to other factors that help shape a country's foreign policy. Let us consider what may represent the most important of these—the international system.

The political environment that every country must operate in consists of diverse phenomena such as global and regional balances of power, international organizations and international law designed to manage or mediate disputes, the ambitions of other state actors, and ideological waves (such as resurgent liberalism today) that have a cross-national impact. The growing global economic interdependence of the second half of the twentieth century (viewed from the debt-ridden states of Latin America sometimes as dependency), taken together with traditional national strategies of forging political and military alliances, signify that few, if any, countries can behave as autonomous actors in the international system.

In the case of Latin America, an international—or more precisely, hemispheric—environment proves at times to be conducive to the supposed latent anti-democratic tendencies existing in much of the region. Military coups in adjoining countries have sometimes followed each other, especially in Central America and the Southern Cone. Similarly, however, there have been times that democracy has "broken out" in a transnational way in Latin America; the second half of the 1980s represents one such period. Figure 2.3 sought to categorize the variety of political regimes in existence in Latin America in long-term perspectives, ranging from stable democratic systems (Costa Rica and Venezuela) through alternating monistic ones (Argentina and Brazil) to stable monistic systems (Mexico, Paraguay, and Cuba). Regardless of the type of regime in power, international environmental factors—in turn produced by such normative agents as great power preferences or such structural ones as technological breakthroughs—can exercise a decisive impact both on a country's political culture and its international relations. For a democratic culture, perhaps the most important difference between the international arena and domestic political conditions is the absence of rule of law in the former.

One normative factor, rooted in a given regime, in a country's history, or even in the international environment, is ideology. Ideological systems have interacted with regional cultures, and the product is another factor affecting foreign policy. Thus, some have argued that the anti-democratic bias of Latin American states is closely linked and entirely consistent with a Catholic and Mediterranean worldview stressing the values of social order, harmony, and end of conflict. The ethical as well as intellectual bases of Catholicism may determine elite attitudes towards the conduct of international politics. While we have not considered the specific relationships among ideology, political culture, and international relations, the spread of a democratizing ideology in the late 1980s represents a major environmental influence acting on individual countries' cultures and external behavior.

In looking at the part played by the international environment in affecting a state's political culture and international relations, an important explanatory paradigm put forward by some Latin American specialists has been modernization theory and, related to it, dependency theory. Modernization theory assumes the existence of a relationship between democratic practice and levels of economic development. According to this theory, the more undeveloped countries of the region are (or should be) most often associated with anti-democratic systems, while the more industrialized ones should be characterized by greater democratic practices. The nature of the political regime is therefore explained by the stage of economic formation attained by that society.

Since, in practice, anti-democratic tendencies in Latin America have afflicted states at differing levels of economic development (for example, relatively developed Argentina and relatively backward Central America), a modified version of modernization theory had to be advanced. This was classic *dependencia* theory. According to the Argentine political scientist Guillermo O'Donnell, at some point in the recent past Latin American economic dependency became a fact of life.

The region's capacity for industrial growth was inherently limited by what we may term "geo-economics": market size, technology, natural resources, and so on. Moreover, whenever economic expansion was threatened as a result of an international economic recession, social conflict was likely to result in the region. Ruling elites—often a coalition of industrialists, middle-class technocrats, the military, and foreign business elites—inevitably chose to squeeze the living standards of the working classes rather than to sacrifice any growth at all. The end result of such political preferences of elites was the regression into political authoritarianism and repression.[4] Dependency theory essentially signified that external economic forces determined both the external politics of Latin American states caught in the web of dependency, as well as political cultural habits at home. The configuration of the political regime (monocratic, repressive, personalist, corporatist, democratic) paled into insignificance as a factor affecting foreign policy given the overwhelming fact of a society's economic dependence on advanced capitalist states.

A more recent variant of *dependencia* theory was developed by Peter Smith. He, too, sought

> to integrate political decision-making with economic determinants. Elites (or others) can select among various responses to economic opportunities; the social structure lays down conditions for plausible (but not necessary) social coalitions; and political strategies and leadership can make or unmake effective alliances. . . . Economic dependency, in short, can delimit the context of decisions and the range of workable options.[5]

The locus of economic power, therefore, is found in the global—not—state—economy, and it sets off a chain of events that ends in the political strategies (domestic and foreign) formulated by leadership teams.

As with any one-factor approach, there is an essential reductionism to this paradigm: international policy and behavior are subjected to a worldwide economic determinism that even Karl Marx would not have contemplated. Nevertheless, recognizing the significant role played by the international environment, to what extent can a nation's indigenous political culture be said to affect its international relations?

Research Findings

Our research design set out to evaluate whether, among so many other important influences, the political culture of a nation is in some measure reflected in its conduct of international relations. We assumed that other explanatory variables were important, but that some could be held relatively constant if we focused on states located in a particular region. We postulated that certain environmental influences are likely to affect all states in a region almost equally: for example, the Monroe Doctrine coupled with American power have been a reality for states in the circum-Caribbean. In addition, certain functional imperatives need to be carried out by all modern states: these include the maintenance of external and domestic security, the management of natural and human resources, the supervision of commerce and trade, and the administration of value and material allocation. Certain institutional arrangements and decision-making processes are required to execute such imperatives, again producing a degree of convergence in states of a given region. These factors added up to what Gray called the "culture-neutral" dimension of behavior in the international arena, and while we acknowledged that not all factors shaping foreign policy could be held constant, we still found that there was room for political culture to prove a meaningful explanatory variable.

Furthermore, in selecting six case studies for our study, we were persuaded that the probability of inadvertently or unconsciously selecting those historical data that would confirm our original hypotheses would be greatly diminished. The fact that the associations to be established were likely to be different since the cases varied from stable democratic to traditional authoritarian regimes militated further aganist committing the self-fulfilling fallacy. Finally, by involving three authors and a small team of graduate researchers in the collection and assessment of data, an additional structural check limited the likelihood of skewing findings to assumptions.

Table 7.1 provides a summary of the basic relationships that we described in the previous three chapters. The six countries are ranked on the basis of their Western Democratic (WD) cultural orientation. Column one gives the WD score for each country (or period of a country's history) based on the aggregate scores from the country's combined WD Value System and Behavior Pattern given in Table 4.2.

Further columns present ratings for each country based on six categories of international behavior: 1) international cooperation; 2) support for democracy and civil rights; 3) support for negotiation and mediation in international conflicts; 4) acceptance of the leadership of an international *caudillo*; 5) anti-Americanism; and 6) use of coercion in international affairs.[6] Categories 1–3 reflect a WD international behavior pattern, while categories 4–6 reflect a Latin American (LA) pattern of international behavior. The ratings are based on 2 points for

TABLE 7.1

Political Culture and International Behavior: Summary of the Relationship for Six Countries
International Behavior Dimension

| Countries Ranked By Culture Type | WD Points* | WD International Behavior | | | | Caudillaje International Behavior | | | | |
		International Cooperation	Support For Democracy and Civil Rights	Support For International Negotiation and Mediation	Total WD Score	Acceptance Of An International Caudillo	Anti-Americanism	Use of Coercion In International Affairs	Total LA Score	Net WD Score**
Costa Rica (1948–88)	41	1	2	2	5	2	0	0	2	+3
Venezuela (1958–88)	36	2	2	2	6	1	0	0	1	+5
Colombia (1974–88)	25	2	1	2	5	1	0	0	1	+4
Cuba (1959–88)	23	0	0	0	0	2	2	2	6	–6
Colombia (1948–74)	18	2	1	2	5	2	0	0	2	+3
Nicaragua (1979–88)	16	1	0	1	2	2	2	2	6	–4
Nicaragua (1934–79)	11	1	0	0	1	2	0	2	4	–3
Cuba (1933–58)	8	0	0	0	0	2	0	0	2	–2
Guatemala 1944–88)	6	2	0	0	2	2	1	2	5	–3

* Points taken from table 4.2, columns 3 and 5
** WD Score minus LA Score

a high rating, 1 point for a medium rating, and 0 points for a low rating. The last column, or "net score," represents the subtraction of the LA score from the WD score.

It is clear from the last column that Western Democratic political culture is broadly associated with Western Democratic international behavior. Costa Rica and Venezuela, as expected, constitute clear cases of democratic cultures which, over thirty years of fairly stable democratic experience, has translated into democratic international behavior. Both nations rank high on support for democracy and civil rights and for negotiation and mediation in international disputes. Costa Rica's overall lower net ranking on WD international behavior than Venezuela's is a reflection of its small size, its limited natural resources, and the fact that the nation always considered itself culturally and politically distinct from the rest of the Central American nations. These factors have had two primary consequences. Costa Rica was reluctant initially to link itself with the Central American Common Market and has been reluctant to join other attempts to create isthmus-wide political institutions. Thus it ranks somewhat lower in "international cooperation" than does Venezuela. Because of its economic and military weakness and the sense of being surrounded by nondemocratic countries (particularly Nicaragua), Costa Rica has been forced to depend on the support and protection of the United States. This gives it a high score in the "acceptance of an international *caudillo*" category.

Because of its greater resource base, Venezuela began to edge out from under the protective wing of the United States once its fledgling democratic system was established in the mid-1960s. With oil as a powerful bargaining chip, it has been able to take a more assertive role in regional economic and political affairs.

More recently, the participation of Venezuela in the various *Contadora* peace initiatives, and Costa Rica's authorship of the Arias Peace Plan for Central America, suggest that both countries are about equal in their orientation toward international cooperation. In taking the peace initiative, Costa Rica has edged away from its *political* dependency upon the United States. However, because of its small size and its lack of a natural resource in global demand such as petroleum, Costa Rica will probably always be subject to a greater degree of economic dependency than Venezuela.

At the LA end of the continuum, Nicaragua and Guatemala both reflect the fact that a *caudillaje* culture tends to translate into a general pattern of *caudillaje* international behavior. Guatemala is an interesting case in that, while hardly enjoying a reputation for supporting democracy and civil rights around the world or taking the lead in espousing the peaceful settlement of disputes (the Belize question, its participation in the Bay of Pigs episode, and the Tuna War with Mexico being three prime examples), it was one of the leaders of the movement toward Central American integration in the 1960s. Of course, its neighbors have sometimes viewed Guatemala's interest in greater Central American integration as a trojan horse for its regional power ambitions.

If it is occasionally perceived as a potential regional *caudillo* in its own right, Guatemala has, until recently at least, seen the United States as the dominant international *caudillo* in the region. To be sure, the country has also experienced bouts of anti-Americanism. Under the Christian Democratic administration of Vinicio Cerezo Arevalo, Guatemala seemed to be altering its international behavior somewhat. It broadened its international contacts to help shore up its weakened economy and supported a peaceful approach toward the settlement of the Central American crisis.

But does one popularly elected regime in a country following thirty years of autocracy constitute a significant change in its political culture? The ambivalent, even two-track, approach Cerezo took toward the URNG guerillas and the human rights movements in the country suggest that some issues continued to be resolved in traditional Guatemalan ways.[7] It will be some time before we know whether Guatemala's first halting steps toward the creation of a more democratic political culture will produce irreversible change. Given its current economic problems, the nation needs all of the international assistance it can get to democratize fully. Obtaining such assistance will require an ongoing change in its image, a fact that will undoubtedly force it to become more involved in regional peace keeping and to move toward greater support for democracy and civil rights—both at home and abroad. The price of an economically viable democratic order will be a less *caudillaje* style of international behavior.

Our caution about Guatemala's road to full democracy seems to be warranted in the case of Nicaragua, too. Although this country has been inching toward a more "Western" (if not democratic) political culture, in early 1990 it still remained essentially *caudillaje* in its international behavior. This reflects the fact that it has been in thrall to an international *caudillo*—either the United States or the USSR—for most of the twentieth century, has suffered from an ongoing insurrectionary problem since the days of Augusto Sandino (1928–1934), and has, under both the Somoza dynasty and the Sandinista regime, continued to exhibit a "combat culture."

International reality, if not political cultural change, may provoke a substantial change in Nicaragua's international behavior. Its "third way" (avoiding orthodox capitalist and communist paths) lost some of its romantic appeal as, ironically, the United States-backed Contras' challenge receded and the grim economic reality became the dominating feature defining Nicaragua under the Sandinistas. By 1990 electors concluded that the country could no longer afford its international economic isolation, nor even a remote and spasmodic insurrectionary threat from the Contras. Evidence for this included its willingness to accept the Arias Plan—even the stationing of U.N. observers on her borders—and a commitment to accelerated democratization, which came as part of the El Salvador agreement concluded by Central American presidents in February 1989. That paved the way for the Presidential election of February 1990. During this time the Sandinistas were also attempting to achieve a tacit truce with the private economic sectors of the nation. Economics may prove to drive both cultural change and a change in Nicaragua's international behavior which had been, up to 1989, aggressively anti-imperialist.

Cuba and Colombia are the slightly more ambiguous of our cases. Colombia's net WD score on international behavior appears to be somewhat higher than its political culture rating. In its post-National Front period (from 1974 onward), Colombia has been the third most Western Democratic of our six countries and second in its Western Democratic international behavior rating. During the National Front period (1948–1974), Colombia also had a WD international behavior rating equivalent to Costa Rica's. Thus, even though its political culture was determined to be more nearly like that of Nicaragua, the stability brought to the country by the National Front Agreement and its willingness to accept the leadership of the United States in international affairs set the style of its international behavior.

Since the ending of the National Front Agreement in 1974, Colombia has edged away from its close relationship with the United States and has become one of the more important actors in circum-Caribbean peace efforts. The nation's ongoing guerilla problem and the "narco-terrorist connection" (linked partially to the Sendero Luminoso insurgency in neighboring Peru) pushed President Virgilio Barco toward greater cooperation with the United States. Talks between the government and the M-19 guerillas were initiated, and Colombia's "mass political culture" may begin to catch up with the more democratic "elite political culture" which is largely responsible for the more Western Democratic character of the nation's international behavior.[8]

Cuba since Castro's revolution is the most "deviant" of our cases. We have argued that the institutionalization throughout the 1970s of what began as a personalist regime gave the nation's culture a Western, if not democratic, cast. Since Castro launched his rectification campaign in 1986 following the Communist Party's Third Congress, however, the regime has displayed signs of returning to rule legitimized by charismatic revolutionary-mindedness in place of Western, Weberian-type principles. What is certain is that Cuba has the highest *caudillaje* score (−6) in international behavior of all the countries studied. Even here, however, a caveat must be recorded: in the late 1980s the country became somewhat more cooperative in its international behavior (a prime example was the agreement with South Africa on resolving the Angolan conflict).

In the more recent manifestations of both its political culture and foreign policy, therefore, there has been a break from traditional Cuban patterns. But "zigzags" in manifestations of political culture (institutionalization followed by rectification) and of international behavior (involvements in Africa, Grenada, and Nicaragua followed by settlement of the Angolan conflict) have not run parallel to each other. Thus, in turning to revolutionary values at home but to peaceful conflict resolution methods abroad, what is the role played by traditional Cuban political culture?

The inconsistency we have detected may, in part, reflect the bifurcated character of Cuba's 1980s political culture. Political westernization occurred, but it was limited in time and scale; most importantly, it did *not* take a democratic direction. But let us go beyond the political culture approach in searching for an understanding of these zigzags. It seems highly probable that nonpolitical cultural factors account for inconsistencies in Cuba's political values and behavior. To begin with, more than any other country in the circum-Caribbean, Cuba has been affected by the major changes in the international environment and, above all, in the strategic relationship between the United States and the Soviet Union that have taken place since 1986. Changes in the superpower relationship and, further, in the domestic policies followed by Cuba's international *caudillo* for the past thirty years, the USSR, have served as a powerful counterweight to the pull of the nation's traditional political culture. The Cuban leadership has, therefore, been forced to re-assess many of the foreign policy assumptions it made over two decades ago.

Apart from changes in the international system, we can also point to Fidel Castro's political need to have a visible enemy in order to maintain a combat ethos in society. This ethos has served as the legitimation of his regime. It also inflates the values of personal charisma and a revolutionary pedigree, values that Fidel claims he alone possesses. This political need may help explain the seemingly schizophrenic international relations pursued by Cuba in the late 1980s. It seems unlikely, therefore, that a dramatic relaxation of tensions with Cuba's "most reliable enemy," the United States, will occur so long as Castro remained in power.

A further reason why Castro was unlikely to undertake wholesale moderation of Cuba's foreign policy was due to his campaign against Mikhail Gorbachev's *perestroika* policies. In rejecting restructuring and reform, Fidel argued that Cuba's political and economic systems never suffered from the problems that afflicted the USSR's political and economic systems. His differences with the Soviet leader over so fundamental an issue put him on a collision course with Cuba's "beneficent *caudillo*," and it could lead to the type of revolutionary adventurism that Cuba undertook in the 1960s, the last time that the two countries disagreed. Fidel's proclamation of Cuba as one of the last "bastions of socialism" suggests this. Finally, Castro is a *caudillaje* personality who seeks to project that personality on the world stage. Thus, a continuation of *caudillaje* international behavior, although modified possibly by the need to function within the current worldwide movement away from doctrinaire Marxism, can be expected.

In short, in the case of Cuba we recognize the shortcomings in following an exclusively political cultural approach. Its explanatory power in offering reasons for lack of congruence between traditional political culture and international relations, and for inconsistencies in domestic and foreign policy courses themselves, is limited. International systemic factors appear to override the pull of culture. Nevertheless, let us note that it is because we adopted a political cultural approach that we are sensitive to the need to search for additional explanatory variables when a regime acts, even if for a short period of time, "out of character." It is, then, very illuminating to draw the contours of such character. For, as Table 7.1 demonstrates, we have established a fairly strong association in five case studies, and in Cuba until the late 1980s, between Western Democratic political cultures and Western Democratic international behavior on the one hand, and between Latin American political cultures and international *caudillaje* behavior on the other.

A Research Agenda

This study confirms that an association exists between Latin American political culture and Latin American international behavior. Political culture is not the sole determinant of foreign policy and international behavior, and it may often not even be the main determinant. But it is *one* determinant, *one* influence, a domestic source of foreign policy and international behavior—one that has received, at most, scant attention in the growing body of literature on the foreign policy of Ibero-American states.

This study focused on six small- and medium-sized Ibero-American countries. The three Central American cases we explored—Costa Rica, Guatemala, and Nicaragua—are small states with limited foreign policy agendas and comparatively restricted international activism, though Nicaragua under the Sandinistas tried to break out of such traditional parameters. Colombia and Venezuela are medium-sized powers with broader ambitions, as evidenced by the roles they have played in transnational organizations such as the U.N. and OPEC respectively. Cuba has exercised an international presence not at all commensurate with its geographical status as a "speck in the Caribbean." All six states are in the orbit of one superpower or the other. Taken individually, each is of limited importance to United States national security interests; taken together, "an 'American Heartland' embracing all of North and Central America and Venezuela and Colombia. . .is a security concept that has considerable immediate, if not necessarily long-term, strategic and economic integrity."[9]

Clearly, substantially more research on the relationship between political culture and foreign policy in other Ibero-American countries would prove illuminating. Case studies of the larger, more developed Ibero-American states that have diverse and complex foreign policy agendas, such as Argentina, Chile, Mexico and Peru, might yield fascinating and contrasting results. The case of Brazil, whose culture was shaped by a different European power, would be of particular importance in cross-cultural research. The complex agendas of the larger states, originating in the need to respond to and interact with a broad range of factors and actors in both domestic and international arenas, might limit the influence of a country's political values and norms, for example. As we see in the case of the United States, a complex foreign policy agenda does often override the impact of political culture, for example, selectively exercising an international *caudillo* role while remaining a democratic political culture.

In short, Latin America represents a unique but complicated laboratory whose cultural styles and political life merit detailed analysis. Peter Smith has colorfully described the impact of a free-wheeling political style on the nature of politics: "In a society where Roman Catholic corporatism coexists and competes with liberal pluralism and radical Marxism, where neofascists fight with socialists, one can hardly afford to dismiss politics as irrelevant or politicians as self-serving."[10]

At the beginning of this chapter, we acknowledged the part that may be played by the international political environment in determining a country's foreign policy. Most international state actors are, we agreed, locked into action-response situations with neighbors or larger powers. What type of systemic changes in the international arena, then, may enhance or diminish the force of political culture in a given country? In the case of Mexico in the 1970s, for example, with oil revenue pouring into state coffers, succesive PRI governments could afford the luxury of manifesting independence from the United States. Independence from U.S. influence has traditionally been a significant element in the country's political culture. Thus, Mexico refused to readmit the Shah of Iran after undergoing medical treatment in New York; then more importantly, it adopted a not unsympathetic policy towards the Sandinista revolution that put it at odds with the Reagan administration. But the massive Mexican debt of the 1980s, so much of it owed to American banks, compelled the country to modify its Central American policy and in other ways to be more cooperative with the United States. A largely systemic factor—economic interdependence and world debt— tempered the influence of a deeply-rooted political culture on international behavior. A study of conditions under which systemic factors promote or undermine political cultural ones would prove significant.

The current resurgence of democratic or quasi-democratic governments in Latin America tends to divert attention from one of the most enduring realities of the politics of most Latin American countries—the alternation at irregular intervals between democratic and authoritarian rule. Using additional case studies, it would be possible to determine more comprehensively the degree of relationship between type of regime—democratic or authoritarian, civilian or military—and the influence of political culture on foreign policy and international behavior. At first blush, it would seem that democratic, civilian regimes are constrained or influenced by political cultural norms to a greater extent than authoritarian, military ones. Being open societies that are not easily susceptible to political manipulation by strong-armed leaders, producing elected governments that are formally accountable to the body politic, and stressing values of deliberation, consultation, rationality, and participation, such countries cannot behave in a radically different way in the international arena, short of becoming a Dr. Jekyll and Mr. Hyde. Undemocratic, military governments, by contrast, may occasionally seek to mask dictatorship and repression at home by behaving in a cooperative fashion with other state actors. This appeared to be true, to some degree, for both Cuba and Nicaragua in the late 1980s. It is true that in our country studies, we found siginificant associations between political cultures and international behavior in both democratic and authoritarian regimes. But from table 7.1 we note that it is Venezuela which most clearly demonstrated the linkage between the two variables: its democratic political culture was most clearly manifest in its international behavior.

Let us depart from our case studies and briefly examine the authoritarian political culture of Argentina. This culture spawned the military governments of the 1970s and 1980s, one of which was headed by General Leopoldo Galtieri. His decision to invade the Falklands/Malvinas in 1982 triggered off the war of the South Atlantic with Britain. The military junta led by Galtieri could be viewed, therefore, as both a product of an authoritarian culture (the internal "dirty war" of the period, with its thousands of *desaparecidos,* was another) and an agent of aggressive military adventurism abroad.

In 1985 the country entered—not for the first time—into a democratic period in its history. The administration of Raul Alfonsin emerged as a result of the Falklands fiasco, political discontent at home, and human rights pressures abroad, but it was in some dissonance with Argentina's authoritarian-prone political culture, evidenced subsequently by sporadic mutinies by military units and leftist attacks on garrisons. A protracted period of democratic rule could go a long way towards transforming the traditional political culture, but the defeat suffered by the Radical party suggested Argentina was returning to its more established Peronist tradition. Whether a democratic regime-type that emerges in an authoritarian culture can fully overcome the state's innate tendency to behave aggressively in the international arena is an open question. We can search for an answer, too, in the reverse experience of Chile, which returned to its established democratic tradition with the inauguration of President Patricio Aylwin in March 1990. The legacy of the Pinochet years on Chilean political culture may, if our thesis holds, be minor. In both these cases it is important for scholars to observe the intervening role played by shifting regime types on foreign policy, and a paradigm seeking to explore this problematic would prove revealing.

Another question meriting further research is to describe the changes, if any, that take place over time in the link between political culture and international orientation. As political cultures evolve or, as in the case of Cuba in the 1960s, are transformed from above, how are patterns of international behavior affected? Among other factors, economic modernization, technological change, and ecological exhaustion compel policy modifications. Longitudinal analysis could focus on the impact of such objective changes on both political culture and foreign policy.

One other important issue is the degree to which short-term national self-interest will win out over traditional political cultural norms and values. We have found some evidence to that effect. Venezuela, from the onset of its democratic period, preferred to associate with other democracies. Yet the perceived benefits to be derived from membership in the OPEC oil cartel led it eventually to associate with some very nondemocratic governments in that organization, such as Saudi Arabia and Iran. Admittedly, the country exhibits Western Democratic values in its dealings with all countries, but it can be argued that even limited cooperation with authoritarian regimes can erode a country's democratic values.

Clearly, much remains to be done in describing the domestic and international contexts of Latin America's international relations. Our focus on political culture has yielded some insights. Elsewhere in the world, especially in the former Soviet bloc, important transformations of long-standing political value systems are being attempted. In the case of the Soviet Union, Mikhail Gorbachev's efforts at democratizing Russian political culture include important changes in foreign policy: military cutbacks, an arms control treaty, the withdrawal of Soviet forces from Afghanistan and parts of Eastern Europe, and a fresh approach to the German unification issue.

The reciprocal relationship between political culture and international relations includes the possibility, therefore, that marked departures in foreign policy can trigger changes in political culture. As we approach the twenty-first century, we need to remain sensitive to the injunction given in the late sixth century by Byzantine Emperor Maurice in his *Strategikon:* to maximize a nation's own security, study the "characteristics and tactics of various peoples."[11] So as to avoid "trouble in our backyard," characteristics of the nations making up Latin America are of particular significance.

Notes

1. Colin S. Gray, *The Geopolitics of Superpower.* Lexington, KY: University Press of Kentucky, 1988, pp. 42–43.

2. Gray, *The Geopolitics of Superpower,* p. 42.

3. Graeme Gill, "Personality Cult, Political Culture and Party Structure," *Studies in Comparative Communism,* XVII, no. 2 (Summer 1984), p. 112.

4. Guillermo A. O'Donnell, *Modernization and Bureaucratic-Authoritarianism: Studies in South American Politics.* Berkeley: Institute of International Studies, 1973.

5. Peter H. Smith, "Political History in the 1980s: A View from Latin America," in Theodore K. Rabb and Robert I. Rotberg (eds.), *The New History: The 1980s and Beyond*. Princeton: Princeton University Press, 1982, p. 17.

6. These six categories were produced by collapsing a larger number of categories. "International cooperation" combines general international activism, support for international bodies, and support for economic integration. "Support for democracy and civil rights" combines support for democracy, support for civil and human rights, and support for socio-economic rights.

7. For a summary of the Cerezo regime, see Roland H. Ebel, "Cerezo and the Transition to Democracy in Guatemala." Paper presented at the Southwestern Political Science Association meetings, Little Rock, Arkansas, March 31, 1989.

8. Diana Gaviria, "M-19, Government Dialogue," *The Times of the Americas* (January 11, 1989), p. 5

9. Gray, *The Geopolitics of Superpower*, p. 47. For an Analysis of what security means for Central America, see Peter Calvert (ed.), *The Central American Security System*. Cambridge: Cambridge University Press, 1989.

10. Smith, "Political History in the 1980s," pp. 4–5.

11. *Maurice's Strategikon: Handbook of Byzantine Military Strategy*. Translated by George T. Dennis. Philadelphia: University of Pennsylvania Press, 1984, p. 113.

Appendix

Works Used in Secondary Analysis

(1) Colombia

Berry R. Albert, Ronald G. Hellman, and Mauricio Solaun (eds.), *Politics of Compromise: Coalition Government in Colombia*. New Jersey: Transaction Books, 1980.

Centro de Investigacion y Accion Social, *Estructuras politicas de Colombia*. Bogota: Centro de Investigacion y Accion Social, 1969.

Garces, Joan E., *Desarrollo politico y desarrollo economico: Los casos de Chile y Colombia*. Madrid: Editorial Tecnos, 1972.

Guillen Martinez, Fernando, *El poder politico en Colombia*. Bogota: Editorial Punta de Lanza, 1979.

Kline, Harvey F., *Colombia: Portrait of Unity and Diversity*. Boulder, CO: Westview Press, 1983.

————, "Colombia: Modified Two-Party and Elitist Politics," in Howard J. Wiarda and Harvey F. Kline (eds.), *Latin American Politics and Development*. Boulder, CO: Westview Press, 1985.

Leal Buitrago, Francisco, "Estudio del comportamiento legislativo en Colombia," *Analysis historico del desarrollo politico nacional, 1930–1970*, Vol. 1. Bogota: Ediciones Tercer Mundo, 1973.

Martz, John D., *Colombia: A Contemporary Political Survey*. Chapel Hill: University of North Carolina Press, 1962.

(2) Costa Rica

Barahona Jimenez, Luis, *Anatomia patriotica*. San José: Publicaciones de la Universidad de Costa Rica, 1970.

————, *Las ideas politicas en Costa Rica*. San José: Departmento de Publicaciones del Ministerio de Educacion Publica, 1977.

Biesanz, Mavis H. et. al., *Los costarricenses*. San José: Editorial Universidad Estala Distancia, 1979.

Booth, John A., "Are Latin Americans Politically Rational? Citizen Participation and Democracy in Costa Rica," in John A. Booth and Mitchell A. Seligson (eds.), *Political Participation in Latin America*, Vol. I. New York: Holmes and Meier, 1978.

————— and Mitchell A. Seligson, "Images of Political Participation in Latin America," in *Political Participation in Latin America*, Vol. I.

Busey, James L., *Notas sobre la democracia costarricense*. San José: Editorial Costa Rica, 1968.

Cerosimo, Gaetano, *Los esterotipos del costarricense*. San José: Editorial Universidad de Costa Rica, n.d.

Denton, Charles F., *Patterns of Costa Rican Politics*. Boston: Allyn and Bacon, 1979.

Lascaris, Constantion, *El costarricense*. San José: Editorial Universitario, 1975.

Seligson, Mitchell A., "Development and Participation in Costa Rica: The Impact of Context," in *Political Participation in Latin America*, Vol. I.

Stone, Samuel, *La dinastia de los conquistadores: La crisis del poder en la Costa Rica contemporanea*, 3rd edn. San José: Editorial Universitaria Centroamericana, 1982.

Vega Carballo, Jose Luis, *Poder politico y democracia en Costa Rica*. San José: Editorial Parvenir, S.A., 1982.

(3) Cuba

Aguilar, Luis, *Cuba 1953: Prologue to Revolution*. Ithaca, NY: Cornell University Press, 1972.

Bray, Donald W. and Timothy F. Harding, "Cuba," in Ronald H. Chilcote and Joel C. Edelstein (eds.), *Latin America: The Struggle with Dependency and Beyond*. New York: John Wiley, 1974.

del Aguila, Juan M., *Cuba: Dilemmas of a Revolution*. Boulder, CO: Westview Press, 1984.

Domínguez, Jorge I., "Revolutionary Politics: The New Demands for Orderliness, " in Jorge I. Domínguez (ed.), *Cuba: Internal and International Affairs*. Beverly Hills, CA: Sage Publications, 1982.

————— , *Cuba: Order and Revolution*. Cambridge: The Balknap Press, 1978.

Farber, Samuel, *Revolution and Reaction in Cuba, 1933–1960: A Political Sociology from Machado to Castro*. Middletown, CT: Wesleyan University Press, 1976.

Horowitz, Irving L. (ed.), *Cuban Communism*. New Brunswick, NJ: Transaction Books, 1977.

Mesa-Lago, Carmelo, *Cuba in the 1970s: Pragmatism and Institutionalization*. Albuquerque: University of New Mexico Press, 1978.

Suchlicki, Jaime, *Cuba: From Columbus to Castro*, 2nd edn. New York: Pergamon-Brassey's, 1985.

(4) Guatemala

Black, George, *Garrison Guatemala*. New York: Monthly Review Press, 1984.

Cambranes, Julio Castellanos, "Origins of the Crisis of the Established Order in Guatemala," Steve C. Ropp and James A. Morris (eds.), *Centeal America: Crisis and Adaptation*. Albuquerque: University of New Mexico Press, 1984.

Davis, Shelton H., "State Violence and Agrarian Crisis in Guatemala: The Roots of the Indian-Peasant Rebellion," in Martin Diskin (ed.), *Trouble in our Backyard: Central America and the United States in the Eighties*. New York: Pantheon Books, 1983.

Jonas, Susanne, "Guatemala: The Land of Eternal Struggle," in Chilcote and Edelstein (eds.), *Latin America: The Struggle with Dependency and Beyond*.

Plant, Roger, *Guatemala: Unnatural Disaster*. London: Latin America Bureau, 1978.

Torres-Rivas, Adelberto, "Seven Keys to Understanding the Central American Crisis," *Contemporary Marxism*, No. 3 (Summer 1981).

Trudeau, Robert and Lars Schoultz, "Guatemala," in Morris J. Blachman et al. (eds.), *Confronting Revolution: Security Through Diplomacy in Central America*. New York: Pantheon Books, 1986.

Weaver, Jerry L., "Guatemala: The Politics of a Frustrated Revolution," in Wiarda and Kline (eds.), *Latin American Politics and Development*.

(5) Nicaragua

Belli, Humberto, *Breaking Faith: The Sandinista Revolution and Its Impact on Freedom and Christian Faith in Nicaragua* Westchester, IL: Crossway Books, 1985.

Black, George, *Triumph of the People: The Sandinista Revolution in Nicaragua*. London: Zed Press, 1981.

Booth, John A., *The End and the Beginning: The Nicaraguan Revolution*, 2nd edn. Boulder, CO: Westview Press, 1985.

Gilbert, Dennis, "Nicaragua," in Blachman (ed.) *Confronting Revolution.*

Millett, Richard, *Guardians of the Dynasty: A History of the U.S. Created Guardia Nacional de Nicaraguay and the Somoza Family.* Maryknoll, NY: Orbis Books, 1977.

Walker, Thomas, *Nicaragua: The Land of Sandino.* Boulder, CO: Westview Press, 1981.

(6) Venezuela

Balorya, Enrique A. and John D. Martz, "Dimensions of Campaign Participation: Venezuela, 1973, " in Booth and Seligson (eds.), *Political Participation in Latin America.*

Blank, David Eugene, *Politics in Venezuela.* Boston: Little, Brown and Company, 1973.

Brewer, Carias and Allan Randolph, *Cambio politico y reforma de estado en Venezuela.* Madrid: Editorial Tecnos, 1975.

Gil Yepes, Jose Antonio, *The Challenge of Venezuelan Democracy.* New Brunswick: Transaction Books, 1981.

Levine, Daniel H., *Conflict and Political Change in Venezuela.* Princeton: Princeton University Press, 1973.

————— , "Venezuelan Politics: Past and Future," in Robert D. Bond (ed.), *Contemporary Venezuela and its Role in International Affairs.* New York: New York University Press, 1977.

Stewart, Bill, *Change and Bureaucracy: Public Administration in Venezuela.* Chapel Hill: University of North Carolina Press, 1978.

Index